Contact in adoption and permanent foster care:
Research, theory and practice

Contact in adoption and permanent foster care

Research, theory and practice

**Edited by Elsbeth Neil
and David Howe**

British Association for Adoption & Fostering
(BAAF)
Skyline House
200 Union Street
London SE1 0LX
www.baaf.org.uk

Charity registration 275689

British Library Cataloguing in Publication Data
A catalogue record for this book is available
from the British Library

ISBN 1 903699 60 6

Editorial project management by Shaila Shah
Cover photographs posed by models;
John Birdsall Photography
Designed by Andrew Haig & Associates
Typeset by Avon DataSet, Bidford on Avon
Printed by Creative Print and Design Group

BAAF is the leading UK-wide membership
organisation for all those concerned with
adoption, fostering and child care issues.

Contents

Foreword

Professor Michael Rutter

Public and professional attitudes to the desirability, or otherwise, of adopted children being able to have contact with their biological families have totally changed over the last few decades. Everyone came to appreciate that the best interests of the child were not necessarily always met by a complete break with the biological family and by the main-tenance of secrecy. As a result, it came to be accepted that, in appropriate circumstances, adopted individuals should be able to make contact with their biological families. In recent years, the expectations have moved even further to a situation in which there is a presumption that contact with the biological parents should be the norm rather than the exception. To a considerable extent, these changes were driven by ideology rather than research evidence, and when research did begin to obtain information on the consequences of contact, the initial findings were somewhat inconclusive on the extent to which contact was necessarily beneficial for the child. As a result, opinions remained divided on the advantages and disadvantages of contact versus no contact.

This important book takes the field forward in a decisive fashion through its bringing together of the systematic findings from both quantitative and qualitative research by several different research groups in both the UK and North America. However, the book does much more than that in indicating that the old style simplistic dichotomy of contact versus no contact is not the right way of thinking about the issues. The individual chapters bring out very well how the matter should be approached, how the research findings should guide thinking, and how these have implications for policy and practice. Let me just highlight some of the main ways in which concepts have advanced. The high quality research reported in the individual chapters should do still more to move the field forward in improving policy and practice. The book gains immensely from the fact that the studies differ markedly in the samples they studied. Thus, some focus on adoptees and some on both adoptees and children in long-term foster care. Some focus on adoptions in infancy of normal babies and others focus on older special needs children. These, and other relevant and important variations, do much to provide the leverage for an incisive analysis of the key considerations.

As is implicit in that description, the first point is that there has been an appreciation that, although the contact versus no contact issue has primarily concerned adoptees, very comparable considerations apply to children in long-term foster care. Second, there has come an appreciation of the need to consider influences on the maintenance and quality of the new placement, whether it be adoption or long-term fostering. This has carried with it the recognition that the crucial issues concern the psychological processes involved for all parties. Children will have feelings about the variety of relationships involved irrespective of whether there is contact or no contact. Although the needs of the child are paramount, both the biological and adoptive families also have needs; but most crucial of all has been the appreciation that there are interconnections and interplay among different relationships. Thus, for example, the child's relationship with both the adoptive parents and with the biological parents will be influenced by the nature and quality of the relationship between the adoptive family and the biological family.

The heterogeneities involved in all of this are both great and important. Thus, the contact with the biological parents may be direct and face-to-face, or it may be through letters or telephone calls, and it may be supervised or unsupervised. In addition, there is heterogeneity with respect to the biological family. Contact cannot be simply reduced to whether or not there is contact with the biological mother, because the biological father, siblings, and grandparents may all be involved. The pluses and the minuses of contact may not be the same for each of these.

It is clear, too, that the children themselves differ in all sorts of ways, including their age at placement, their temperamental qualities, their prior experiences within the biological family, the degree to which the children are impaired in their functioning, and their views on what they want with respect to contact. Similarly, parents differ in all sorts of ways, including whether or not the biological parents supported or opposed adoption, whether they are currently impaired in their psychological functioning, and whether contact might involve a risk of abuse – either physical or psychological.

These considerations must take into account the fact that the views and the wishes of all parties (the children, the adoptive families and the biological families) may well change over time and what is possible, or what seems important, at one point may look rather different at a later point. Clearly, it follows from all of these considerations that the handling of the contact needs to be carefully managed in relation to the details of the specific situation and the qualities, attitudes and feelings of the different participants. There is not, and cannot be, one standard approach that suits everyone and each situation needs careful, considered attention to what is likely to work best with this individual child and these adoptive and biological families. Of course, that should be absolutely standard in any form of clinical practice or social fieldwork, but if this is to be done, it is necessary for there to be evidence-based guidance on how to make these difficult decisions.

This book does much to provide just such guidance. It ought to be required reading for all who are concerned with adopted or long-term fostered children and it will be of equal interest to researchers concerned with the psychological development of children in these situations.

August 2004

Acknowledgements

We should like to thank The Nuffield Foundation for the generous support they gave to help run and organise the original "contact seminar" held at their London headquarters in October 2003. In particular, we are grateful to Sharon Witherspoon, Deputy Director, The Nuffield Foundation for her encouragement, guidance and advice, which helped make the event an unqualified success.

Elsbeth Neil
David Howe
August 2004

1 Introduction

Elsbeth Neil and David Howe

Permanently placing a child with new adoptive or foster parents removes a child physically from their birth family, but should not be expected to remove the birth family from the child's mind. Whether or not a permanently placed child has any actual contact with their birth family, and whether or not the child's legal ties to the birth family are severed or curtailed, we now understand that while a permanent placement creates new relationships it cannot entirely eradicate old ones. Permanent family placement may be first and foremost about creating "new" families for children, but children who are fostered or adopted do have thoughts and feelings about their birth family that are not easily extinguished by either physical or legal distance, or by the satisfaction of finding love and security with adoptive or foster parents. Post-placement contact between birth families and adoptive and foster families is where the interconnectedness of all parties is made real. Questions about the desirability, frequency and type of post-placement contact that adopted and long-term fostered children should have with their birth family are currently a major consideration for families and social and legal practitioners. Finding the right balance between the needs and wishes of all parties, but keeping the child's needs uppermost, is the challenge practitioners and families face on a daily basis.

The past twenty years have been a time of rapid change when it comes to thinking about post-placement contact. Of a large sample of children permanently placed in foster care or for adoption in the early 1980s, 30 per cent of children had plans for some form of ongoing contact with their birth relatives, and those who did were mainly older placed fostered children (Fratter *et al*, 1991). Of those placed under age five, only eight per cent had any birth family contact. In contrast, a number of studies of children placed more recently has shown that birth family contact of some type is now usual for the majority of both adopted and fostered children (Performance and Innovation Unit, 2000; Cleaver, 2000; Neil, 2002; Neil *et al*, 2003; Lowe *et al*, 1999).

Changes in thinking about contact have come about for a number of reasons. The placement of older children in new permanent families took off in the 1980s and required a shift in thinking. Many older placed children had established relationships with their birth family which they were reluctant to relinquish. Secrecy and severance made less sense for these children. Changes in views about post-placement contact for children in public care were reflected in the Children Act 1989 (England and Wales) and the Children (Scotland) Act 1995, the effect of which was to give an additional impetus to more open placements (Cleaver, 2000). Concerns about the need for and effects of closed placements also stemmed from research which suggested that a complete severance model could leave adopted children struggling to resolve identity concerns (Triseliotis, 1973; Haimes and Timms, 1985) and could complicate the grieving process of birth mothers (Winkler and van Keppel, 1984). Early studies of the impact of contact on permanent placements suggested that birth family contact did not increase, and might even reduce, placement breakdown rates. It seemed that requiring children to sever established relationships could actually get in the way of helping them make new relationships (Fratter *et al*, 1991; Barth and Berry, 1988; Borland *et al*, 1991).

In New Zealand the philosophy and practice of adoption within the Maori community challenged the orthodoxy of the need for secrecy in adoptive placements (Rockel and Ryburn, 1988; Mullender, 1991), an outlook which began to have a growing influence on practice in the UK. In the USA, openness in adoption was in part driven by the wishes of birth mothers and concerns about the long-term consequences of sealed records (Henney *et al*, 2003). Research which showed that openness could work well in the placement of infants also began to appear (e.g. McRoy *et al*, 1988; Rockel and Ryburn, 1988; Grotevant and McRoy, 1998), suggesting that contact could serve the needs of children who did not know or remember their birth family, as well as those of older children who had an established relationships with their birth family.

The cumulative effect of these shifts in philosophy and outlook has resulted in an acceptance of the limitations of "clean break" models of permanency and a willingness to explore alternatives. However, what continues to be a major problem is the lack of a theoretical bridge allowing links to be made between the empirical evidence currently available on contact and the need to make specific decisions in particular cases. The long-term impact on children's development of different types of birth family contact is not yet available. In fact, research into the effects of contact has largely followed changes in practice, not created them. Arguments about the value or otherwise of contact have often been driven by ideology rather than science. And when protagonists have appealed to the findings of research, they have found themselves drawing on different studies with contrasting results. For a while, no clear consensus about the value or otherwise of contact could be found (Quinton *et al*, 1997; Quinton and Selwyn, 1988; Quinton *et al*, 1999; Ryburn, 1998, 1999).

Simple formulae are not helpful. "No contact for anyone" denied many children a range of developmental opportunities. However, although contact did seem to offer many advantages, in practice maintaining successful contact turned out to be not always easy, and birth family contact is not necessarily appropriate or even achievable in all cases (Macaskill, 2002). As practitioners recognise, how contact works out in practice depends on many different factors, not least of which are the characteristics of the individuals involved. Different types of contact or particular kinds of support can lead to a variety of outcomes. What works for one party may not work for another and what seems a good plan at one point in time may need to change at a later date. Easy and straight-forward answers to the problems of contact will not be found in this book. What you will discover are a series of well-designed studies by leading research authorities which tease out key factors that need to be taken into account when thinking about and planning contact.

The idea for this book arose from a seminar on research into contact. It was held at The Nuffield Foundation's London headquarters in October 2003 and chaired by Professor Sir Michael Rutter. The seminar, 'Contact in permanent family placement: the research evidence reviewed', was organised by the University of East Anglia's Centre for Research on the Child and Family and was built around the visit to the department of Professor Harold Grotevant of the University of Minnesota. Professor Grotevant was acting as a consultant to Elsbeth Neil on her "Contact after

3

Adoption" project. Harold Grotevant, a key researcher into openness in adoption in the USA, seemed too good a person to keep all for ourselves and so the idea of a seminar germinated. We thought it was a good time to stop and take stock of the research evidence on contact, and to look at a number of key studies and arguments alongside each other. In addition to Harold Grotevant's research on contact for children placed in infancy, and Elsbeth Neil's study of children adopted under age four, we wanted also to consider the impact of contact on children placed at older ages and in more difficult circumstances. With this in mind we invited additional papers from David Howe and Miriam Steele, David Quinton, and June Thoburn. The Nuffield Foundation generously sponsored the day and we were able to invite key representatives of birth and adoptive family groups and networks, adoption agencies, the judiciary, the research community and policy-makers.

The seminar proved to be both stimulating and an agreed success. Looking at findings from very different groups of placed children allowed us to identify a number of common themes as well as relevant and key differences. We also wanted to include in the book a wider range of research than it was possible to contain in the seminar. In particular, we were keen to address the needs of children permanently placed in foster care, as well as those who were adopted. With this in mind we broadened the scope of the compilation to include papers from Mary Beek and Gillan Schofield, Kate Wilson and Ian Sinclair, and Janette Logan and Carole Smith.

We hope that readers will gain an up-to-date and accessible account of contact research and the thinking it is generating. The concluding chapter reviews the main research findings, outlines a way of assessing whether or not contact is indicated in any particular case, and builds in a model of support based on the recognition that placed children have a special set of developmental needs.

References

Barth, R. P. and Berry, M. (1988) *Adoption and Disruption: Rates, risks and responses*, New York: Aldine de Gruyter.

Borland, M., O'Hara, G. and Triseliotis, J. (1991) 'Placement outcomes for children with special needs', *Adoption & Fostering*, 15(2), pp. 18–28.

Cleaver, H. (2000) *Fostering Family Contact*, London: The Stationery Office.

Fratter, J., Rowe, J., Sapsford, D. and Thoburn, J. (1991) *Permanent Family Placement: A decade of experience*, London: BAAF.

Grotevant, H. D. and McRoy, R. G. (1998) *Openness in Adoption: Exploring family connections*, Thousand Oaks: Sage.

Haimes, E. and Timms, N. (1985) *Adoption, Identity and Social Policy: The search for distant relatives*, London: Gower.

Henney, S. M., McRoy, R. G., Ayers-Lopez, S. and Grotevant, H. D. (2003) 'The impact of openness on adoption agency practices: a longitudinal perspective', *Adoption Quarterly*, 6(3), pp. 31–51.

Lowe, N., Murch, M., Borkowski, M., Weaver, A., Beckford, V. and Thomas, C. (1999) *Supporting Adoption: Reframing the approach*, London: BAAF.

Macaskill, C. (2002) *Safe Contact? Children in permanent placement and contact with their birth relatives*, Lyme Regis: Russell House Publishing.

McRoy, R. G., Grotevant, H. D. and White, K. L. (1988). *Openness in Adoption: New practices, new issues*, New York: Praeger.

Mullender, A. (1991) *Open Adoption: The philosophy and the practice*, London: BAAF.

Neil, E. (2002) 'Contact after adoption: the role of agencies in making and supporting plans', *Adoption & Fostering*, 26(1), pp. 25–38.

Neil, E., Beek, M. and Schofield, G. (2003) 'Thinking about and managing contact in permanent placements: the differences and similarities between adoptive parents and foster carers', *Clinical Child Psychology and Psychiatry*, 8(3), pp. 401–418.

Performance and Innovation Unit (2000) *The Prime Minister's Review of Adoption*, London: The Cabinet Office.

Quinton, D., Rushton, A., Dance, C. and Mayes, D. (1997) 'Contact between children placed away from home and their birth parents: research issues and evidence', *Clinical Child Psychology and Psychiatry*, 2, pp. 393–413.

Quinton, D. and Selwyn, J. (1998) 'Contact with birth parents after adoption: a response to Ryburn', *Child and Family Law Quarterly*, 10, pp. 349–361.

Quinton, D., Selwyn, J., Rushton, A. and Dance, C. (1999) 'Contact between children placed away from home and their birth parents: Ryburn's 'reanalysis' analysed', *Clinical Child Psychology and Psychiatry*, 4, pp. 519–531.

Rockel, J. and Ryburn, M. (1988) *Adoption Today: Change and choice in New Zealand*, Auckland: Heinemann Reed.

Ryburn, M. (1998) 'In whose best interests? post adoption contact with the birth family', *Child and Family Law Quarterly*, 10(1), pp. 53–70.

Ryburn, M. (1999) 'Contact between children placed away from home and their birth parents: a reanalysis of the evidence in relation to permanent placements', *Clinical Child Psychology and Psychiatry*, 4, pp. 505–518.

Triseliotis, J. (1973) *In Search of Origins*, London: Routledge and Kegan Paul.

Winkler, R. and Van Keppel, M. (1984) *Relinquishing Mothers in Adoption: Their long term adjustment*, Melbourne: Institute of Family Studies.

2 Contact after adoption: Outcomes for infant placements in the USA

*Harold D. Grotevant, Ruth G. McRoy
and Susan Ayers-Lopez*

We acknowledge, with gratitude, funding support from the William T. Grant Foundation; the National Institute of Child Health and Human Development; the Office of Population Affairs; U.S. Department of Health and Human Services; the Hogg Foundation for Mental Health; the John D. and Catherine T. MacArthur Foundation; the Minnesota Agricultural Experiment Station; the Center for Interpersonal Relationships Research, University of Minnesota; and the University Research Institute of the University of Texas at Austin. We extend special thanks to the adoptive parents, adopted children, birth parents, and adoption agency staff members who generously gave their time to share their experiences with us. Correspondence should be directed to Harold D. Grotevant, University of Minnesota, Department of Family Social Science, 290 McNeal Hall, 1985 Buford Ave., St. Paul, Minnesota 55108 USA; Tel: (612) 624 3756; email: hgrotevant@che.umn.edu

*   *   *

Contact between members of a child's adoptive family and birth family is becoming a significant issue to consider in adoption planning. Early debates focused on whether contact was "good" or "bad" overall. The dialogue has now shifted to ask more subtle questions about what type of contact might be advisable, for whom, and when.

We have been following 190 adoptive families and 169 birth mothers since the mid-1980s, when adoption agencies in the USA began offering options that included contact between members of the child's families of adoption and birth. The children were voluntarily placed for adoption by their birth mothers in the late 1970s and early 1980s. The mean age of placement was four weeks (range: immediately after birth to 44 weeks). Ninety per cent of the children were placed by nine weeks. Because of this restricted range, age of placement was not an important contributing factor to child outcomes and will not be discussed further in this chapter.

Families and birth mothers were recruited through 35 private adoption agencies across all regions of the USA. We limited the sample to infant placements in order to remove one possible source of variation in adoption outcomes. The sample intentionally did not include transracial, inter-national, or special needs placements so that the clearest possible conclusions about openness could be drawn. Families and birth mothers were first interviewed between 1987 and 1992, when the children were between 4–12 years of age (mean age = 7.8 years) and again between 1996 and 2000, when the children were adolescents (mean age = 15.7 years.) For further information about the birth mothers, see Henney *et al* (Chapter 3). For a more detailed description of the entire sample, see Grotevant and McRoy (1997, 1998).

The sample included 190 adoptive fathers, 190 adoptive mothers, 171 adopted children, and 169 birth mothers at Wave 1. Almost all families were white, and all placements were "same race". At Wave 2, the longitudinal sample included at least one member of 177 of the originally participating 190 adoptive families (173 adoptive mothers, 162 adoptive fathers, 156 adopted adolescents), and 127 of the original 169 birth mothers.

Families from across the full range of openness participated. Four major categories were used to differentiate among levels of openness:

- **confidential adoptions** in which no information was shared between birth and adoptive parents after six months post-placement (at Wave 1: N = 62 adoptive families, 52 birth mothers; at Wave 2: N = 51 adoptive families, 31 birth mothers);

- **mediated – stopped adoptions** in which information was transmitted between adoptive parents and birth mothers by agency caseworkers, but the information sharing had stopped by the time the partici-pants were interviewed (at Wave 1: N = 17 adoptive families, 18 birth mothers; at Wave 2: N = 31 adoptive families, 29 birth mothers);

- **ongoing mediated adoptions** in which indirect exchange of letters, pictures, or gifts was mediated by the agency and was continuing (at Wave 1: N = 52 adoptive families, 58 birth mothers; at Wave 2: N = 19 adoptive families, 23 birth mothers);

- **fully disclosed adoptions** in which direct sharing of information occurred between the adoptive parents and the birth mother, usually accompanied by face-to-face meetings. For 57 adoptive families and 41 birth mothers, this contact was *ongoing* at the time of the Wave 1 interview; for two adoptive families, the contact had ceased and the parties did not intend to resume contact (*stopped*). At Wave 2, there were 67 adoptive families and 43 birth mothers with ongoing fully disclosed arrangements as well as nine adoptive families and one birth mother with fully disclosed adoptions in which contact had stopped. The frequency and intensity of contact in the fully disclosed adoptions ranged widely, from occasional letters or phone calls to several meetings per year. The exchange of phone calls, letters, and holiday and birthday gifts was more typical. When the adoptive family lived far away from the birth mother, visits were less frequent, although letters and phone calls may have been exchanged more frequently. In some cases, contact with the birth mother was infrequent, but there was more contact with other members of her extended family.

The project has studied changing family relationships within the context of changing social policies and practices. (For details about changing adoption agency practices that occurred during the study, see Henney *et al*, 1998; Henney *et al*, 2003.) This project is the largest nationwide study in the USA involving personal interviews and standardized questionnaires with adoptive parents, birth parents, and adopted children experiencing a range of post-adoption contact and followed longitudinally.

Study design and methodology

At Wave 1, adoptive families were interviewed in their homes in one session that lasted three to four hours. The session included separate interviews with each parent and with the target adopted child as well as a joint couples interview with the adoptive parents. Several questionnaires were administered, including the Understanding of Adoption Scale (Brodzinsky *et al*, 1984); Self-Perception Scale for Children (Harter, 1985); and Child Adaptive Behavior Inventory (CABI: Miller, 1987). Eight years later at Wave 2, participants were once again interviewed in their homes. The session lasted four to five hours and included individual interviews with each parent and the target adopted child, as well as a family interaction task. Several questionnaires were also administered, including the Child Behavior Checklist (CBCL: Achenbach and Edelbrock, 1983), Youth Self-Report (YSR: Achenbach and Edelbrock, 1987), and Brief Symptom Inventory (BSI: Derogatis, 1993). For further information about the methods used with the birth mothers in the study, see Henney *et al* (Chapter 3).

Findings

This chapter focuses on the key findings concerning outcomes for the adopted children and adolescents. The issues to be discussed include socioemotional adjustment, adoptive identity development, satisfaction with contact, curiosity about and searching for birth parents, and changes in openness.

Socioemotional adjustment

At Wave 1, there was no relation between level of openness and the children's socioemotional adjustment, as measured by the CABI (Grotevant and McRoy, 1998). However, adjustment was predicted by the quality of relationships between the adoptive parents and child's birth mother, which we have called *collaboration in relationships* (Grotevant *et al*, 1999). This emergent property of the adoptive kinship network is characterised by the ability of the child's adoptive and birth parents to work together effectively on behalf of the child's well-being. It involves collaborative control over the way in which contact is handled and is based on mutual respect, empathy and valuing of the relationship.

We rated collaboration on a 10-point scale for a subsample of 12 adoptive kinship networks. In networks rated low on collaboration, the adults often had very different perceptions about how open the adoption actually was. The needs and fears of the adoptive parents and birth relatives took precedence over their consideration of the children's interests in knowing more about their adoption and background. One adoptive parent wishing to minimise contact stated, 'and so you kind of put up your protection walls. And you think, OK, once I adopt my child, he's mine and I should have the choices.' Kinship networks that were rated high in collaboration were characterised by mutual respect, caring and affection. The adults were committed to making contact work, because they viewed it as being in their child's best interest in the long run. The adults were sensitive to each others' control needs – who would initiate contact, how communication would be handled – and took these needs into account. Although more collaborative networks were not entirely free of concerns or fears, the adults found ways to deal with their concerns while still valuing the network relationships. We correlated these ratings of collaboration with children's scores on the CABI. Higher ratings on collaboration were associated with lower scores on problematic adjustment (Grotevant et al, 1999).

We were also concerned with the issue of "goodness of fit" or perceived compatibility between parents and their adopted children. Since adoptees are not genetically related to their adoptive parents, the sense of fit must be socially constructed by the family rather than assumed because of biological similarity or kinship. In a prior study of adopted adolescents in residential treatment for emotional disorders, we found that many of the adoptive families had not succeeded in developing a perception that the child fitted well within the family (Grotevant et al, 1988). At Wave 1, we found that a strong predictor of problematic adjustment (internalising and externalising) during middle childhood was the adoptive parent's perception of the child's incompatibility with the family (Ross, 1995). At Wave 2, we found that patterns of change in perceived compatibility predicted adolescent adjustment outcomes. A greater sense of compatibility maintained longitudinally from middle childhood to adolescence was associated with lower incidence of problem behaviour and greater sense of attachment to adoptive parents. The results were similar for male and female adolescents and regardless of whether compatibility change patterns were derived from mothers' or fathers' perceptions (Grotevant et al, 2001).

At Wave 2, adjustment scores for the entire group of adopted adolescents did not differ significantly from gender-specific national norms on the CBCL (mother or father report). Males in the study showed fewer symptoms than the norm group on the BSI. With regard to openness, we compared two groups of adolescents: those who had been in confidential adoptions since placement and those who had been involved in some form of contact since placement or soon thereafter. There were no differences between the groups in child adjustment, as reported by parents on the CBCL.

In summary, our data show that this sample of adopted adolescents, on average, is no different in levels of adjustment from the national norms developed on a set of well-validated measures. In addition, level of openness by itself was not a major predictor of adjustment outcomes at Wave 1 or Wave 2. However, relationship qualities such as collaboration in relationships and perceptual qualities such as perceived compatibility were predictive of adjustment across openness levels.

Adoptive identity development

Adopted adolescents face the challenge of making meaning of their beginnings, which may be unknown, unclear, or otherwise ambiguous. The meaning-making process varies for children adopted under different circumstances. Children adopted as infants may wonder: Where did I come from? Who were my birth parents? Why was I placed for adoption? Do I have siblings? Children adopted at older ages may wonder: Do my birth parents think about me? What are my birth parents' daily lives like now?

All adoptees are challenged to construct a story about themselves that attempts to answer some of these questions and clarify the meaning of adoption in their lives. This narrative helps the adolescent to make sense of the past, understand the self in the present, and project himself or herself into the future (Grotevant, 1993). Constructing this narrative is about the development of adoptive identity, the evolving answer to the question: 'Who am I as an adopted person?' (Grotevant, 1997; Grotevant et al, 2000). It is part of the larger process of identity development, an important task of adolescence that lays a foundation for adult psychosocial development (Erikson, 1968).

The interviews administered to adolescents during Wave 2 examined issues of adoptive identity development. A number of dimensions were coded from these interviews, and adolescents' narratives were ultimately categorised into four types by using cluster analysis (see Dunbar, 2003; Dunbar and Grotevant, 2004, for details about the dimensions coded).

In the first group, *unexamined adoptive identity*, the adolescent had undertaken little or no exploration of the personal meaning of adoption, adoption had low salience, and little positive or negative affect around adoption was expressed. For example, one adolescent stated, 'Because I feel like it's over and that I'm happy where I am and I just don't want to mess with that other part.' Another noted that: 'I don't really think about adoption that much so it's just – I probably don't even realise that I am.'

In the second group, *limited identity*, adolescents were beginning to actively explore ideas. As one young woman stated, 'Sometimes it's important to me and sometimes it isn't.' One young man noted that conversations he has with others are infrequent and unemotional. However, he also noted that 'you have to be like a strong person, to be able to, like, take all the questions that people ask you'. When he talks with his friends, he tries to explain adoption as well as he can, but he says he would rather 'just like to have fun'. In general, adolescents in this group did not see adoption as being different from not being adopted: 'There's no difference between whether I was their child, their real child, or theirs like I am now.' 'You know you're adopted, you're adopted, you know. It's not any different than if you were not adopted.' Adoption in general does not appear to be very salient in their daily lives: 'I don't think too much about adoption. It's not a big issue in my life. I feel it's happened, you can't change that.' 'I'm fine with it [adoption] and it's just a thing of the past.'

Adolescents in the third group, *unsettled identity*, had narratives showing strong negative affect; however, their narratives were also coherent and integrated, marked by high exploration of adoptive identity and high salience of adoption. One adolescent stated, 'My mom [adoptive] and I aren't very close and I know that's [adoption] the reason. I mean if, I'm sure if I lived with my real mom we'd be a lot closer, we'd talk about it and that's just hard because all my friends can talk to their moms.' Another noted that he would never adopt a child: 'Well, hopefully, I won't have to adopt because I know what it is like for kids and the parents. Because, I mean, I feel different than them, and so I don't want my kids to feel different than me . . . I don't want to have my kids be adopted, because then I guess I would just feel less and less complete.'

Finally, adolescents demonstrating *integrated identity* had coherent narratives in which adoptive identity was highly salient and viewed positively. For example, one teenager said, 'When I was little I worried I was placed because she didn't want me. Now I know I was placed because she cared enough.' Another said:

> My dad [adoptive] *and I had a conversation once about if she* [birth mother] *thinks about me or if she just tried to forget about me. He just told me, he's like, 'don't worry about that. Ninety-five percent of the people that we've talked with still have never forgotten about their kids whether they be eighty years old or whether it just happened a week ago.' So, it makes me feel really good knowing that, you know, maybe she is – and especially right now being my birthday and everything. I wonder if she's thinking about me now because, like, she had me, you know, so . . .*

Although patterns of adoptive identity differed widely across adolescents, more positively resolved patterns were found among older rather than younger adolescents and girls rather than boys (Dunbar and Grotevant, 2004). Girls' levels of preoccupation about adoption (as measured by the Adoption Dynamics Questionnaire) were higher than those of boys, on average. However, differences in degree of preoccupation with adoption were not related to level of openness (Kohler *et al*, 2002).

Satisfaction with contact

The majority of adoptive family participants reported that they were either satisfied or very satisfied with the level of openness they were experiencing with the child's birth mother: 51.3 per cent of the adopted adolescents, 80.0 per cent of the adoptive mothers, and 82.3 per cent of the adoptive fathers. The teenagers reported that they hoped their contact with the birth mother either stayed the same (55.8 per cent) or increased (41.9 per cent) in the future. Only one adolescent (2.3 per cent) hoped it would decrease.

Adolescents who had contact with their birth mother reported greater satisfaction with their level of adoption openness than did adolescents having no contact. Satisfaction with openness was lower during middle adolescence (ages 14–16) than during early or late adolescence

(Mendenhall *et al*, 2004). Table 1 summarises rationales for levels of satisfaction held by adolescents having and not having contact. For example, one adolescent who was having contact and was satisfied stated:

I love her, she's awesome, and she's really supportive, really nice. Oh, it's like having another close older role model, like my parents. Yeah, it's a blessing I think, and it's really nice having an open adoption because you can just interact with her and like, know what she's like instead of wondering throughout your life what your birth mom's like and everything. And I know her personality and so, it's good. It's also like having another family, sort of. I get lots of support from both of them. You'd want that, no matter what happens in my life, I'll know I have a lot of support.

In contrast, some adolescents were not satisfied with their level of openness, typically because they wanted more contact and felt unable to bring it about:

I'm curious to ask my birth mother about, like, if she still cares or thinks about me . . . or is interested in the things I am doing. That's one of the main reasons I want to meet her, I guess.

Other adolescents had no contact but were satisfied with that situation. One adolescent stated, 'Birth mothers should not know the location of the children they give up . . . the child is better off not knowing her . . . it would feel funny, you know, to meet her.' Another noted, 'Information exchange should not occur, it would confuse the kid.' And another said, 'My birth parents should not even care about, or contact me. It could mess up my life.'

In summary, the reasons behind levels of satisfaction coded from the adolescents' interviews provide an important window into how adopted adolescents think about contact. The ways of thinking are very diverse, as are the contact arrangements themselves.

Table 1
Adolescents' satisfaction with birth mother contact: reasons for those having and not having contact

	Contact	*No contact*
Satisfied	45.5% of sample • provided an opportunity for a relationship to emerge that would provide additional support for them • positive affect toward birth mother • felt that contact helped them better understand who they are • made them interested in having contact with other members of their birth family, such as siblings	17.1% of sample • felt that adoption was not an important part of their lives • felt it was not necessary to have contact • had generally positive felings about being adopted • feared contact might be a bad experience for them • felt they were better off where they were than had they been raised by their birth parents
Dissatisfied	16.3% of sample • wanted more intensity in the relationship than they currently had, but were not able to bring it about • felt that they could have good relationships with both adoptive and birth family members – did not have to choose one over the other • grateful to birth mother for making adoption plan for them	21.1% of sample • had negative feelings toward birth mother (such as anger, sadness, hurt, disappointment) • desired to have contact to answer identity-related questions about themselves • assumed birth mother had not made an effort to search for them • worried that adoptive parents or birth mother might feel bad about their pursuing contact • their own efforts to search had been unsuccessful

Percentages are based upon the 123 participants who indicated they were either satisfied or dissatisfied with contact; cases indicating "neutral" or "mixed/ ambivalent" were not included in this analysis.
From Berge *et al* (in press)

Curiosity and searching

Much of the literature about searching for birth parents has focused on adult adoptees. Interviews with the adopted adolescents in our study have allowed us to gain insight into their thinking and actions regarding searching (see Wrobel *et al*, 2004, for details). This analysis involved the 93 adolescent participants who did not have ongoing direct contact with their birth mother. We divided them into four groups, based on their interview responses: a) those who said they would definitely not search or left open a very small possibility that they might search (34.4 per cent); b) those who said they might search in the future (24.7 per cent); c) those who would definitely search in the future (28 per cent); and d) those who had already embarked on a search (12.9 per cent).

Those most likely to search were among the older adolescents who experienced some contact (usually indirect) and were the least satisfied with the degree of openness. Search intentions or behaviour were not related to family functioning (as measured by the Family Assessment Device: Epstein *et al*, 1983) or adolescent problem behaviour (on the YSR or CBCL), contradicting reports in the literature that adoptees search for their birth parents because of their own adjustment difficulties or unsatisfactory relationships with their adoptive parents (Wrobel *et al*, 2004). Our data suggest that decision-making about searching is part of the normative developmental process for adolescent and young adult adoptees.

Curiosity about one's origins is a strong theme in this and other adoption studies. As one young woman stated, 'It's basic curiosity you know, wanting to know what they are like and wanting them to tell me why they gave me up for adoption, that sort of stuff. Just curiosity, basic curiosity. I think that explains it.'

However, some adolescents are less interested:

Other than the fact it would make sense to find out some medical history, I'm not in a big hurry [to meet birth parents]. *It would be kind of weird and I don't know what they could offer me other than just being new people to meet and that's how I would consider it, just new people to meet.*

The following quote, from an adolescent in a mediated adoption, illustrates how curiosity about birth parents and a strong desire to meet them does not negate the adolescent's positive views about her adoptive family.

I want to see what it's like. I want to see them. I want to meet them. I want to see what it's like to have a little brother. I think after I have contacted them once, I'd talk to them more frequently. You know, I mean, I'd never ditch the family I have now for them.

Changes in openness

A number of changes in openness occurred between placement and our first wave of data collection. Almost two-thirds of the fully disclosed adoptions did not begin that way: 51 per cent began as mediated and 15 per cent began as confidential adoptions. In many of these cases, trust and mutual respect were gradually established between the adoptive parents and birth mother, until they made the decision to share identifying information (Grotevant and McRoy, 1998).

The majority of adoptive families (71.8 per cent) remained within the same major openness level from Wave 1 to Wave 2. Smaller, and roughly equal, proportions of adoptive families increased in openness level (14.7 per cent) or decreased in openness (13.6 per cent). Of those families in fully disclosed arrangements at Wave 1, only 13.2 per cent stopped contact by Wave 2. Among adoptive families with ongoing mediated adoptions, almost equal numbers continued in this category (36 per cent), stopped contact (34 per cent), and increased to fully disclosed (30 per cent). Within the group of adoptive families in confidential arrangements at Wave 1, the majority (89.5 per cent) continued in confidential arrangements at Wave 2.

When there were decreases in openness in adoptive kinship networks, the birth mothers and adoptive parents tended to have both incongruent accounts regarding who initiated discontinuation of contact and divergent understandings about why contact stopped (Dunbar *et al*, 2000). In addition, adoptive parents were more satisfied when birth mothers respected their family's boundaries and let the adoptive family initiate most of the contact.

Members of adoptive kinship networks involved in ongoing contact found that their relationships were dynamic and had to be re-negotiated over time. Early in the adoption, meetings were especially important for the birth mothers, who were very concerned about whether they had made the right decision, whether their child was safe, and whether the adoptive parents were good people. After a while, birth mothers' interest in contact sometimes waned, especially as they were assured that their child was thriving. With the passage of time, many birth mothers became involved in new romantic relationships, sometimes taking attention away from the adoptive relationships. According to the adoptive parents, the ability of birth mothers to provide information when requested was not always in tune with the timing of the request (Wrobel *et al*, 2003). Adoptive parents tended to become more interested in contact as they became more secure in their role as parents. As the children grew older and understood the meaning of adoption (see Brodzinsky *et al*, 1984), their questions tended to put pressure on the adoptive parents to seek more information or contact (Wrobel *et al*, 1998, 1999).

The maintenance of open adoptions is a complex dance in which the roles and needs of the participants change over time, affecting the kinship network as a whole (Grotevant *et al*, 1998). Even though most adoptions that involved fully disclosed contact remained that way, there was no uniform pattern for change or continuity in the details of daily contact – kinship networks have contact by different means, among different people, at varying rates, and with varying degrees of interest. Successful relationships in such complex family situations hinge on participants' flexibility, communication skills and commitment to the relationships.

Discussion

We have drawn several consistent general conclusions from this project with implications for practice and policy. First, one type of adoption arrangement is not "best" for all adoptive kinship networks and further, within a kinship network, what works well for one party at one point in time may not be the best for other parties (Grotevant and McRoy, 1998). Most child outcomes we have studied (e.g., child self-esteem, child adjustment, adolescent adjustment) are not significantly related to the level of openness in the child's adoption. Instead, family process variables, such as the adoptive parents' perceptions of child compatibility, appear to have greater implications for adjustment outcomes than openness levels *per se*. We are continuing to explore processes such as empathic understanding, communication, and collaboration in relationships that are related to outcomes for adoptive kinship network members.

Second, contact brings with it additional relationships with their attendant joys and complexities. Deciding what kind of contact to have, how frequently to have it and with whom requires consideration of the needs and desires of different kinship network members (Grotevant and McRoy, 1997; Grotevant *et al*, 1998). And because relationships are not static, it means that these considerations must be re-visited periodically.

Implications for practice

Since there are such wide individual differences in children's and adolescents' adaptation to adoption, school personnel and clinicians should be acquainted with the diversity of ways in which adoptive identity may be explored. Support groups for adolescents exploring identity issues should be normalised and available. Similarly, professionals who work with parents of more than one adopted child (particularly with different openness arrangements) should help them see that their children may not experience identity development in the same way.

Second, while agency staff might try to match birth mothers and adoptive parents by their openness preferences at the time of placement, our findings suggest that no one can predict what the parties' preferences will be in the future. Practitioners can educate adoptive kinship network members to expect and prepare for change over the course of the adoption, since changes in type, frequency, mode of contact, and relationships seem to be the rule rather than the exception. Agency staff can help kinship members negotiate any difficulties that may derive from changes in openness or in relationships. They can develop appropriate ways to assist the contact process and can offer post-adoption services in the event that issues surrounding openness arise. These services should be designed to respond to a diversity of needs. In order to provide effective services, agency staff need training and knowledge about the issues encountered in different openness arrangements as well as the outcomes most commonly associated with them.

Further, the needs of children themselves – unknowable at placement in the case of infant placements – will also be likely to differ. At adolescence, for example, some young people desire contact but do not actively seek it for fear they might offend their adoptive parents. In this case, agency staff could facilitate the process by helping the adoptive parents and adopted child talk about their feelings concerning contact with birth relatives. Other adolescents desire no contact with birth family members and are happy with their lives as they are. Agency staff and adoption professionals should be aware that desire for contact can be influenced by many factors including developmental level, understanding of adoption, prior experiences of the child with birth parents, and current circumstances. Therefore, it should not be assumed that either a desire to search or a desire not to have contact is problematic (Wrobel *et al*, 2004). Both are legitimate feelings and highlight the fact that openness arrangements may differ across the lifespan.

Finally, agency staff serving as the link in mediated (indirect) adoptions have a very special responsibility, since they serve as information gatekeeper between the adoptive and birth family members. Prompt responsiveness to clients' communications is essential, as is communication with kinship network members about impending changes at the agency (e.g., staff or workload) that may affect the information flow in their adoption.

Implications for policy

Now that a growing body of research about openness is being published, legal and policy initiatives should be based on scientifically credible findings about openness rather than myths, suppositions or traditions. In the case of the present research, policy should be guided by our findings suggesting that openness is not inherently problematic or harmful for children and that many participants in open arrangements consider them to be very positive. Legal procedures related to initiating and maintaining openness should provide mechanisms for voluntary agreements, for the ability of agreements to be re-negotiated, and for the availability of professionals who can assist kinship networks experiencing difficult transitions. The formulation of effective policy also requires further ongoing research aimed at revealing how adoption processes play out over time in the lives of adoptive kinship network members.

Summary headlines

Three main aims
- To examine consequences of variations in openness in adoption for adopted children across time.
- To examine patterns of change and continuity in contact over time.
- To elucidate the family processes in adoptive kinship networks in which contact was occurring.

Three main findings
- Contact between adopted children and their birth mothers does not appear to be harmful to the children.
- Contact may be helpful, and child outcomes are better when the adults involved in the contact interact in a collaborative manner, with the child's best interests in mind.
- Each type of openness arrangement presents distinctive challenges and opportunities.

Three main implications
- The level of openness should be decided on a case-by-case basis.
- Adoptive kinship network members should anticipate the possibility of changes in openness over time.
- Legal procedures related to initiating and maintaining openness should provide mechanisms for voluntary agreements, for the ability of agreements to be re-negotiated, and for the availability of professionals who can assist kinship networks experiencing difficult transitions.

References

Achenbach, T. M. and Edelbrock, C. (1983) *Manual for the Child Behavior Checklist and Revised Child Behavior Profile*, Burlington, VT: University of Vermont Department of Psychiatry.

Achenbach, T. M. and Edelbrock, C. (1987) *Manual for the Youth Self-Report and Profile*, Burlington, VT: University of Vermont Department of Psychiatry.

Berge, J. M., Mendenhall, T. J., Wrobel, G. M., Grotevant, H. D. and McRoy, R. G. (in press) 'Adolescents' feelings about openness in adoption: implications for adoption agencies', *Child Welfare*.

Brodzinsky, D. M., Singer, L.M. and Braff, A. M. (1984) 'Children's understanding of adoption', *Child Development*, 55, pp. 869–878.

Derogatis, L. R. (1993) *Brief Symptom Inventory: Administration, scoring, and procedures manual*, Minneapolis: National Computer Systems.

Dunbar, N. (2003) *Typologies of Adolescent Adoptive Identity: The influence of family context and relationships*, Unpublished doctoral dissertation, St Paul: University of Minnesota.

Dunbar, N. and Grotevant, H. D. (2004) 'Adoption narratives: the construction of adoptive identity during adolescence', in M. W. Pratt and B. H. Fiese (eds.), *Family Stories and the Life Course: Across time and generations*, Mahwah, NJ: Erlbaum.

Dunbar, N., van Dulmen, M. H. M., Ayers-Lopez, S., Berge, J. M., Christian, C., Fitzgerald, N., Gossman, G., Henney, S., Mendenhall, T., Grotevant, H. D. and McRoy, R. G. (2000, November), *Openness Changes in Adoptive Kinship Network Connections*, Paper presented at the meeting of the National Council on Family Relations, Minneapolis.

Epstein, N. B., Baldwin, L. M. and Bishop, D. (1983) 'The McMaster Family Assessment Device', *Journal of Marital and Family Therapy*, 9(2), pp. 171–180.

Erikson, E. H. (1968) *Identity: Youth and crisis*, New York: Norton.

Grotevant, H. D. (1993) 'The integrative nature of identity: bringing the soloists to sing in the choir', in J. Kroger (ed.), *Discussions on Ego Identity* (pp. 121–146), Hillsdale, NJ: Erlbaum.

Grotevant, H. D. (1997) 'Coming to terms with adoption: the construction of identity from adolescence into adulthood', *Adoption Quarterly*, 1(1), pp. 3–27.

Grotevant, H. D., Dunbar, N., Kohler, J. K. and Esau, A. L. (2000) 'Adoptive identity: how contexts within and beyond the family shape developmental pathways', *Family Relations*, 49, pp. 379–387.

Grotevant, H. D. and McRoy, R. G. (1997) 'The Minnesota/Texas Openness in Adoption Research Project: Evolving policies and practices and their implications for development and relationships', *Applied Developmental Science*, 1, pp. 166–184.

Grotevant, H. D. and McRoy, R. G. (1998) *Openness in Adoption: Connecting families of birth and adoption*, Thousand Oaks, CA: Sage.

Grotevant, H. D., McRoy, R. G. and Jenkins, V. Y. (1988) 'Emotionally disturbed adopted adolescents: early patterns of family adaptation', *Family Process*, 27, pp. 439–457.

Grotevant, H. D., McRoy, R. G. and van Dulmen, M. H. (1998) 'The adoptive kinship network: putting the perspectives together', in H. D. Grotevant and R. G. McRoy, *Openness in Adoption: Connecting families of birth and adoption* (pp. 173–194), Thousand Oaks, CA: Sage.

Grotevant, H. D., Ross, N. M., Marchel, M. A. and McRoy, R. G. (1999) 'Adaptive behavior in adopted children: predictors from early risk, collaboration in relationships within the adoptive kinship network, and openness arrangements', *Journal of Adolescent Research*, 14, pp. 231–247.

Grotevant, H. D., Wrobel, G. M., van Dulmen, M. H. and McRoy, R. G. (2001) 'The emergence of psychosocial engagement in adopted adolescents: the family as context over time', *Journal of Adolescent Research*, 16, pp. 469–490.

Harter, S. (1985) *Manual for the Self-perception Profile for Children*, Denver: University of Denver.

Henney, S. M., Onken, S. J., McRoy, R. G. and Grotevant, H. D. (1998) 'Changing agency practices toward openness in adoption', *Adoption Quarterly*, 1(3), pp. 45–76.

Henney, S., McRoy, R. G., Ayers-Lopez, S. and Grotevant, H. D. (2003) 'The impact of openness on adoption agency practices: a longitudinal perspective', *Adoption Quarterly*, 6(3), pp. 31–51.

Kohler, J. K., Grotevant, H. D. and McRoy, R. G. (2002) 'Adopted adolescents' preoccupation with adoption: impact of adoptive family dynamics', *Journal of Marriage and the Family*, 64, pp. 93–104.

Mendenhall, T. J., Berge, J. M., Wrobel, G. M., Grotevant, H. D. and McRoy, R. G. (2004) 'Adolescents' satisfaction with contact in adoption', *Child and Adolescent Social Work Journal*, 21, pp. 175–190.

Miller, N. B. (1987) *Scales and Factors of the Child Adaptive Behavior Inventory*, Unpublished manuscript, Becoming a Family Project, Berkeley, CA: University of California.

Ross, N. M. (1995) *Adoptive Family Processes that Predict Adopted Child Behavior and Self-esteem*, Unpublished master's thesis, St Paul: University of Minnesota.

Wrobel, G. M., Grotevant, H. D., Berge, J. M., Mendenhall, T. J. and McRoy, R. G. (2003) 'Contact in adoption: the experience of adoptive families in the USA', *Adoption & Fostering*, 27(1), pp. 57–67.

Wrobel, G. M., Grotevant, H. D. and McRoy, R. G. (2004) 'Adolescent search for birth parents: who moves forward?', *Journal of Adolescent Research*, 19, pp. 132–151.

Wrobel, G. M., Kohler, J. K., Grotevant, H. D. and McRoy, R. G. (1998) 'Factors related to patterns of information exchange between adoptive parents and children in mediated adoptions', *Journal of Applied Developmental Psychology*, 19, pp. 641–657.

Wrobel, G. M., Kohler, J. K., Grotevant, H. D. and McRoy, R. G. (1999) 'The family adoption communication model (FAC): identifying pathways of adoption-related communication', in M. Johnson (ed.), *Proceedings of the 29th Annual Theory Construction and Research Methodology Workshop of the National Council in Family Relations*.

3 A longitudinal perspective on changes in adoption openness: The birth mother story

Susan M. Henney, Susan Ayers-Lopez,
Ruth G. McRoy and Harold D. Grotevant

This study was supported by grants from the National Institute of Child Health and Human Development, DHHS Office of Population Affairs; the Hogg Foundation for Mental Health; and the University Research Institute of the University of Texas at Austin. Manuscript preparation was supported by a grant from The Lois and Samuel Silberman Fund, New York, NY. The authors also wish to thank the birth mother participants who generously gave of their time and willingly shared their experiences in this longitudinal study. Correspondence should be directed to Ruth G. McRoy, University of Texas, School of Social Work, 1 University Station D3510, Austin, Texas 78712-0359; Tel: (512) 471 0551; email: r.mcroy@mail.utexas.edu

* * *

The life course of an open adoption has been minimally addressed in the adoption literature. This chapter presents the Wave 2 findings of a nationwide, longitudinal study of birth mothers' perceptions of and experiences with openness in adoption in the USA. One hundred and twenty-seven birth mothers completed telephone interviews that produced a rich array of data providing substantive information and insight into the experiences of this sample of women who placed their children for adoption 12–20 years ago. These data were analysed both quantitatively and qualitatively, resulting in a unique picture of these women's satisfactions and dissatisfactions with their openness arrangements and the course of their adoption openness.

In the USA, the decreasing societal stigma against, and increasing support systems for, single parenting, along with the wider availability of abortion, have been associated with a concurrent reduction in the number of children placed for adoption (Bachrach *et al*, 1992; Donelly and Voydanoff, 1991; McLaughlin *et al*, 1988). Although recent data are not available, during 1982–1988 about two per cent of unmarried women in the USA placed their child for adoption (Bachrach *et al*, 1992). This decision occurs for all birth mothers within their own developmental context and within the framework of their perceived current and future life tasks, whether the adoption choice is made as an adolescent, young adult or older adult.

For many women the adoption decision today has the added dimension of the possibility of openness. Openness in adoption can be broadly defined as a purposeful act of contact or communication between adoptive parents, adopted persons and birth families. Openness in an adoption can begin at any time prior to placement or after placement. In this research, openness is conceptualised as a spectrum involving differing degrees and modes of contact and communication between adoptive family members and the child's birth parent(s). At one end of the openness continuum are *confidential* adoptions, in which non-identifying information is shared between adoptive and birth family members and is never transmitted directly; any exchange of information typically stops with the adoptive placement or shortly thereafter. In the middle are *mediated* adoptions, those that are ongoing and those in which contact has stopped. Non-identifying information is shared between parties through adoption agency personnel. Sharing could include exchanges of pictures, letters, gifts, or infrequent meetings at which identifying information is not revealed. At the other end of the continuum are *fully disclosed* adoptions, which involve direct communication and full disclosure of identifying information between adoptive and birth families. These adoptions may involve face-to-face meetings, phone calls, letters sent directly, email, and sometimes contact with extended family members.

The act of communication in open adoptions may, for some birth mothers, unlock a satisfying and mutually agreeable long-term relationship with the adoptive family. For others, the communication is equally satisfying but is of short duration and is utilised to fill a void of knowledge about the adopted child. Still other birth mothers yearn for communication, but have none, and are dissatisfied with their lack of knowledge about the child or relationship with the adoptive family. The factors leading to satisfaction and dissatisfaction with adoption openness, or the lack thereof, are as varied as the life experiences of those involved in the adoption. This chapter explores various issues related to birth mothers' experiences of and attitudes about openness in adoption.

Study design and methodology

At Wave 1 (W1), 1987–1992, birth mothers and adoptive families were recruited for the study through 35 agencies located in 31 different states in all regions of the USA. A small number of birth mothers (15) were recruited through advertisements in newspapers and periodicals. For further information on the W1 sample, see Grotevant and McRoy (1997, 1998).

At Wave 2 (W2), 1995–2000, 127 birth mothers from the original sample participated again. The average age of the birth mothers at the W2 interview was 35.42 years (ranging from 29 to 54). The birth mothers' average family income was about $30,000 per year, with a range of less than $3,000 to more than $50,000. Slightly more than a third of birth mother participants had family incomes greater than $50,000. Birth mothers reported an average of 14.16 years of education (e.g., between two and three years of college), ranging from 10 to 20 years of education. One hundred-and-twenty-three birth mothers (97 per cent) were white/ Caucasian; two (two per cent) were Hispanic/Mexican American: one (one per cent) was Black/African American and one (one per cent) did not provide ethnicity information. Eighty-four birth mothers (66 per cent) were married, 25 (20 per cent) divorced and 18 (14 per cent) single.

All birth mothers in the study placed their children as infants voluntarily for adoption through private adoption agencies in the USA. None of the children in the study had been involuntarily removed from their birth mothers' homes. About half of the 127 reparticipating birth mothers (48 per cent) had their children when they were teenagers. Their age at delivery ranged from 14 to 36 (mean age = 19.3). At delivery, more than 90 per cent were single (never married). A majority of these birth mothers (76.4 per cent) did not believe they were ready to be parents. The most typical reason for placement was that the birth mother sought a better life for her child than she believed she could provide. Many of the birth mothers believed that adoption placement with a two-parent family would give the child more opportunities (75.6 per cent) or a more stable financial situation (62.7 per cent) than the birth mother could offer. Birth mothers also cited their marital status (55.2 per cent), age and lack of emotional maturity (54.8 per cent), problems with the birth father (44 per cent) or their own family (34.4 per cent), and a desire to complete their education (34.4 per cent) as factors in their decision to place. About half (53.2 per cent) reported personal beliefs against abortion that contributed to their unwillingness to terminate the pregnancy and subsequent placement decision.

At both waves, birth mothers were interviewed using a structured interview schedule and were administered several standardised question-naires. The four major topics assessed in the interview include birth mothers' adjustment to the adoption decision, changes in openness, relationship with the adoptive parents, and relationship with the adopted adolescent. In reference to openness, each birth mother described, via a structured openness checklist, the degree to which there has been identi-fied or non-identified information sharing and contact between the birth mother and the adoptive parents and/or the adopted child.

The birth mother interview was coded using several discrete and qualitative codes to achieve different levels of specificity as to the nature of the openness arrangement and changes in openness. The most detailed code is the openness changes code, wherein information from the inter-view was used to create a list of each change that occurred in the adoption arrangement from the time of the placement through the W2 interview. These openness changes included changes in frequency, category, persons involved in contact, etc. Each change was then rated as an increase, decrease, mixed (an aspect of openness increased and another decreased simultaneously), or stable (not technically an increase or decrease) open-ness change. Each birth mother was also assigned a specific, descriptive nine-category openness code for both W1 and W2, the primary purpose of which is to allow descriptive analysis of birth mothers' openness situations. The definitions provided in Table 1 are standard across all triad members. Finally, the broadest conceptualisation of openness is represented by a four-category openness code. This code represents a reduction of the nine-category openness code for the purpose of statistical analysis. See Grotevant *et al* (Chapter 2) for a description of the four categories of openness.

Table 1

Nine-category openness definitions

Confidential	No information is shared between triad members beyond six months post-placement. Any information shared before six months is non-identified.
Confidential with updates	Information is given to update agency files after placement, and this information is not necessarily intended for current transmission.
Mediated stopped	Any contact has stopped for at least one year past the point when it normally should have occurred. Before the stop, all contact was arranged through the agency or agency personnel and occurred beyond six months after placement. Information shared was intended for the other party and was perceived as received.
Mediated stopped with updates	All criteria for mediated stopped adoptions are met, plus file updates have occurred at the agency.
Mediated paused	Contact has occurred through the agency, but there has been a temporary cessation of a regular pattern of contact without an agreement or a conscious decision to stop.
Mediated ongoing	Contact is occurring through the agency. Contact could be reciprocal or one-way only. The party sending believes the information is being received, and the party receiving believes it was transmitted with the other party's knowledge and approval.
Fully disclosed stopped	The parties have shared identifying information and/or contact directly, without agency mediation. The same rules for stopped contact that apply to mediated cases apply here.
Fully disclosed paused	The parties have shared identifying information and/or contact directly, without agency mediation. The same rules for paused contact that apply to mediated cases apply here.
Fully disclosed ongoing	The parties are or have shared identifying information and/or contact directly, without agency mediation. The same rules for ongoing contact that apply to mediated cases apply here.

Findings

Changes in birth mothers' openness arrangement over time

Using a broad conceptualisation of openness, birth mothers experienced changes in openness from W1 to W2. These changes were primarily experienced by the birth mothers who were in ongoing mediated adoptions at W1. Of the 44 birth mothers involved in an ongoing mediated adoption at W1, 52.3 per cent had experienced an increase to fully disclosed or a decrease to mediated stopped at W2. Using only the four-category code, only 8.7 per cent of those involved in a confidential adoption at W1 had experienced a change in openness category to mediated or fully disclosed at W2, and one birth mother involved in a mediated stopped adoption at W1 had resumed contact so her adoption changed to the ongoing mediated category at W2.

The more descriptive nine-category openness classification of the 127 reparticipating birth mothers is presented in Table 2. Overall, 50 of the 127 birth mothers (39.4 per cent) in our sample experienced a change in openness category from W1 to W2. Of these birth mothers, 29 (58 per cent) experienced an increase in openness and 21 (42 per cent) experi-

Table 2
Birth mothers' nine-category openness at Wave 1 and Wave 2

	Wave 1 (N = 127)	Wave 2 (N = 127)
Confidential	23 (18.1%)	8 (6.3%)
Confidential with updates	11 (8.7%)	23 (18.1%)
Mediated stopped	14 (11%)	22 (17.3%)
Mediated stopped with updates	1 (.8%)	7 (5.5%)
Mediated paused	2 (1.6%)	6 (4.7%)
Mediated ongoing	42 (33.1%)	17 (13.4%)
Fully disclosed paused	0	0
Fully disclosed stopped	0	1 (.8%)
Fully disclosed ongoing	34 (26.8%)	43 (33.9%)

enced a decrease in openness. Most increases were from confidential to confidential with updates (41.4 per cent of increases) or from ongoing mediated to ongoing fully disclosed (31 per cent of increases). Most decreases were from ongoing mediated to mediated stopped (52.4 per cent of decreases) or from ongoing mediated to mediated paused (28.6 per cent of decreases).

Fluctuations in contact for birth mothers with experiences of openness

As the analysis of birth mothers' openness in adoption progressed, it became clear that changes in openness category did not tell the full story of the course of birth mothers' openness across time. Many birth mothers who had contact at W2 or had contact sometime between Waves 1 and 2 had experienced fluctuations in that contact. Fluctuations in contact are conceptualised as changes in frequency, person(s) contacted, or mode of contact (i.e., beginning phone calls in an already fully disclosed adoption), and can be within-category increases in contact, decreases in contact, mixed, or stable.

Of the 58 birth mothers in mediated and fully disclosed adoptions who had not changed their openness category from W1 to W2, most did experience some fluctuations in contact within those categories. Fourteen birth mothers (24.1 per cent) experienced no fluctuations in contact within their openness category from W1 to W2. Birth mothers in ongoing fully disclosed adoptions experienced the most fluctuations overall, accounting for two-thirds of all fluctuations within openness category. Thus, although birth mothers in fully disclosed adoptions cannot technically make many changes in terms of openness category (i.e., they can only move to fully disclosed paused or stopped), they do experience more "action" or movement within their openness category than do birth mothers in mediated adoptions.

Overall, most of the birth mothers in this sample had experienced some type of openness change or fluctuation over the course of their adoption. Only 13 birth mothers (10.2 per cent) experienced no changes in openness of any type from the time of placement through W2. Those experiencing changes had an average of 2.4 changes over the history of their adoption.

Satisfaction with openness

It is clear at W2 that the birth mother's satisfaction with openness is related to her four-category openness (See Table 3). Specifically, 52 per cent of birth mothers involved in confidential adoptions were dissatisfied or very dissatisfied with their openness arrangement, and 32 per cent were satisfied or very satisfied. The situation is dramatically different for those in fully disclosed adoptions. Seventy-nine per cent of those in a fully disclosed arrangement were satisfied or very satisfied with their openness at W2, and only one fully disclosed birth mother reported being dissatisfied or very dissatisfied.

Table 3

Relationship between birth mothers' openness category and satisfaction with openness at Wave 2

	Dissatisfied or very dissatisfied	Mixed	Satisfied or very satisfied
Confidential	16 (51.6%)	5 (16.1%)	10 (32.3%)
Mediated stopped	12 (41.4%)	5 (17.2%)	12 (41.4%)
Mediated ongoing	10 (43.5%)	7 (30.4%)	6 (26.1%)
Fully disclosed	1 (2.3%)	8 (18.6%)	34 (79.1%)

*Note: Percentages are by openness category, not as a per cent of total sample.

We also found that W2 satisfaction with openness is related to whether the birth mothers' openness category had increased, decreased, or remained the same from W1 to W2. Specifically, those whose openness category had decreased or increased were less satisfied with their current openness than were those whose openness category remained stable. Of the 21 birth mothers (42 per cent) who experienced a decrease in openness from W1 to W2, 11 (52 per cent) were dissatisfied or very dissatisfied with their current openness, while only seven (33 per cent) were satisfied or very satisfied and three (14 per cent) reported mixed satisfaction. In contrast, 44 (58 per cent) of birth mothers who remained stable in their openness category from W1 to W2 were satisfied or very satisfied with their current openness. Those who experienced an increase were fairly evenly distributed across the satisfaction continuum.

Satisfaction and problems with current openness

In an effort to understand which aspects of each openness arrangement were satisfying or dissatisfying to the birth mothers in this sample, we analysed birth mother responses to the following two questions: 'What are some of the satisfactions you've encountered in the current type of adoption you have?' and 'What are some of the problems you've encountered in the current type of adoption you have?'

One-hundred-and-thirteen birth mothers (89 per cent) responded with 291 satisfying aspects of their current openness arrangement, while 13 birth mothers in the sample (10 per cent) indicated there were no satisfying aspects, and one birth mother did not answer the question. When birth mothers were asked about problems they had experienced in their openness arrangement, 97 (76 per cent) responded with 185 problems. Twenty-nine birth mothers (23 per cent) responded that they did not have any problems or issues with their openness, and one birth mother was not asked the question.

Confidential adoptions

When asked about satisfying aspects of their openness arrangement, the most frequent response for birth mothers in confidential adoptions was that they experienced no satisfactions in the adoption (35 per cent). When a satisfaction was stated, it was most frequently the belief that the adoptive parents are good people or good parents (19 per cent). Birth mothers felt this way for a variety of reasons, including the belief that the agency screened the adoptive parents thoroughly, being told that the parents wanted a baby very badly, or being told that the agency had chosen the type of family that the birth mother wanted. Birth mothers who had received updated information through the agency were pleased with the information they received or happy that if there is an emergency, the parties can contact each other through the agency. Nine birth mothers (29 per cent) felt that confidential adoptions are best for the adoptive parents, the adopted adolescent or themselves. They believed that the adopted adolescent and the adoptive parents would not experience confusion about who the parent is, adoptive parents feel safer, and that birth mothers are better able to handle a confidential adoption.

Birth mothers in confidential adoptions considered their primary openness-related problems to be worry about the adopted adolescent (52 per cent) and having no (39 per cent) or not enough (23 per cent) information. Some of the birth mothers worried about the health of the adopted adolescent because their parented children had developed serious medical problems, some of which had been fatal. Others worried that the adopted adolescent would inherit family characteristics that would give them trouble, such as being overly sensitive or thrill seeking. However, the majority of the birth mothers had generalised worries about the adopted adolescent's well-being because they had no information, rather than having a specific reason to be worried. A common fear was that the adopted adolescent may die or become seriously ill and that the birth mother would not be told. One birth mother checked back with the agency, and she was told that she would not be notified if something happened to the adopted adolescent. This birth mother stated, 'I could be waiting to meet her and she could already be gone [dead].' Twenty-three of the 31 birth mothers in confidential adoptions had either left medical updates in their file at the agency or had requested that agency personnel check with the adoptive family to let them know if the adopted adolescent was alive and healthy.

Mediated stopped

Birth mothers in mediated stopped adoptions most frequently mentioned the letters and information they received in the past as the most satisfying aspect of their adoption (26 per cent). It should be noted that some birth mothers who were thankful for the letters they received in the past were dissatisfied about the letters stopping. The next most frequent satisfactions mentioned were feeling that this type of openness was best for her (23 per cent), feeling that the adoptive parents are good people/parents (20 per cent), knowing the adopted adolescent is alive and thriving (17 per cent), and believing that the agency handled the adoption well (17 per cent). Birth mothers who believed that a mediated stopped adoption was best for them were happy with the information they received in the beginning, but felt that they didn't need it anymore. Several used the term "closure". Only one birth mother felt that she had no satisfactions in this openness arrangement.

As with the birth mothers in confidential adoptions, worrying about the adopted adolescent (23 per cent) was a concern for birth mothers in mediated stopped adoptions. One birth mother expressed her worries:

I think I have the common worries. Every once in a while it'll cross my mind – Is she alive? Did she die of cancer? Has she been in a car accident? Did she die in a car accident?

Several birth mothers in mediated stopped adoptions felt that they did not have enough information about the adopted adolescent and one birth mother said she had no information.

Twenty per cent of birth mothers in mediated stopped adoptions stated that one of their greatest problems was that the adoptive parents had not upheld the agreement for contact or had discontinued contact in situations where there was no stated agreement. Some birth mothers felt the agency guaranteed a certain amount of contact, such as a letter with pictures once a year. Other birth mothers had no expectations of the amount of contact that would occur but were disappointed, just the same, when the adoptive parents discontinued it. Some were mildly disappointed, yet were able to empathise with the adoptive parents, while others were hurt and angry.

Mediated ongoing

Eighty-two per cent of birth mothers in mediated ongoing adoptions reported satisfaction in knowing about the adopted adolescent's life – what goes on, milestones, interests, etc. They also expressed satis-faction about receiving letters (76 per cent), in knowing that the adopted adolescent was alive and thriving (71 per cent) and in receiving pictures (71 per cent). Forty-one per cent mentioned that mediated ongoing adoption was best for the birth mother. Birth mothers described a sense of peace from knowing that the adopted adolescent was developing normally and was happy. Only one birth mother felt that she had no satisfaction in this openness arrangement.

Some birth mothers in mediated ongoing adoptions had problems similar to birth mothers in mediated stopped adoptions. Forty-one per cent believed that the adoptive parents had not upheld the contact agree-ment or wanted to stop the contact. In some cases, the birth mothers were disappointed that the frequency of contact had declined, for example, from receiving one letter per year to receiving one letter every three years. Others continued to write to the adoptive parents, even though they had stopped responding. Birth mother responses ranged from acceptance to feelings of betrayal. Birth mothers who felt that a clear agreement was violated by the adoptive parents tended to be angrier.

> . . . *it helps you to know you're going to get letters and pictures all her life. And then you don't. And there's nothing you can do about it . . . it makes you mad.*

Waiting for the adoptive parents to respond to their correspondence was difficult for 29 per cent of the birth mothers in mediated ongoing adoptions. Twenty-nine per cent of the birth mothers also believed they did not have enough information about the adopted adolescent. These birth mothers desired things like recent photos, rather than photos of the adopted adolescent as a baby, or to know the first names of the adoptive parents and the adopted adolescent.

Fully disclosed

The 44 birth mothers in fully disclosed adoptions reported a total of 118 satisfactions in their openness arrangement. The primary satisfaction for birth mothers in fully disclosed adoptions was getting to know the adopted adolescent and developing a relationship with him or her (57 per cent). One birth mother described this as, 'the sheer happiness at being able to interact with him'. Another said, 'That I know who she is.' Also frequently mentioned was knowing what was going on in the adopted adolescent's life (45 per cent) and knowing the adopted adolescent is alive and thriving (34 per cent). Thirty-two per cent of the birth mothers in fully disclosed adoptions felt that this type of openness was best for them. No birth mothers in fully disclosed adoptions felt they had no satisfactions.

Problems reported in confidential and mediated adoptions were more similar to each other in type and frequency than to problems reported in fully disclosed adoptions. Twenty-five per cent of the birth mothers in fully disclosed adoptions felt that their primary problem was in their role and relationship development with the adoptive family. This issue was not mentioned in any other openness arrangement. Some birth mothers talked about situations in which they did not know what to say and what not to say, did not know when they were overstepping their boundaries, and did not know what their role should be with the adopted adolescent. 'Well, there wasn't a map. That's probably the biggest [problem] . . . we were real pioneers with that.' Sixteen per cent of the birth mothers mentioned issues so unique to their situations that they could not be grouped. For example, one birth mother was anxious about the interactions between her own parents and the adoptive parents. Another birth mother wondered if the adopted adolescent would lose interest in their relationship as she matured.

Birth mothers in fully disclosed adoptions also reported that they worried about the adopted adolescent (14 per cent), but their worry stemmed from issues that they knew about, such as difficulties the adolescent is having in school, rather than what isn't known, as is the case in mediated and confidential adoptions. Some similarity can be found in fully disclosed and ongoing mediated adoptions in the interactions they have with the adoptive parents. Eighteen per cent of the birth mothers in fully disclosed and paused/ongoing mediated adoptions reported that personality or parenting style differences created some issues for them in the adoption, as compared to nine per cent in stopped mediated adoptions.

Discussion

We have found it necessary to look at openness through a variety of lenses at different levels of "resolution" to get the full picture of openness for these women. Although 60 per cent of birth mothers were stable in their four-category openness arrangement from W1 to W2, only 10 per cent of the birth mothers did not experience a change *of any kind* from W1 to W2. This means that using the broadest conceptualisation of openness, stability is evident, but when looking at the specifics of birth mothers' actual, day-to-day contact, change is quite apparent. Therefore, stability in openness overall was not the experience of most birth mothers *in practice*, indicating that one of the important aspects of the "life course" of an adoption is change in openness.

Openness itself is not a static concept. Adoption agency support of openness, societal opinions about openness, and triad members' willingness or demand to participate in openness have changed considerably over time (Baumann, 1997; Henney *et al*, 2003; Sachdev, 1989; Weir, 2000). Even the manner in which we have defined openness has changed and become more sophisticated as our understanding of the multiple categories and facets of open adoption has evolved. Openness is also not static in practice. In most adoptions there is a range of opportunities for parties in the adoption to initiate, decrease, or increase openness over time. However, opportunities for change may be passed by or declined for many reasons, even in adoptions in which changes in openness ultimately do occur.

Most birth mothers did experience changes in openness from W1 to W2, with 50 per cent experiencing within-category fluctuations in frequency, person contacted and mode of contact, and about 40 per cent experiencing a categorical change in openness, with slightly more than half of these changes being increases. The largest increases in openness were from confidential to confidential with updates and from mediated ongoing to fully disclosed. The largest decrease in openness was from mediated ongoing to mediated stopped. Regarding the move from confidential to confidential with updates, this indicates that many birth mothers are either actively seeking or actively providing updated information later in their adoptions – possibly as much as 21 years after the placement. These birth mothers are not necessarily seeking current contact, but rather may be interested in providing the means by which the adopted adolescent could contact them if so desired (i.e., by the birth mother updating her contact information at the agency) or by accessing the files for any updates from the adoptive family that may be available within the confines of confidentiality.

These findings may also have their roots in the developmental course that occurs over the lives of birth mothers and adoption. For example, the same developmental issue – the aging into adolescence of the adopted person – can be the catalyst for both increases and decreases in openness. For some women in confidential adoptions, the pre-teen and teen years of the adopted adolescent are a period of renewed interest in establishing contact, updating files with contact or personal information, and/or requesting information about the well-being of the adopted adolescent. For birth mothers in historically mediated adoptions, some have experienced an opening of the adoption to full disclosure, which is indicative of the relationship, trust and sense of connectedness that was built over the course of the mediated contact. For these women, the pre-teen and teen years of the adopted adolescent are times of opportunity for increased contact. Their ongoing connection with the adoptive family causes themselves, the adopted adolescent or the adoptive family to dispense with the barriers of mediated contact and request a more personal, one-on-one relationship. These birth mothers tend to believe that the adopted adolescent is at an age when he or she can emotionally and cognitively handle contact, although most are still careful and thoughtful about not interfering in the adopted adolescent's life or family.

On the other hand, for birth mothers who have experienced a stop or reduction in their mediated contact, the pre-teen and teen years of the adopted adolescent can be a time of increased activity and/or turmoil for the adoptive family and for themselves because of family commitments. These stresses may cause either one or all parties to cease or reduce contact. Indeed, many of the birth mothers reported remembering their own adolescence as a turbulent and emotionally difficult time, and they do not want to burden the adopted adolescent or adoptive family with more contact than they can handle. It appears that these critical adolescent years may be turning points in openness, with busy lives, dissatisfaction with openness, family concerns and other situations for both birth mothers and adoptive parents causing decreases in openness for some. For others, similar circumstances may lead to increased comfort with openness and renewed interest in finding out more about the adopted adolescent.

Satisfaction with openness was one of the most interesting areas of inquiry regarding birth mothers at W2. Birth mothers were insightful about their desires regarding openness and were able to describe their satisfactions and dissatisfactions in this area. Although satisfaction with openness was not related to openness category at W1 of this study, by W2 birth mothers in fully disclosed adoptions were significantly more satisfied with their adoption arrangements than those in other openness categories. At W2, birth mothers in fully disclosed adoptions reported that being in direct contact with the adoptive family provided them with the satisfaction and pleasure of personally observing the adopted adolescent's development, happiness and adjustment, and of generally getting to know the adopted adolescent and being a part of his or her life. These birth mothers also enjoyed the specific knowledge they had about the adopted adolescent, such as talents and achievements.

In contrast, birth mothers in confidential adoptions were the most likely to report "no satisfactions" with their openness arrangement and were also the most likely to report worrying about the adopted adolescent due to their lack of contact. It is important to note, however, that some birth mothers were able to list satisfactions with their confidential adoptions. Birth mothers in mediated stopped adoptions were most likely to report worrying about the adopted adolescent due to lack of information, to report dissatisfaction with the amount of information they received, and to perceive that the adoptive parents had not upheld their contact agreement. Some birth mothers in mediated ongoing adoptions were also dissatisfied due to their perception that the adoptive parents were not upholding their contact agreement. These women also tended to indicate that they were not receiving enough information and were dissatisfied with the amount of time it took for the adoptive parents to respond to their contact. Many birth mothers in fully disclosed adoptions were enjoying a level of intimacy with and knowledge about their birth children that women in other openness categories cannot and do not have. Issues raised by some birth mothers in fully disclosed adoptions revolved around role and relationship development with the adoptive family. The women in other openness categories, perhaps influenced by media portrayals of increasing trends towards openness, were by W2 more aware of what they were missing in their lack of contact, particularly face-to-face contact, with the adoptive family.

Another substantial finding in terms of satisfaction is that birth mothers whose openness category remained stable from W1 to W2 were significantly more satisfied with openness than those whose openness category increased or decreased. Note that this only applies to openness category changes, not to non-categorical fluctuations in frequency, mode or person. There are several important facets to this finding. First, although change is a part of life in general and openness in particular, it is still stressful. Change requires adjustments, modifications and transitions, not only in the adoption, but also in the birth mothers' psyche, emotions, family life, and schedule. Although birth mothers initiate many changes in openness, initiating a change can add stress even if it is wanted and/or needed. Changes that are positive and work out as expected still require adjustments, and changes that have negative or unintended consequences (e.g., birth mother gives her phone number to the adoptive parents and gets more phone calls than anticipated) can require more emotional and behavioral adjustments and time for the adjustments to take root and become comfortable, if in fact they ever do.

Second, major changes, such as categorical changes in openness, probably require more time and energy for birth mothers to adjust, and the birth mothers' satisfaction is influenced by the perceived or actual difficulty of the change. When openness category is stable, there is comfort in the fact that one knows what will be happening into the future. This makes life planning easier and lowers the emotional upheaval of continual change. At a relatively young age, these women experienced the major life events of pregnancy, childbirth and adoption placement. Following this type of personal upheaval, the value of predictability and stability may increase. Many of these women are trying to maintain intimate relationships and possibly manage children and a career, and the upheavals of openness changes can divert their attentions from their own developmental pathways and cause emotional, familial and relational issues in their lives. Finally, these women have an ongoing concern for the well-being of the adopted adolescent. They may believe that stability in openness is beneficial for the adopted adolescent and wonder whether the stresses associated with openness changes will impact the adopted adolescent negatively.

These findings regarding openness 12–20 years after the adoption placement support findings from our earlier study that there is no one type of openness that fits every person's wants and needs. It is important to note, however, that this chapter focuses on the birth mother's perspective, and the corresponding adoptive parents and adopted adolescents might see the openness scenario in their adoptions quite differently. Nonetheless, birth mothers in the current study can list satisfactions and dissatisfactions with all adoption categories. Each openness arrangement comes with both high points and issues for all parties to cope with or work through. Some birth mothers in this study are satisfied with exactly the amount of contact they currently have – whether confidential, mediated or fully disclosed. Birth mothers who are satisfied with their confidential adoptions tend to be protective of their privacy and do not desire the emotional or relational complications that they perceive would be involved in opening contact with the adoptive family. On the other end of the openness continuum, many birth mothers in fully disclosed adoptions could not imagine their lives without fully disclosed contact with the adoptive family, particularly with their birth child, and are committed to maintaining that contact and to working out any problems that might arise.

It is also the case that other birth mothers desire a change to either more or less contact than they have, but are either reluctant to institute a change or are somehow blocked from making the desired change. This speaks to the importance of recognising, expecting and preparing for change in openness. Adoption practitioners need to be aware of the issues involved in matching birth mothers and adoptive parents by their openness preferences at the time of placement. No one has a "crystal ball" to see what the desires and needs of any adoption participant will be in the future. Any openness agreement negotiated, whether legally binding or not, should have provisions for negotiating changes in the future. Adoption professionals must provide counselling and training about how openness needs will most likely change for participants over time and discuss with them techniques to use when these needs diverge.

Summary headlines

Three main aims

- To examine patterns of change and stability in birth mothers' contact with the adoptive family over time.
- To trace birth mothers' satisfactions and dissatisfactions with their openness arrangement and the course of openness in their adoptions.
- To explore the practice factors associated with birth mothers' perspectives about, and needs related to, openness in adoption.

Three main findings

• Birth mothers experienced significant changes in openness from W1 to W2, both in terms of openness category and fluctuations in contact, when openness was defined in its most specific terms.

• Satisfaction with openness is related to openness category, with birth mothers in fully disclosed adoptions being more likely to be satisfied with their openness category than those in any other openness category.

• Birth mothers can list satisfactions and dissatisfactions with all openness categories.

Three main implications

• Adoption professionals should be aware of the importance of matching birth mothers and adoptive parents by their desire for openness, while assisting birth mothers to recognise, expect and prepare for both change and stability in openness.

• Through comprehensive education and counselling, birth mothers should be made aware of the prospective challenges and satisfactions that may be experienced in each openness arrangement.

• Adoption professionals should be available to birth mothers and other adoptive kinship network members over the life course of adoption to assist in renegotiation of contact agreements, resolution of contact-related difficulties, and adoption and openness-related counselling.

References

Bachrach, C. A., Stolley, K. S. and London, K. A. (1992) 'Relinquishment of premarital births: evidence from national survey data', *Family Planning Perspectives*, 24(1), pp. 27–32 and 48.

Baumann, C. (1997) 'Examining where we were and where we are: clinical issues in adoption 1985–1995', *Child and Adolescent Social Work*, 14(5), pp. 313–334.

Donelley, B. W. and Voydanoff, P. (1991) 'Factors associated with releasing for adoption among adolescent mothers', *Family Relations: Journal of Applied Family & Child Studies*, 40(4), pp. 404–410.

Grotevant, H. D. and McRoy, R. G. (1997) 'The Minnesota/Texas openness in adoption research project: evolving policies and practices and their implications for development and relationships', *Applied Developmental Science*, 1, pp. 166–184.

Grotevant, H. D. and McRoy, R. G. (1998) *Openness in Adoption: Exploring family connections*, Thousand Oaks, CA: Sage.

Henney, S. M., McRoy, R. G., Ayers-Lopez, S. and Grotevant, H. D. (2003) 'The impact of openness on adoption agency practices: a longitudinal perspective', *Adoption Quarterly*, 6(3), pp. 31–51.

McLaughlin, S. D., Pearce, S. E., Manninen, D. L. and Winges, L. D. (1988) 'To parent or relinquish: consequences for adolescent mothers', *Social Work*, 33(4), pp. 320–324.

Sachdev, P. (1989) *Unlocking the Adoption Files*, Lexington, MA: Lexington Books.

Weir, K. N. (2000) 'Developmental, familial, and peer deterrents to adoption placement', *Adoption Quarterly*, 3(3), pp. 25–50.

4 The "Contact after Adoption" study: indirect contact and adoptive parents' communication about adoption

Elsbeth Neil

Introduction

Indirect contact provides an opportunity for all parties to deal with the special challenges that adoption can bring. It is a potential route for the child and adopters to learn more about the birth family and can be a way for the child to learn that he or she is still cared about by birth relatives. Adoptive parents can use exchanges of information to introduce or ease communication about adoption, or to show their child they care about the birth family. For the birth family, indirect contact can provide much valued information about the welfare of their child. These are the kinds of reasons why indirect contact is planned for adopted children, but are these hopes realised in practice? Using data from the University of East Anglia (UEA) "Contact after Adoption" study, this chapter explores how indirect contact works (or doesn't work) in helping adoptive parents to help their child with identity issues. It also explores how adopters communicate about adoption, how indirect contact is viewed and used by adopters and how this relates to broader parenting characteristics, and how effective this type of contact is as a means of information exchange.

The "Contact after Adoption" study: key findings from Phase 1

Phase 1 of the "Contact after Adoption" study began in 1996, and it focused on children placed for adoption under the age of four years. Ten adoption agencies participated in the research and a cohort of children, placed for adoption or adopted during 1996–7, was identified. Social workers provided detailed, non-identifying information about 168 children by means of a postal questionnaire. The main aims of the questionnaire were to determine current practice in relation to openness in adoption and to consider whether contact arrangements bore any relationship to other characteristics of the cases. The results of the survey revealed that some form of post-adoption contact was planned for almost 90 per cent of children, the most common arrangement being infrequent, agency-mediated letter contact, in most cases with the birth mother. Face-to-face contact was planned for 17 per cent of the sample, although wide variations between agencies were noted. Such contact was largely planned for children adopted from public care, as opposed to children relinquished for adoption (Neil, 2000). In other words, it was the children with the *easiest* personal histories and the birth parents in the best psychosocial situations for which agencies were the *least* likely to plan face-to-face contact. The general view that came across from social workers about contact planning was that face-to-face contact is only appropriate in situations where a child has an established relationship with birth relatives, and that, in the absence of such a relationship, this type of contact was counter-productive or unnecessary. Although children's longer-term needs such as making sense of their identity and understanding their adoption story were acknowledged, face-to-face contact was rarely considered as a resource to the child in addressing these issues. The "standard" contact plan for children in the "Contact after Adoption" study was for letterbox contact, and the reason most commonly given for setting up this contact was to help the child with identity issues.

In the first phase of our research, we looked in detail at face-to-face contact with adult birth relatives. An interview study involving the adoptive parents of 35 children and the birth relatives of 15 children was conducted. In all these cases, it was planned for the child to have ongoing face-to-face contact with an adult birth relative. This study revealed a largely positive view of this type of contact, but outcomes varied from case to case. In all the variations as to how contact could be set up and managed, as well as all the differences between children and birth relatives, one thing stood out as being important in predicting how contact seemed to work out: the overall approach of adoptive parents to the whole issue of adoption and contact after adoption. Other authors have discussed differences between adoptive parents. Kirk (1964) argued that adopting differs in important respects to parenting by birth, and that adoptive parents vary in terms of the extent to which they acknowledge or deny these differences, with acknowledgement being the healthier position. Fratter (1996) reported that direct contact was most likely to succeed when adoptive parents approached it with an "openness of attitude". Grotevant and colleagues (1999) identified differences in the ability of adoptive parents to collaborate with birth parents. We found all of these ideas useful in understanding differences between adoptive parents in our sample. Some adopters seemed very keen on contact and were prepared to carry on trying to make it work, even if meetings were difficult: they were motivated by a strong belief in the value of the contact for the child and by an inclusive and understanding view of the birth family's situation, and they tended to have a secure but non-possessive view of their relationship with the child. Other adoptive parents did not feel so strongly that contact was important for adopted children – instead, relationships in the adoptive family were emphasised. They could find it hard to feel sympathetic towards birth relatives, especially when children had been poorly cared for, and they would prefer to stop contact rather than tolerate any difficulties in the arrangements. Obviously people did not fit neatly into two "types" of adopters, but we did find that adoptive parents had different capacities to imagine the viewpoints of the other parties in adoption – i.e., to empathise with the child as an adopted person and with the birth relatives (Neil, 2003). Parents who had higher empathy ratings were those who were more likely to feel positive about contact and to sustain face-to-face contact over time even when contact meetings could be difficult. The capacity to understand how other people might feel helped adopters to see beyond the immediate situation they were faced with. For example, an adopter would understand that, although contact meetings may mean very little to their young adopted child, in the future the child might feel upset or curious about their birth family and may want and need the contact.

We found that adoptive parents' characteristics could affect what type of contact arrangement they chose. About one-third of adoptive parents having face-to-face contact had definitely wanted this type of contact, and had fought to get it, sometimes in the face of disagreement from the adoption agency (Neil, 2002). People who had specifically wanted face-to-face contact, or who had agreed willingly to have such contact, were more likely to sustain contact and find it positive than were those who agreed to it reluctantly (Neil, 2002, 2003), as also reported in other research studies (e.g., Fratter, 1996; Berry et al, 1998). We also found that successful contact could help adopters to become more understanding of the birth family and to develop more empathic attitudes. Positive experiences of face-to-face contact won over some adopters who were initially anxious about having such contact. The experience of getting to know birth relatives as real people helped many adopters to feel less threatened about their own position and more understanding of the birth relatives' points of view (Neil, 2003). This implies that although adoptive parents have different attitudes, beliefs and values, these can be altered by experience.

"Contact after Adoption": Phase 2

Phase 2 of the study, funded by The Nuffield Foundation, began in 2001. We followed up the families having face-to-face contact who were interviewed in Phase 1, this time including interviews with the children: almost all the families who took part in Phase 1 were again included. Using a similar number of cases, we also explored indirect letter contact, by interviewing adopters, birth relatives and adopted children from the original questionnaire sample who had experience of this type of contact. At the time of this second phase, the adopted children ranged from age five to twelve, with most being aged seven to nine. We conducted 45 adopted child interviews, 62 adoptive parent/couple interviews, and 61 interviews with birth relatives. In all three groups, roughly half of the sample had been having face-to-face contact and half indirect (mediated letter) contact. We also used a range of standardised measures of child and adult adjustment.

The outcomes that are being considered in this second phase of the study include (for children) their understanding of and feelings about being adopted; their feelings of closeness to adoptive parents and birth relatives; feelings about contact and curiosity about birth relatives; self-esteem; and emotional and behavioural development. With adoptive parents the outcomes we have been focusing on are: empathy for the child as an adopted person; empathy for the birth relatives; relationships with the adopted child; satisfaction with and feelings about contact; stability of contact arrangements over time; and communication about adoption within the adoptive family. In this chapter we focus on indirect contact from the point of view of adoptive parents, based on our 33 interviews with the adoptive parents of 48 children.

How contact works (or doesn't work) to help parties understand each other

The extent to which one party in adoption can understand another is likely to be influenced by the amount, type and accuracy of information available about the other person. In other words, whether or not contact helps or hinders people's understanding of each other is likely to depend on the quality of information exchange that takes place. Information exchange can work on a number of levels. Firstly, there is the communication between the adoptive parents and the birth family. Secondly, there is the communication between adoptive parents and the child about the birth family. Thirdly, there is the direct involvement of the child in communication with the birth family. From our interviews with adopters, children and birth relatives, we would argue that the type of contact people were having (face-to-face or indirect) is less important than the quality of information exchange that takes place between parties. In some cases in our sample, indirect contact was working really well to facilitate communication on all three levels. When communication between adopters and birth relatives was good, adopters tended to identify the following types of benefits for themselves and their child:

- being able to answer child's questions, fill in gaps for their child;
- gaining a deeper, richer understanding of the birth history of their child;
- being able to show their child – either now or in the future – that they are not forgotten or rejected by their birth family.

For example, Darren was adopted at age three, and he had been physically abused when at home with his birth parents. The adopters and the birth mother had maintained indirect contact twice a year, and at the time we interviewed the family, Darren was ten. Darren's adoptive mum had been initially apprehensive about contact:

I didn't know if it was good or bad at that stage, because I'd never done it. I didn't really know much about how it would affect him or anything like that, so I thought, well, I'll see and we'll just see how it goes.

Over the seven years of Darren's placement, the twice-yearly contact had been kept up on both sides. Darren's birth mum sent news about her life and her other children. She included photos of the family and vouchers or a book for Darren's birthday. She was even able to talk in her letters about some of the difficult events that had led to the need for Darren to be adopted. She wrote her letters partly to Darren directly, and partly to the adoptive parents. For their part, Darren's adopters wrote letters of about two or three pages, talking about Darren's progress, his likes and dislikes and his personality. They included news about, and photos of, their whole family. When it was time to write to his birth mum, they invited Darren to be part of the process, and sometimes he wrote a few words or drew a picture.

The communication about adoption that was aroused by the contact had created some ups and downs over the years. At the age of about six or seven, Darren started to find the letters from his birth mum upsetting. They raised the question of "why" he was removed from home, and he had to take on board difficult information about his birth parents.

Within his own mind, he'd put his mum on this pedestal, which is OK to a certain extent, but . . . I thought he was making her into this grand person and he was blaming everything on his dad . . . and I was saying, 'we don't know' . . . In the end, the letters were quite upsetting him as well when he got them . . . I didn't know then whether to stop reading him the letters, but by that time he knew he got letters so he was expecting them.

Reading the letters and talking to his adoptive mum about them raised lots of questions and feelings for Darren. He and his mum often had long conversations, usually at bedtime. Darren's mum's view was that in the long term it would be helpful for him to have had these issues out in the

51

open, rather than living in fantasy or ignorance and finding out difficult information when he was older.

We had quite an emotional time of it, but I think my personal view is, in the long run it's going to be easier for him. Because when he grows up, and if he does ever want to find her, he'll always know what had happened and how [his birth mother's] life has gone on. I think more than anything else . . . it won't be a shock, it will just be something that he's always known . . . I feel that . . . yes, it has upset him, but it's also been quite a positive thing and he can talk about it and I think it's very important for them to talk about it and to be able to be quite comfortable. He knows pretty much all of it really, because it's come out gradually.

Darren's adoptive mum said that now he was older and understood more, he found the letter contact easier and he looked forward to hearing from his birth mother. In particular, she felt he took away from the letters a sense that his birth family still cared about him:

It's quite clear that she loved him and still loves him really and still thinks of him, so I think that's a positive thing. I mean, it's hard for a child to understand, but I think it's good for him to know that. I think that's a real, positive thing that comes out of the letter contact.

We also interviewed Darren, a highly articulate and well-adjusted boy. His view of contact fitted very much with that of his mum. He told us about how his feelings had changed over time:

The first letter I, I didn't know what it was about because, I was about four. And when I was about six . . . the letter I got from her, I started crying because my mum explained it all to me.

At age 10 he now thought getting the letters was good:

It is a nice feeling that she is actually able to contact me. 'Cause I feel, I still feel part of her if you know what I mean, I still feel that she is my mum and that, she, she still loves me because at the bottom of the letters, it says 'love from your dear mum'.

We found that both face-to-face and indirect contact could, as happened in Darren's case, be an effective means of facilitating understanding between parties and communication with the child about adoption, but this outcome was certainly not inevitable. We found that quality of information exchange could vary within both types of contact; as Grotevant *et al* emphasise (see Chapter 2), there is no one arrangement that is best for everyone. However, we did think that overall there were some important links between contact type and the quality of information exchange that people were able to achieve. In particular, it seemed that indirect contact, although it could result in good information exchange between all parties, presented many challenges along the way.

Barriers to achieving good-quality information exchange in indirect contact

We identified four issues that could hamper indirect contact acting as a means of effective information exchange between adoptive parents, birth relatives and adopted children. In outline these were:

- the rules and mechanics of letter exchange;
- birth relatives do not respond;
- the child is excluded;
- knowing what to write in letters.

The rules and mechanics of information exchange

In some cases no contact was ever established: indirect contact was the stated plan, but no letters had ever been sent by either party. We found great variation between agencies in terms of whether or not planned contact had occurred, this seeming to relate to the extent to which agencies actively facilitated such contact. Some agencies had one person clearly "in charge" of letterbox contact, while in other agencies responsibility for following up on post-adoption contact appeared much more haphazard. Some agencies intervened when planned contact was not initiated or maintained, other agencies did not.

Indirect contact was managed in a huge variety of ways. Variations included factors such as whether letters were automatically sent on to the

53

birth relatives, or if they had to be requested or collected; whether or not photographs or presents were allowed to be exchanged; whether or not letters were acknowledged, opened and read, copied and kept on file by the agency; and whether or not agencies involved themselves when a letter was late or did not arrive. Some adopters found these various rules and systems confusing or inefficient. Some people told us they experienced considerable delay in letters being forwarded on to or from the other party:

In the past there's been stuff sitting on a file that hasn't come to me and I know that because of the postmarks on the envelopes and I'm thinking 'well I'm sorry, this has been in your file for a year'.

In other cases, people did not receive acknowledgement of the receipt of their letter, or were not informed as to whether the letter had been collected or sent on to the other party. For some people this led to a sense that they were sending letters off into a void. Other people were mystified about why agencies did not automatically forward letters to birth relatives.

They don't even actually physically make a point of contacting her to say there's a letter. It's up to her to ring in and say 'is there anything for me?' . . . So I don't know if my letters are still sitting there . . . the procedure isn't the same each time which I find frustrating and a bit in-efficient . . . at the moment I think my letters are sitting there. Which is sad . . . I do truly want her to get the letters . . . I'm writing them for her . . . I want her to have them but there is nothing I can do about it.

In other cases, interviewees told us that it was hard to establish a dialogue with the other party, because letters were sent at the same time of year (e.g., at Christmas) and crossed over, rather than one person writing and then the other person responding. At the point of writing, therefore, the latest information they had on the other person was about a year old. For some people it felt hard to write a "response" with such a time gap: the letters became bulletins from each party to the other, rather than a responsive exchange. As Grotevant *et al* highlight in Chapter 2, mediated contact arrangements are reliant on the efficiency of agency procedures.

Birth relatives do not respond

A common problem with the sending and receipt of letters was that one party had sent letters but the other party had not responded (in almost all cases the non-responding party was the birth relative) or had only responded erratically (this could be either the adoptive parents or the birth relatives). The difficulties birth relatives can experience in beginning or maintaining letter contact are discussed in Chapter 4, so here we focus on adopters' views of one-way contact. In Phase 1, when we were looking at face-to-face contact, we found that different adopters responded quite differently to very similar situations. This also appears to be very much the case with indirect contact, and this can be seen in adopters' views about non-responding birth relatives. What adopters felt about birth relatives who did not respond seemed to depend heavily on the purpose they hoped that contact would serve and their expectations about the birth relative's response. Some adoptive parents had been prepared from the beginning that birth relatives would be unlikely to respond, and they accepted this and tried to imagine why people couldn't write back:

No I'm not expecting it because I couldn't ask her to do that . . . She can't give any more – she's given everything.

I just think she wanted to get on with her life, because it must have been painful for her.

In some cases where contact was one-way to birth relatives, adoptive parents still felt the contact could be a beneficial activity for themselves, the child or the birth family. For example, in some cases adoptive parents said that they thought contact could benefit themselves and the child because it was a symbol to the child of their acceptance of the birth family. As one adoptive mother put it:

I wanted him to see that I did want, I do want, his mum to know about him . . . I want him to know that's it alright. I want him to know that I want his mum to know about him. I want him to know that I do really have compassion for his mum.

In other cases, adopters said they felt that indirect contact was primarily to help the birth family, to reassure them that the child was OK. Some adoptive parents were quite happy to undertake writing letters, sending photographs, etc. for this purpose alone: they neither expected nor hoped for any reply. Some adopters were even glad or relieved that the contact was only one way. A letter would have made them feel uncomfortable or they worried that it might have upset the child. One adoptive father said:

I'd feel a lot less keen [if the birth mother wrote back] *'cos you'd almost feel like temporary parents. I would feel that . . . you know this sort of shadow family were there waiting to come back again at some stage and I don't think for a child that's good.*

Another mother said that she was "a right mess" every year when she had to write to the birth mother. It seemed to undermine her feelings about her own position as mum:

She's my daughter. Not her daughter. . . why should I have to tell her what she is up to and doing when she couldn't look after her. . . with all this contact, this one letter and whatever, you feel as though she is not yours. At all. And all you are doing is just looking after her for them.

In this case, the adoptive mum said she did regret that the birth mother did not reply to letters, as she would have liked something on file in case her daughter went looking for more information later. But she would not have wanted any letters from the birth mother *sent on* to her or her daughter, as she thought this would be unsettling for both.

From the point of view of other adoptive parents, when birth relatives did not write back this could be confusing, disappointing and in some cases undermining of positive feelings. Some adoptive parents had entered into the contact arrangement in the hope that they and the child would receive information about the birth family and/or reassurance that the child was still cared about. When this was adoptive parents' understanding of the purpose of contact, then obviously they hoped for and expected replies. If none came, it was not knowing why that was difficult. Most of the time when this happened there was simply no information to go on. In the absence of alternative explanations some adoptive parents concluded things like, 'I think that after a while they lose interest', 'She just can't be bothered' or 'I actually do wonder how much she wants it . . . I'm fairly certain that she doesn't want to communicate with us'. Worries about how the child would feel about their birth parents not writing back were also expressed: 'The thing that worries me mostly . . . about the letterbox, is in the long term how the child feels knowing there's no reciprocation, isn't that a little bit hurtful?' Some adoptive parents told us that they had given up writing letters to the birth family because they were discouraged by the lack of response. For example, one adoptive mother told us that she thought letterbox contact was a good idea:

> *I agree with the whole thing in principle, the action is hard but we did try . . . we used to send a big thing of photographs as well. We composed a nice letter saying all about her achievements, what she had done at school, she had learned to ride a bike, all that sort of thing and the photographs.*

However, when the birth parents did not respond to several letters, she stopped sending anything herself:

> *It hasn't worked because there's been no comeback and you get to the point where you think 'I haven't got the energy for this any more because I've got too many other things on'. I think we did it three times . . . it just sort of drifted. There was nothing to push it. If something comes back, you think let's make an effort.*

The child was excluded from contact

Indirect contact gives choices to adopters about what to disclose to the child and when to disclose it, and adoptive parents did not necessarily or automatically involve their children in contact. Whether or not adopters included their child in contact seemed to be part of a general pattern of views and behaviours on the part of adopters, especially how they handled communication about adoption within the family. Not surprisingly, it was those adoptive parents who talked about adoption more with their children who tended to involve their child in indirect contact.

Adoptive parents have the important role of helping their child understand and come to terms with their adoptive status (Trisleiotis *et al*, 1997). It is important for the child's adjustment that adopters can create an open and positive atmosphere around the subject of adoption and the birth family (Raynor, 1980), without making the child feel insecure by over-emphasising their adoption (Kaye, 1990). This can enable the child to freely express their feelings and questions without worrying that their adoptive parents will be upset and without being made to feel their background is shameful or unspeakable. We asked adoptive parents about their communication with their child about adoption: How often did they talk about adoption? Who brought the subject up? What, how much and in what tone did the parents tell the child about the birth family? We have called this behaviour "empathic communication about adoption" and we are planning to analyse and code this variable using our interview data. The first thing we found, when looking at patterns of communication, was great variation between different adopters. Some people talked about adoption a lot; they brought the subject up themselves, and they felt it was important to keep adoption as an open subject within their family. For example, one adoptive mother said:

I talk about it when they bring things up . . . I try and do it that way and sometimes you might be watching a film or reading a book and you get a context so you get a bit of conversation about it. I always talk about when we adopted the children so I always bring the word adoption in wherever I can . . . and we have adoption day every year where we have presents and cake . . . So hopefully that tries to give them an opportunity to talk about things . . . I think I've done a reasonably good job of having it slipped into the conversation so often that they have sort of absorbed the reasons for it . . . we have never had a big bang conversation about 'why was I adopted'. Because they know they are adopted and we talk about it regularly, but not in a big emotional way.

Implicit in this mum's description of talking about adoption is a view that adoption is a subject that should be kept open, that children need to understand why they are adopted and that adopters must take responsibility for raising the subject.

Others took a different approach. Some adopters had a general policy of responding openly to any questions the child might ask, but not initiating discussion themselves. As one adoptive father put this, 'We don't so much say "well, we are going to talk about adoption today" but if they bring something up, then we will go over it and we will talk about it as much as they want.' Underlying this dad's description is a view that talking about adoption is not necessarily required: it should be led by the child's *expressed* needs and if the child doesn't express a need then it may be better to leave the subject alone. Other adopters were different again, they felt it was better for their child to keep talk about adoption to a minimum: 'Just why introduce the issue . . . it's a nonsense really. They need a happy, carefree childhood. They don't want to have to think about those kind of things . . . why should you?' In this final example, what seems to underlie the adoptive parent's approach to talking about adoption is a belief that adopted children don't need to think about being adopted, in fact having to talk about adoption could be a burden.

Child characteristics also seemed to influence the decisions that some adopters made about talking to their child about adoption and involving their child in contact. Some children wanted to talk about adoption a lot either out of curiosity, sadness or anxiety. Other children shied away from the subject. For example, one mother described how her daughter was very reluctant to consider anything to do with her life before she was adopted. She avoided talking about adoption and was upset by any reminders from the past:

> She won't ever talk about anything to do with pre-adoption . . . She will never ever speak about [her birth parents], never ever in all the years now – she has never spoken about them and she wouldn't even let me stay in contact with the foster parents, and they were good to her.

Because her daughter was so against anything to do with her birth family or her past, the adoptive mother worried that involving her in the indirect contact would just upset her more:

> No, to be honest her reaction had been so bad pre-adoption, and remember it didn't all settle down and become rosy straightaway, even now I would be cautious about throwing her off balance . . . It might upset her and worry her.

Cases such as this serve as reminders of the complexity of concepts such as sensitivity and empathy in adoptive parenting: an adoptive parent needs to think about their child's need to know about their birth family, but sometimes they need to balance this with the child's need *not* to think about their family (at least for a while). Other adoptive parents didn't include their child because they were worried that the erratic response or non-response of birth relatives would upset him or her. For example, one adoptive mother said that although the birth mother did sometimes send a birthday card, this was not every year and was often not on time.

> *It's not been every year so I can't guarantee that he will receive a card so I can't let him know that I'm receiving cards . . . I don't think he needs to know right now 'cos you are opening yourself wide up for a year when a card doesn't come and I think that will be just so awful for him. So this way you are cushioning the blow . . . And also they don't come* [on time] *. . . so you can't tell him that's there's been cards because he will be now literally waiting for the post.*

When children are not involved in contact it raises the question of whether they might feel betrayed or excluded when they do find out about the contact: the decisions that adoptive parents have to make are very difficult. Adoptive parents who facilitate face-to-face contact meetings between their child and the birth family do not face the same kind of issues about whether and how to include children in contact: they are by definition included. Instead, they may face issues about how to manage children's feelings about being included in contact. As many adopters described it, face-to-face contact necessitated communication about the birth family. If a meeting is to take place with birth relatives, adopters *have* to talk to the child beforehand and afterwards. The meetings themselves promote reactions from children, which can be positive or negative. The adoptive parents have to manage children's responses in the here and now. In contrast, letterbox contact can (both literally and metaphorically) be put away in the drawer or cupboard.

Knowing what to put in the letters

Another common problem we found with indirect contact was that, although exchanges of letters were taking place, either one or both parties were dissatisfied with the quality of information contained in the letters: this type of contact was ineffective in creating a useful dialogue between parties. In particular, some adopters wanted more information about birth relatives' past and current lives. One adoptive mother told us that she did receive regular letters from the birth mother, but that these letters talked almost exclusively about the birth mother's other child who lived at home with her. The adopters were quite keen to hear 'wee bits and things of what her life is now, whether she's met somebody else, whether she would let us know, or let us know to let [our daughter] know if she re-married. I mean we've got no idea about how her life's moved on since then.' Adopters also talked about their difficulty in knowing what to put in letters, especially how to talk about all the good things in the child's life, without making the birth parents feel bad about not being able to offer the child similar opportunities. As one father put it,

We're lucky that we've got a comfortable lifestyle and we can go on holiday, so I'd feel sort of guilty if she was getting letters and she was in a difficult situation and, you know, no income, difficult to find food and well, not even able to think about a holiday . . . writing the letters I've found that so hard about what to put in them . . . Because it sounds as if you're boasting, but on the other hand I want her to know that Kirsty has got what she wanted, she wanted her to have nice holidays, to have a nice time, do the things which she couldn't give her.

In cases where we were able to interview both adoptive parents and birth relatives we could see that quite serious misunderstandings had arisen because people found it hard to communicate effectively by letter. Such misunderstandings about the other party's feelings or intentions were far less common in face-to-face contact situations, as this type of contact provided immediate and direct opportunities for exchanges of information, and theories about the other party could be easily tested against reality.

Conclusions

Our survey data showed there is a widely held assumption that face-to-face contact is not necessary, and maybe not desirable, for young adopted children who have not established an attachment to their birth relatives. Face-to-face contact is not considered as a means of helping the child with longer-term issues of loss and identity. Indirect contact is the usual type of contact planned for young adopted children, and in most cases the intention in establishing such contact is to help the child with issues of identity. Although indirect contact is the usual plan for young adopted children, it is rarely a straightforward option. Indirect contact will be experienced very differently in different cases, and how things work out in practice will depend on the behaviours and feelings of adopters, children and birth relatives. Whether indirect contact has any benefits to the child in understanding their background will depend firstly on whether planned contact actually takes place. It is clear from our research sample that it cannot be taken for granted that indirect contact is "easy" and will automatically happen. In many cases, clear and sensitive involvement from the agency is required to get contact started and keep it going. Assuming contact is actually initiated, the next question is whether or not it is reciprocated by birth relatives. Contact that is one-way to birth relatives may have the advantage of helping the child know the adopters care about the birth family, and it may be of benefit to birth relatives. Without dismissing the importance of either of these outcomes, if contact does not involve information coming to the adopters and the child, it is unlikely to help the child with identity issues. Even when contact is two-way, how effective it is as a means of the birth family and the adoptive family getting to know one another is another question. For indirect contact to develop into real and meaningful dialogue between the two families, a high level of ability and commitment are required. Both parties, but especially birth relatives, may need long-term support. Letterbox contact is unlikely to run smoothly in most cases without the devotion of resources from agencies to ensure that letters are exchanged efficiently and support is offered when problems arise. As with face-to-face contact, some adoptive parents will find managing contact easier than will others, and the capacity of adoptive parents to understand how adoption affects their child and the birth family is a crucial consideration.

Three main aims

- To look at what contact is planned for young adopted children.
- To explore how indirect contact works out, especially from the perspective of adopters.
- To consider differences between adoptive parents in how they manage indirect contact.

Three main findings

- Indirect contact is the "standard" plan for young adopted children.
- Indirect contact can be an effective means of all parties learning more about each other, but many hurdles have to be overcome for this to happen.
- Adopters who can put themselves in the place of their child and the birth family are those who are more likely to sustain contact, involve their child in the contact, and communicate openly with their child about adoption.

Three main implications for practice

- Indirect contact should not be considered an "easy" option.
- All parties may need ongoing support to maintain contact and communicate effectively.
- Systems for managing letterbox contact need to be clear, efficient and appropriate to the case.

References

Berry, M., Cavazos Dylla, D. J., Barth, R. P. and Needell, B. (1998) 'The role of open adoption in the adjustment of adopted children and their families', *Children and Youth Services Review*, 20(1–2), pp. 151–171.

Fratter, J. (1996) *Adoption with Contact: Implications for policy and practice*, London: BAAF.

Grotevant, H. D., Ross, N. M., Marcel, M. A. and McRoy, R. G. (1999) 'Adaptive behaviour in adopted children: predictors from early risk, collaboration in relationships within the adoptive kinship network, and openness arrangements', *Journal of Adolescent Research*, 14(2), pp. 231–247.

Kaye, K. (1990) 'Acknowledgement or rejection of difference?', in D. M. Brodzinsky and M. D. Schechter (eds.) *The Psychology of Adoption*, New York: Oxford University Press.

Kirk, H. D. (1964) *Shared Fate*, New York: Free Press.

Neil, E. (2000) 'The reasons why young children are placed for adoption: findings from a recently placed sample and implications for future identity issues', *Child and Family Social Work*, 5(4), pp. 303–316.

Neil, E. (2002) 'Contact after adoption: the role of agencies in making and supporting plans', *Adoption & Fostering*, 26(1), pp. 25–38.

Neil, E. (2003) 'Understanding other people's perspectives: tasks for adopters in open adoptions', *Adoption Quarterly*, 6(3), pp. 3–30.

Raynor, L. (1980) *The Adopted Child Comes of Age*, London: George Allen and Unwin.

Triseliotis, J., Shireman, J. and Hundleby, M. (1997) *Adoption: Theory, Policy and Practice*, London: Cassell.

5 The "Contact after Adoption" study: face-to-face contact

Elsbeth Neil

Introduction

This chapter is the second one in this volume to consider findings from the UEA "Contact after Adoption" project, and readers are referred to Chapter 4 for a summary of the aims and methods of the study. In this chapter the focus is on face-to-face contact with adult birth relatives, and how this was working out over time, especially from the perspective of adopters and children. The chapter explores what had happened to contact plans in the four years since we first talked to families, and how adopters felt when plans changed. Children's reactions to contact meetings and what children said about their experiences of having contact are also explored.

The children included in the study were all under age four when placed for adoption, and most of those having face-to-face contact were adopted from care. Previous research on contact has tended to focus on either relinquished infants (see Chapters 2 and 3), or older children with established relationships with birth relatives (e.g., Macaskill, 2002; Lowe *et al*, 1999; Rushton *et al*, 2001). The children in our sample are different to both these groups. They do not have the *relatively* easy life history (e.g., absence of abuse, early placement) and backgrounds (e.g., birth parents who are relatively free of major problems like addictions, consenting to adoption) of relinquished infants, yet they mostly did not have established relationships with their birth relatives. Children adopted between the age of one and four years constitute the largest group currently being placed and it is important to consider the impact of contact on children of this age. In making such consideration it cannot be assumed that what is known about contact for relinquished infants also applies to young children adopted from care. By the same measure it also must not be assumed that what applies to older children adopted from care also applies to children from similar backgrounds, but placed at younger ages.

Who was having face-to-face contact?

One of the aims of the project was to consider how contact plans related to case characteristics. As already discussed (see Chapter 4) we found that children adopted from care were significantly more likely to have a plan for face-to-face contact with birth relatives than were children relinquished for adoption. We were interested to know, of all the children in our sample who were adopted from care (n = 104), whether those for whom it was planned to have face-to-face contact differed from those with other contact plans. For example, were they the "easier" cases, that is, children from more benign backgrounds? Or were they children who were older and who had spent more time with their birth relatives before adoption? We compared children adopted from care having face-to-face contact with their counterparts not having such contact on a range of variables including birth parents' difficulties (mental health problems, learning difficulties, drug/alcohol problems), history of maltreatment, length of time spent in care of birth family, and amount of contact pre-adoption. None of these case characteristics predicted who did or did not have face-to-face contact. We concluded that probably the single most powerful influence in determining who did or did not have face-to-face contact after adoption was the adoption agency placing the child (Neil, 2002a).

The families in our sample

In the first phase of our study we interviewed the adopters of 35 children (living in 31 adoptive families) for whom it was planned to have face-to-face contact with an adult birth relative. We also interviewed the birth relatives of 15 of these children. Seventeen children (49 per cent) had contact with one or both birth parents, 13 children (37 per cent) were seeing a birth grandparent but not a parent, and five children (14 per cent) were seeing grandparents *and* one or both birth parents. Some children seeing more than one relative had separate arrangements with different relatives, while other children would see all their relatives together on one occasion. The mean age at placement of the 35 children was one year eight months, and their mean age when the adopters were interviewed was four years five months. Most children (n = 26, 74 per cent) had been adopted from care, and 21 children (60 per cent) were reported to have experienced neglect or maltreatment prior to adoption. Thirty-two of the children were white and three were of mixed parentage, having one white birth parent and one parent of mixed African-Caribbean and white ethnic origin. All the children were placed with white adoptive parents. The children came generally from birth families experiencing high levels of both social deprivation and psychological difficulties such as mental health problems, learning disabilities and drug and alcohol misuse problems (Neil, 2000; Neil *et al*, 2003).

In Phase 2 of the project (now on average six years after placement), we managed to locate and involve all the original adoptive parents, with the exception of three families (taking the number of children down to 32). We were able to include nine additional children having face-to-face contact. Three of these were other children of adopters already in the sample, two were children from our survey sample whose contact arrangements had changed from indirect to direct, and four were new cases recruited in Phase 2. In Phase 2, we also sought to interview the children themselves, and we negotiated access via adoptive parents. We obtained interview data about 41 children. We interviewed the adopters of 38 children (living in 29 families), 24 adopted children and the birth relatives of 27 children (living in 23 different adoptive families). In 14 cases we interviewed all three parties. Only seven of the children in our face-to-face contact sample had been placed for adoption at the request of their birth parents: all the other children had been adopted from care. Of these seven, only one child was a "straightforward" baby relinquishment: the other children were placed in very complex circumstances by their birth parents, and in many of these cases, had the parent(s) not requested adoption, it is likely that their consent to adoption may have been dispensed with.

Face-to-face contact in the early stages

Our first follow-up of the face-to-face contact cases revealed a largely positive picture of this type of arrangement, contact being most successful when adopters entered into it willingly and where all parties were supported when they needed help (Neil 2002a; 2002b; Neil *et al*, 2003).

67

Face-to-face contact took many forms, ranging from frequent, directly negotiated meetings on home ground through to brief, once a year supervised meetings held on agency territory (Neil, 2002a; Neil *et al*, 2003). Adoptive parents were generally positive about having contact, reporting that it did not negatively affect their relationship with their child and that it gave them better access to information about the child's background (Neil, 2003a). As has been discussed (see Chapter 4), how adopters felt about contact was related to their empathy for the adopted child and the birth family, rather than to the characteristics of the birth relatives or the type or frequency of meeting. Birth relatives involved in face-to-face contact showed high levels of acceptance of the child's placement, and most reported that they had been helped to accept the adoption because they had seen for themselves that the child was getting on well and that the adopters were nice people (Neil, 2003b).

In terms of children's reactions to contact, we assessed this through the reports of adopters, as the children were too young to talk to us themselves. The majority of children were reported to respond to contact meetings without any problems, most children appearing to be either unconcerned or neutral about the meetings, or positive (Neil, 2002b; Neil *et al*, 2003). About a quarter of the children showed a mix of positive and negative reactions to contact, but severe negative reactions were not reported. Children who appeared to feel some anxieties about contact meetings were those who were older at placement and had more difficult pre-placement histories. Such children tended to find adjusting to many different situations difficult (for example, going to school, making friends and meeting people) and contact meetings were no exception to this general pattern. At the time of our first follow-up, many children had either no understanding of adoption or only a very basic understanding. Hence it was difficult for children to understand the significance of contact meetings with birth relatives and many adopters said that children reacted no differently to when they saw any other adult friend or acquaintance of the family.

Changes in contact arrangements over time

At the time of our follow-up, the children in our study were aged between five and thirteen, with most being aged seven to nine. This second round of interviews took place approximately four years after the first study, when children had been in their adoptive families for about six years on average. One of our first questions was whether contact arrangements had been kept up over time. In line with the outcomes of other studies, we found that in some cases face-to-face contact had not continued (e.g., Berry *et al*, 1998; Millham *et al*, 1986). Of the 43 children we were following up, there were six pairs of siblings placed together and having the same contact: these were counted as one placement. Thus, there were 37 placements and a total of 43 contact arrangements (31 placements involved one contact arrangement and six placements involved two separate contact arrangements, e.g., parents *and* grandparents, or maternal *and* paternal grandparents). Of the 43 different face-to-face contact arrangements, contact had stopped in nine cases (21 per cent), was very erratic in four cases (9 per cent) and was ongoing (and in many cases had increased) in 30 cases (70 per cent).

Contact that had stopped or become erratic

The reasons why contact had ceased or became erratic were very varied, and often more than one factor was at play in each case. The main reasons why contact had stopped or been erratic in 13 cases were:
- death of the birth parent (two cases);
- birth parents' lifestyle or ill-health prevented meetings happening (four cases);
- birth parents had decided to stop contact (two cases);
- adopters had decided to switch to indirect contact (one case);
- contact meetings had stopped, and neither party had attempted to reinstate them (three cases);
- ill-health in the adoptive family had prevented meetings happening (one case).

Two main points are clear about contact that had stopped or become erratic. The first is that birth relatives were more likely to be the ones dropping out of contact than were adopters. The second point is that birth *parents* were less able to maintain contact than were *grandparents or other relatives*. As the above list shows, there was only one case where the adopters had actively decided to end face-to-face contact. There were three more cases where adopters had allowed contact to lapse, but where there had not been a definite decision that it was stopped for good. In the remainder of cases, contact had stopped because the birth relatives had difficulties in maintaining it. Of the 43 contact plans, 21 involved contact with birth parent(s) and 22 were with grandparents or other relatives. Contact with grandparents or other relatives was ongoing in 86 per cent of cases (19 of 22), but contact with birth parents had only endured in about half of cases (52 per cent, 11 of 21). This fits with our finding that birth parents were more likely to have serious mental health difficulties than were other birth relatives (see Chapter 6). In many cases it was clear that problems such as mental illness, depression and drug and alcohol problems contributed to the difficulties for birth relatives in keeping up contact over time.

In the 13 cases where contact had stopped or been erratic, adopters had a range of feelings about how things had gone. In many cases where meetings had stopped, adopters regretted the ending of contact and indicated their willingness to resume it, should this be possible at a later date. Many people felt that overall there had been more advantages than disadvantages in having contact, even though it had not worked out as planned. One advantage identified by some adopters was that they (and the child) had gained some knowledge about and memories of the birth family. For example, in one case where the birth mother had died, the adopter said:

> *I can't see that there were any downsides to what we did and there were just plusses so I think we all agree that it was beneficial all the way through . . . It might not be a nice thing because it isn't happening any more [but] . . . I think it was actually better to have had something that was warm, friendly and memorable than nothing at all.*

Although contact had not been straightforward in many cases, adopters often said that the unpredictable frequency of meetings had not caused children any concerns. For example, Damien's birth mother had a lot of mental and physical health problems related to her misuse of drink and drugs. For the first three years or so, contact meetings happened as planned. Then Damien's birth mum moved away, her problems worsened, and there were long periods when the adopters could not track her down or when she was not well enough to see Damien. A contact meeting had happened when Damien was six, but the adopters were not sure if or when there would be any further meetings. Damien did not have an established relationship with his birth mother and he accepted whatever contact happened as "normal". His adoptive mum's views about the effect of contact on Damien were:

> *I don't feel that it bothered Damien in the slightest . . . you know he didn't dwell on it, he just accepted it . . . I think it was very healthy that he's seen her and got a memory at five or six . . . you know, he has that memory whereas at three he didn't have it and he would never have had it . . . I mean if you asked him to describe [his birth mum] I'm sure he could now, whereas he couldn't before.*

Some adoptive parents regretted that contact had stopped: they had hoped that contact would help their child in the longer term. For example, Bethany was adopted from care at age two. The plan was for her to have contact with her birth mother twice a year, but soon after the adoption the contact went awry. A couple of meetings happened after which the birth mother cancelled the next contact and did not respond to a letter from the adopters asking if she wanted to continue. Bethany was seven at the time we interviewed her adopters, and at that stage they did not feel that the lapse in contact was a problem. They explained that, although Bethany knew she was adopted, the subject of adoption and her birth family held little importance for her. But looking to the future, they thought that some contact would be a good idea.

> *There's no interest from her point of view . . . I don't think her adoption bothers her . . . And she doesn't ask too much about it at all . . . I don't really feel anything particularly about [contact stopping] . . . at the moment I don't mind either way. Bethany doesn't seem to mind and that's OK. I think for Bethany's sake that at some point we will probably want to continue it. Just so she's got this picture in her mind I think . . . from Bethany's point of view later on she might want to know things.*

That's why I think we may need to go back to [the birth mother]. At the moment it seems OK without it. But if ever Bethany did say she would like to know again what she really looks like, or to see if she has changed or anything, then I would phone up and see if she would meet us again.

Some adopters had quite mixed feelings about the contact that had taken place. For example, Tyrone's adopters said that meetings with his birth mother had not been very comfortable. The birth mum had a lot of problems and needs. She did not pay much attention to Tyrone, other than wanting to take lots of photos of him. Instead, she spent a lot of time talking to the adopters about her life. When Tyrone was about six, his birth mum decided she did not want to have face-to-face contact anymore, as she found it too painful. The adopters were in some ways relieved, as they too had found meetings difficult. Tyrone's adoptive mum said:

But I am not sorry that they have stopped really, the way that it was going . . . you know I don't think anyone would really benefit now, well I don't even think [his birth mum] was really benefiting . . . I think she has got her own problems she needs to sort out and not really bring our family in to try and sort her problems out.

However, they felt that Tyrone had enjoyed the meetings ('He was fine. I mean he came away with his toys and that and at that age . . . it is like seeing, seeing a nice aunt who spoils you'), and they were concerned that he would feel bad about not seeing his birth mother anymore. In particular, they worried that he may feel rejected or unwanted. Tyrone had asked if he could see his mother again and the adopters explained, 'That's been the hardest thing, him saying he wants to see her and what do you keep saying . . . [your birth mum] doesn't want to see you, obviously you can't say it like that . . . I just say at the moment it is too upsetting for her.'

Contact that was ongoing

In 70 per cent of cases, face-to-face contact was still taking place steadily. In some cases the contact arrangements had changed very little from the time of the first interviews: everything was much as it was before. But in many cases the arrangements had broadened out in one way or another. Ways that contact had broadened could be quite modest, or quite extensive and they included:

- A greater disclosure of identifying information between parties, e.g., exchange of phone numbers, email addresses, home addresses. This enabled people to arrange contact directly, rather than via the agency, and to add phone, letter or email contacts to face-to-face contact.
- Meetings took place on neutral or home ground, rather than on agency territory.
- Contact became more frequent or meetings lasted longer. This could include the child spending time alone with birth relatives, including overnight stays.
- More birth relatives were introduced to the child, e.g., newly born siblings, aunts, uncles and cousins, grandparents.
- The two families shared important events like weddings, christenings, parties.

The reasons why contact arrangements had altered were varied, and often it was a number of factors in combination that brought about changes. In many cases, moves towards a different type of face-to-face contact resulted from the growth of trust between parties. For example, Zena had contact twice a year at the family centre with her grandmother, Diane. At the time of the first interview (when Zena was four) the adopters said they found the meetings stilted and uncomfortable, 'like if you imagine in a doctor's surgery'. They felt Diane didn't interact much with Zena ('She will be just looking at her rather than getting up and going "what are you doing Zena? Shall I help you build that?" '). Zena seemed to get little out of contact: 'To be honest she doesn't really know who she [grandmother] is. She can't piece together . . . how she fits into her life'. By the time Zena was eight, the contact seemed much more positive. The adoptive mum explained how over time she felt more trusting of Diane, and more convinced of her genuine interest in Zena: 'I thought, well, each time obviously she had got to ring up for this contact otherwise there would be no contact, and she has not let me down once: so she genuinely wants this contact.' Because she felt more trust, Zena's adoptive mum let Diane have her home phone number, so that meetings could be arranged independently of the agency. They met a few times in public places like the shops and a play centre, then after one meeting, Zena's mum decided to invite Diane to their home:

The weather wasn't too cracking so I said, 'Well, if you wanted to come back to ours'. I thought at that time I have got to make it easier for myself in the future. Well, there is nothing wrong with it, she isn't going to hurt nobody: she wouldn't hurt a fly. And so I said, 'There is a nice park next door' and I said, 'If you wanted to go, if you wanted to come back and have a cup or tea or whatever'.

Having the contact at the house seemed to allow people to relate to each other on a different level. As Zena's mum explained:

She could see where Zena lived really and Zena entertained her with her dancing in front of her. So she saw Zena in a different way you know, in her home, and she was being Zena and nanny Diane was being nanny Diane. And she talks about nanny, she knows who she is talking about now . . . she will remember it . . . this real person.

As had happened in Zena's case, for some people mediated or supervised arrangements began to feel uncomfortable or difficult. Although many people had wanted and needed the agency to be quite involved in contact in the beginning (and this remained vitally important in many cases), in some situations the logistical disadvantages of involving a third party started to outweigh the advantages. Kelly was also having contact with her grandparents once a year at the agency. As in Zena's case, meetings hadn't been particularly relaxed or enjoyable for anyone. At the time of follow-up (when Kelly was seven), the adopters explained that they had moved to meeting in public places away from the agency, this suggestion first coming from the grandparents. Kelly's adopters felt that it was becoming cumbersome to go through the agency, saying, 'It is awkward having to write through somebody all the time because by the time you get replies you know you are talking weeks later.' Having met the grandparents on several occasions they also felt confident that they posed no threat: 'We were secure in the fact that we didn't think they were going to snatch her.' For their first meeting away from the agency, the two families decided to meet at a family pub with a children's play area and they brought all their children along. Kelly's dad felt she was more comfortable on this occasion:

She was more herself. . . I mean she could play in the play area and . . . then keep running back and bits and pieces and with [our other children] there as well made a difference as well, they all played happily together. So yes it was a lot better. I think she was a little bit more herself. . . I think she will benefit – it will be a more relaxed atmosphere and she will be able to develop a relationship with them as family members.

He added that he felt the meetings went better for everybody:

You know, it is more flexible now and both sides admit it is easier and it was a better meeting. And it is a nicer meeting as well because you don't mind, you know, if you are going to go to the zoo, or you are going to go here, because you know the kids are going to enjoy themselves anyway and we are going to enjoy ourselves as well . . . I mean, when we come back, when we have had the contact, in past contacts you have come away from it and you think, well, 'that was OK and that is over for another year sort of thing' but I mean this last one was so much more relaxed . . . We came back and said, 'well wasn't that lovely, that was a really nice meeting!'

Adoptive parents' views about expanding contact depended on what they were hoping to get out of the meetings. Some adopters clearly wanted the contact to help their child with identity issues: a chance for both families to establish some communication so that if and when children asked questions, these could be answered more easily. In such cases adopters did not necessarily want contact to be of any great frequency. This was not because they found meetings difficult or unpleasant, but because they had busy family lives. They were not looking for extra family members or to develop close relationships between the child and the birth family: they saw the child's relationship needs as being met within the adoptive family. For example, to return to Kelly's situation, after meetings started to feel more comfortable, her parents did think about having slightly more contact, say twice a year instead of once, but it would have been difficult practically for them to have more contact than this. As Kelly's dad

explained, it would be hard to fit it in with both Kelly's individual activities
and their life as a family:

*Kelly has her friends and she goes with her friends and, you know, so it
is a busy life and time just disappears, you don't realise it. Yes and
there's the DIY. . . ! But I mean weekends and stuff like that with
children, it is more or less planned because you know, [my wife's]
parents, my parents, or seeing friends or, you know, it just disappears.*

Kelly had grandparents in her adoptive family. Although her adoptive
parents said they hoped Kelly would relate to her birth grandparents as
'*family members*', they didn't really envisage her developing a similar
relationship to that she enjoyed with her adoptive grandparents:

They are not, like, they are not the same age as her [other] *granddad
and her granny, so I think that is more on the lines of an aunt and uncle
really. A sort of, a distant sort of uncle and aunt lines really rather than
grandparents.*

In other families, face-to-face contact had started to involve a wider circle
of birth relatives, and the child had an active life within the birth family
network. For example, Peter (age seven) had contact with his grandmother.
Although his grandparents were divorced, they remained in touch, and so
the grandfather was able to ask, via the grandmother, if he could also see
Peter. Peter's adoptive mum's response to this was, 'It was good, I mean
I . . . that's good the more people who are involved with Peter . . . I don't
mind at all really'. Peter's adoptive mum had fostered him as a baby and
had gone on to adopt him. She had birth children, but they were much
older than Peter and her life no longer revolved around "family" activities.
Her own parents had died and she saw benefits for both Peter and herself
in him developing close relationships with his birth family.

*It's perfectly fantastic having his nan and granddad because it gives
me, it gives me a break now and again when he goes off with them, you
know, that's fine, that's very good. I am hoping as more times goes on,
the more time he can spend with his granddad quite honestly. Well,
other children do, don't they? They go off with their grandparents. I
haven't got any parents so it is quite nice.*

Peter was having visits to his grandma's house on Sunday afternoons every six weeks, and his mum said she'd like this to develop this so that he could spend the whole day with her. Contact with his grandfather also went well, and had included overnight stays. This kind of face-to-face contact where the birth relatives became an important part of the child's extended family network, did work well for some people, but was not for everyone. In Peter's case the success of contact was predicated on a number of factors. One was the trust that had been established over the years with the birth family. Another was Peter himself: he didn't stay on his own with grandparents until he was of an age where the separation from his adoptive mum was comfortable and his behaviour was manageable. A third factor was that Peter's adoptive mum was very happy to "share" him with birth family members. The contact with the birth family did not make her feel threatened. She had looked after Peter since he was a few days old, and he was 'like her own', but at the same time she said 'I don't own him'.

Children's reactions to contact

By the time of our second study, most of the children now had some level of understanding of adoption. As a consequence, children were more able to understand their relationships with birth relatives, and contact meetings took on more significance: it wasn't just anybody they were going to see, it was *somebody to do with them*. A lot of the children who were "neutral" about contact at our first follow-up now seemed to feel quite positive about meetings. Where contact was comfortable and relatively frequent, children's relationships with birth relatives could be close, and similar to relationships with extended family members in the adoptive family. Where contact was less frequent, a more usual pattern described by adopters was that children looked forward to meetings, but their relationship with the birth relative was not necessarily that close. For example, Millie was placed when she was one, and she saw her birth mother, Sally, once a year. When she was a toddler, her mum said that to Millie, Sally was 'just like another person, another person who wanted to play'. When Millie was seven, her adoptive mum said that when a contact meeting happened, 'I suppose she gets a little more interested in checking bits and pieces out about her family and you know what happened and that kind of thing'. Millie seemed to be comfortable during contact meetings, but her relationship with her birth mother wasn't close: more like 'an affectionate aunt':

> *So it's like a family outing and it's not like, Millie doesn't make a beeline for Sally and wants to be doing things with her and Sally doesn't make a beeline for Millie either. . . . Sally is kind of like one step removed.*

As in the first study, some adoptive parents said that contact meetings could raise questions or anxieties for children, but severe negative reactions were not reported. For example, Kasey was placed for adoption when she was three-and-a-half. Her birth mother was not able to care for her because she had a mental illness. Kasey has contact in a neutral place with her birth mum once a year. Her adoptive mum described Kasey's reactions before, during and after contact meetings.

> *Well, she is quite keen to go, she is quite exuberant, you know and there are always presents and it's opening the presents. And it's always . . . a bit of a nightmare because . . . Kasey will be whizzing about at like ninety miles an hour . . . I suppose she was a bit hyper really, a bit over-excited . . . On the way back she is usually very sad, very quiet and I usually try to make it all as calm as possible, we just have a nice tea, and then we watch telly . . . She just needs a couple of hours to get over it really and I don't ask her questions because that would just set her off. [But] she is not one to be badly behaved after or even better behaved. It's just the sadness of the occasion and then she gets herself back together and then she will be alright. I have not really had sleepless nights or anything like that.*

We interviewed 24 children having face-to-face contact, and we asked them what they thought about meetings with their birth relatives. Again, in line with other research studies, most children said that they were glad they were having contact, and that they enjoyed meetings (e.g., Thomas *et al*, 1999; Fratter, 1996; Macaskill, 2002). When we asked children what was good about contact, they tended to express this simply in terms of it being good to see their birth family, as the following quotes show:

See her lovely smiley face. Um . . . giving her a big cuddle . . . Seeing her. (Girl, aged 8, once-yearly contact with birth mother)

I like seeing their faces. (Girl, aged 7, contact with birth parents in school holidays)

'Cause if you haven't seen your brother for a while you would probably miss them and probably want to see them. (Boy, aged 8, occasional contact with grown-up brother)

Eleven-year-old Suzanne gave a more sophisticated explanation as to what she liked about seeing her grandparents twice a year:

I enjoy going out with [my grandparents] because they are just really kind and they talk to me about lots of things and they make me laugh and feel happy.

In some other cases, it was aspects of the event of contact that children remembered, rather than the birth relatives themselves. For example, Jason, who was only just seven when we interviewed him, said the best thing about contact was 'getting the presents'.

A few children expressed mixed feelings about having contact. Eight-year-old Declan had been seeing his birth mother three times a year. He said that he felt a 'little bit excited and a little bit worried' when he went to contact meetings. He had mixed feelings about seeing his birth mother. In particular he was unhappy that she did not seem to even remember his age: 'I quite liked it, quite didn't like it. The *didn't like* bit is "what age are you?" like that. I quite liked it when we was sitting down and talking and that.' He felt that the presents his birth mum gave him were too young for him: 'When it was Easter we'd go there and she would give us a Thomas the Tank Engine and Tweenies Egg . . . We said, this is babyish, like that.' Declan also saw his younger brother (who lived with his birth mum) at some meetings, and he worried if he was OK: 'He was very dirty, his hair looked like it wasn't washed for two weeks . . . and it looked very dirty with grease in it and all his dinner in it.' In Declan's case his adopters had decided to change to letterbox contact because they felt that contact meetings were not very positive any more, and again he had very mixed feelings about this. On the one hand, he very clearly said that it was 'my idea' to write letters and send photographs instead, but when we asked him if he was glad that he did not see her anymore, he said 'a little bit, and a little bit not'.

Summary

The overall message from our study is that face-to-face contact was generally a benign or positive experience for these young placed children. This concurs with the research findings about relinquished infants (Grotevant *et al*, Chapter 2) but is at odds with research on other samples of children which suggest that the outcomes of contact can be more mixed (e.g., Chapters 8, 9, 10, 12; Macaskill, 2002). The kinds of problems that have been identified as happening in a minority of cases when children are adopted from care include:

- birth relatives undermine the placement;
- interactions between children and birth relatives can be poor or even abusive;
- children can be very disturbed after contact and need time to recover;
- birth relatives do not maintain contact.

In our sample of children we did find that about half of birth parents were not able to maintain regular contact with their adopted children in the six years or so since their child had been adopted. In most cases these were birth parents who had serious health, social and psychological problems and who were without either formal or informal support. Birth parents who were able to maintain contact with their children were those who had a supportive partner, parent, friend or relative or who were helped by a social worker. In one or two cases the adoptive parents themselves took on a supportive role with birth parents. Our study therefore supports the view of others (e.g., Crank, 2002) that, when children are adopted from care, birth parent contact needs to be actively supported.

The other problems listed above were very uncommon in our sample. Why should this be so when the birth families of these children are very similar to the birth families of older placed children? We would suggest that the relative success of face-to-face contact in our sample of children could be explained in a number of ways.

The lack of an established relationship between the child and birth relatives

The lack of attachment relationships between children and birth relatives seemed to account for the ease of contact meetings for the child. This pattern had not changed since the first interviews, despite the fact that children now understood more about their adoption. Although many children had lived with birth relatives, and many had experienced poor care, often children had no conscious memories of this. Other children had contact with birth relatives they had not lived with in the past. In general the children in our study were not emotionally entangled with the birth relatives they saw on contact meetings, therefore meetings did not arouse strong feelings.

Birth relatives' acceptance was high

As we reported after Phase 1 of the study, most birth relatives showed high levels of acceptance of the child's adoption (Neil, 2003b) and were keen not to do anything to upset the child or the adopters (see Chapter 6). Again this seemed to be at least in part related to the lack of established relationships between children and birth relatives: contact was a first-hand illustration of the child's attachment to adoptive parents, and children's behaviour did not reinforce any fantasies the birth parents might have about being the preferred parent. Contact meetings also helped birth relatives to accept the adoption because they saw for themselves that the child was thriving in their new family, and because they felt they still had a continuing role in the child's life.

Percentage of children having face-to-face contact was small

It needs to be remembered that it was only a small percentage of children from our wider sample of children placed under age four that were having face-to-face contact. Although we found no evidence that the children having contact were from "easier" backgrounds than those not having contact in terms of broad case indicators (if anything, the opposite was the case), it may be that social workers had (on the basis of their more

subtle knowledge of the people involved) screened out potentially problematic cases at an earlier stage, e.g., where it seemed likely that
birth parents would remain hostile to the adoption. Because most young
adopted children do not have established relationships with birth relatives,
practitioners may feel that, while contact could be desirable, it is not
necessary. In such a climate, social workers may reject the idea of contact
where they have the slightest doubt about whether it may work. For older
children, contact may be attempted even when people have doubts about
it: it may be considered worth trying because people will be aware of the
costs to the child of cutting contact.

Family-friendly meetings with adopters "in control"

Much of the success of face-to-face contact in our sample seemed to be
that everybody had a clear sense that it was adoptive parents who had the
ultimate control over contact arrangements (Neil, 2002b; Neil *et al*, 2003),
a point also identified as important in Logan and Smith's study of direct
contact (see Chapter 7). From the adopters' perspective, this sense of
control reduced anxieties. From the birth relatives' point of view, boundaries were very clear. In almost all cases contact was a whole-family event:
the child always had their adoptive parents there as a "secure base".

In summary, our study suggests that face-to-face contact for young
adopted children can work very well and to the satisfaction of all parties.
In most cases the dynamics of such contact will be easier than when
contact takes place between an older child and a birth parent with whom
they have a difficult relationship. Grandparents were more likely to be
able to sustain contact than were birth parents, and it was often grandparent contact that evolved over time into a more informal, directly
negotiated form of contact.

Three main aims

- To look at whether face-to-face contact with adult birth relatives was
  sustained over time, in cases where children were adopted under age
  four.
- To consider changes in contact arrangements over time.
- To examine the adopters' views about changes in contact and to look
  at aspects of the children's reactions to contact.

Three main findings

- Contact had been maintained in 86 per cent of cases where it was with a non-birth parent, and in just over half of cases where it was with birth parents.
- Contact that had been maintained often broadened over time as the two families developed trust.
- Contact meetings were generally positive or unproblematic for children.

Three main implications for practice

- Support for all parties involved in face-to-face contact needs to be available. This is especially so for birth parents.
- The contributions that grandparents can make should not be lightly dismissed: outcomes of face-to-face contact with grandparents were particularly positive.
- The complexity of face-to-face contact for young adopted children should not be considered equal to the complexity of such contact for older placed children.

References

Berry, M., Cavazos Dylla, D. J., Barth, R. P. and Needell, B. (1998) 'The role of open adoption in the adjustment of adopted children and their families', *Children and Youth Services Review*, 20(1–2), pp. 151–171.

Crank, M. (2002) 'Managing and valuing contact with contesting birth families', in H. Argent (ed.) *Staying Connected: Managing contact arrangements in adoption*, London: BAAF.

Fratter, J. (1996) *Adoption with Contact: Implications for policy and practice*, London: BAAF.

Lowe, N., Murch, M., Borkowski, M., Weaver, A., Beckford, V. and Thomas, C. (1999) *Supporting Adoption: Reframing the approach*, London: BAAF.

Macaskill, C. (2002) *Safe Contact? Children in permanent placement and contact with their birth relatives*, Lyme Regis: Russell House Publishing.

Millham, S., Bullock, R., Hosie, K. and Haak, M. (1986) *Lost in Care*, Aldershot: Gower.

Neil, E. (2000) 'The reasons why young children are placed for adoption: findings from a recently placed sample and implications for future identity issues', *Child and Family Social Work*, 5(4), pp. 303–316.

Neil, E. (2002a) 'Contact after adoption: the role of agencies in making and supporting plans', *Adoption & Fostering*, 26(1), pp. 25–38.

Neil, E. (2002b) 'Managing face-to-face contact for young adopted children', in H. Argent (ed.) *Staying Connected: Managing contact arrangements in adoption*, London: BAAF.

Neil, E. (2003a) 'Understanding other people's perspectives: tasks for adopters in open adoptions', *Adoption Quarterly*, 6(3), pp. 3–30.

Neil, E. (2003b) 'Accepting the reality of adoption: birth relatives' experiences of face-to-face contact', *Adoption & Fostering*, 27(2), pp. 32–43.

Neil, E., Beek, M. and Schofield, G. (2003) 'Thinking about and managing contact in permanent placements: the differences and similarities between adoptive parents and foster carers', *Clinical Child Psychology and Psychiatry*, 8(3), pp. 401–418.

Rushton, A., Dance, C., Quinton, D. and Mayes, D. (2001) *Siblings in Late Permanent Placement*, London: BAAF.

Thomas, C., Beckford, V., Lowe, N. and Murch, M. (1999) *Adopted Children Speaking*, London: BAAF.

6 The "Contact after Adoption" study: The perspective of birth relatives after non-voluntary adoption

Julie Young and Elsbeth Neil

Introduction

In the UK, the majority of birth parents whose children are placed for adoption will have neither wanted nor chosen this to happen. This chapter explores the contact experiences of parents and other relatives in non-consenting adoption, using data from 42 interviews with birth relatives whose children were adopted from care. While there has been some systematic research on the effects of contact on relinquishing birth mothers (Chapter 3), little is known about the perspectives of non-relinquishing mothers, and even less about other birth relatives such as birth fathers and grandparents. It is important to consider how much of what we now know about the adoption and contact experiences of relinquishing mothers also applies to the relatives of children adopted from care. As our survey of 168 children adopted under age four showed (Neil, 2000), there are important differences between consenting and non-consenting birth parents, the latter group having significantly more difficulties likely to affect their parenting capacity (i.e., mental health problems, learning difficulties, drug and alcohol problems, poverty). These difficulties will have played a large part in the processes which resulted in the removal of the child from their parents' care, and may also affect people's ability to cope with the experience of the loss and to maintain successful contact after adoption.

An interest in the experience and welfare of birth relatives is not only a subject for consideration in its own right but also has implications for the outcomes for the adopted child. Contact is more likely to be of benefit to the child if the birth relative can participate in contact with an acceptance of their new role and a supportive position with regards to the child and their adoptive parents (Lowe *et al*, 1999; Festinger, 1986; Smith and Logan, 2004).

Methodology and sample

This chapter refers to findings from interviews with adult birth relatives who had a child from their family adopted via the care system. The sample was drawn from the pool of birth relatives who had a plan for either direct or indirect contact as identified by Neil's original survey. Out of those approached, a positive response was received from nearly two-thirds of "face-to-face contact" birth relatives and just less than one-third of "indirect contact" birth relatives. Mirroring the proportion of enforced adoptions typically taking place in the UK, the majority (69 per cent) of interviews were with relatives who had children from their family adopted following care proceedings and the 42 interviews that took place with this subgroup is discussed here. Couples were interviewed together; altogether 52 relatives took part in the 42 interviews. As Table 1 shows, 30 of our interviews were with birth parents (more commonly mothers) and 12 were with other relatives (in 11 cases grandparents).

Table 1
Number of interviews undertaken with each birth relative type (n = 42)

Birth relative type	Number of interviews undertaken
Birth mothers	16
Birth fathers	5
Birth parent couples	9
Birth maternal grandparent individuals/couples	7
Birth paternal grandparent individuals/couples	4
Adult birth sibling	1

Interviews usually took place in the birth relatives' own home, and lasted two to three hours. The interviews explored several aspects of the birth relatives' experience, attitudes and feelings following the child's adoption; however, in this chapter the focus is on birth relatives' feelings of comfort and satisfaction associated with the contact experienced. Most (approximately 80 per cent) of the birth parents we interviewed had cared for the children in their early weeks, months or years of life and the majority of the grandparents had regular contact with their children up to the time of placement. Over 40 per cent of the birth relatives had more than one child or grandchild adopted. The interviews focused only on those children who were placed under four years (as targeted by this study), most of whom were placed for adoption on average at around two years old (range one to 50 months). At the time of interview, approximately six years had elapsed since the child's placement. The birth relatives had a range of contact arrangements. Table 2 crudely divides interviewees into the broad categories of letterbox and face-to-face contact arrangements planned for them at the time of the adoption. However, the interviews revealed a wide range of individual differences between, and unique developments of, each contact plan. There had also been some movement between the two basic contact types.

Table 2
Type of contact planned for interviewees at the time of the adoption (n = 42)

Birth relative type	Indirect contact	Face-to-face contact
Birth parents	19	6
Other birth relatives (grandparents & adult siblings)	6	11

The Brief Symptom Inventory (Derogatis, 1993), a self-report measure that screens for nine primary psychological symptom dimensions including depression and anxiety, was used with participants in this current stage of our research and produced some interesting results. We found that 56 per cent of birth parents scored in the clinical range on this measure, as compared to only 20 per cent of other birth relatives (n = 47). This is an interesting finding when one considers that grandparents and other relatives are not as frequently included in contact plans as are birth parents.

Findings: indirect contact

Our survey of 168 cases found that indirect contact was the most common plan for adopted children under four. In most cases this contact was with birth mothers. Birth fathers were included 30 per cent of the time, and grandparents in 19 per cent of cases. We interviewed 25 birth relatives who were having indirect contact. As discussed in Chapter 4, some indirect contact was one-way – from adopters to birth relatives – and in other cases it was two-way. We discuss what birth relatives said about receiving information from the adoptive family and then go on to discuss their views about the sending of letters or information to adopters and the child.

Receiving information from adopters

It was clear from our interviews that in most cases the more information birth relatives received from the adoptive family, the more satisfied they were with contact. Quite a few of the letterbox contact plans had not really become established. Some people had only received one or two brief paragraphs from the agency, but otherwise had not heard about the child for several years. A great deal of dissatisfaction with the lack of information was expressed:

> *I think it would put me more at ease if I knew what was going on . . . Letter information, photographs, anything that the adoptive parents wished.* (Birth mother, very minimal information from adopters)

The lack of information could be a considerable and ongoing worry. Birth relatives could be left wondering whether the child was alive or well. The interviews showed how the horror of tragic events involving children can take on a different dimension when you do not know where your child is and whether your child might be involved:

> *When Dunblane started you think, oh, it's my kid in there, and that really did my head in . . .* [and] *like last time with that Sarah Payne . . . when it says like an eight-year-old kid and that's how old our [child] was at the time, you think 'is it my kid or not?'* (Birth father, very occasional/minimal one-way indirect contact)

The feeling that the child had just disappeared or died was quite common. One birth mother had a child who was adopted into a family where regular two-way letterbox contact had been established. There was a striking comparison between the way she spoke about her son in that family, clearly pleased to hear of his progress and developing character, and about her daughter, where there had been only minimal contact:

She is out there somewhere and I don't know how she is getting on. It is as though she don't exist . . . because I don't hear nothing about her really or get any photos. It is just like, it is just a name. (Birth mother, very occasional/minimal one way indirect contact)

The view that 'anything is better than hearing nothing at all' was often voiced. Birth relatives who had even a minimal amount of information were glad they had something that could fill the void ('At least I'm still getting photos of her growing up through the years and what she's doing and everything'). Others who received a regular flow of information from the adoptive family, updating the birth relative with the progress of the child, could voice many satisfactions about being on the receiving end of these letters. The letters were clearly a reassurance that the child was developing happily and healthily. The child's enriched life opportunities could be a source of comfort that something good had come out of bad. Birth parents sometimes contrasted the life that they would have been able to give the child, and the life that they were reading about. One birth father, very against his daughter's adoption at the time, spoke of his amazement on reading a short letter from his daughter's adopters that she could use a computer at the age of nine. He felt pleased to know that his youngest daughter had life opportunities he knew he could not have given her:

Well, at first I . . . I really disagreed with it, I didn't feel like it should have happened. But now as I said she is . . . those letters I have had . . . I think she is getting a good life there, you know. She is a happy girl and that is all I wanted to see her do. I want her to be a happy child, not in the environment where there is trouble, problems . . . she goes abroad, on holidays and that, good holidays, and which I can't give her. (Birth father, one-way letterbox contact)

Interestingly, interviews with adopters had revealed their reluctance to write that openly about, for example, expensive holidays or riding lessons (see Chapter 4). They worried that the birth relative might feel they were "showing off" riches and affluence, and that this would stand in too great a contrast to the lack of opportunities and the poverty of the birth family. Two birth mothers did wonder if the adopters were 'rubbing their nose in it' or 'trying to buy the child's love' when their letters referred to holidays in Florida, but at the same time it was clear that they were pleased to hear their child had such opportunities:

> *I know she'll be getting treated lovely because the photos of where she is tells you that they've got money . . . she's obviously with a rich family so I don't think she's got to want for anything . . . I think to myself now have the adopted parents done that for spite like 'oh, she's with us, we can take her all this way and if she was with you you couldn't' . . . they've done that to prove to me that they've got money and I haven't. Things like that did go in my head but* [the photographs] *are nice.* (Birth mother, one-way letterbox contact)

It was surprising to find that virtually all these birth relatives (with the exception of some grandparents) were very unhappy – sometimes furious – about the adoption in the first place, but could see that good things had resulted from the adoption for them or the child; they often felt the adopters were good parents or felt the environment was better for the child. They were glad the child was settled and happy. They expressed that they would not want to upset what the child now had. As we found with face-to-face contact in the first wave of our study, reassurance about the child helped birth relatives to accept the adoption (Neil, 2003). For example, one birth father, still showing a great deal of anger and a desire to have his children returned at the time of the interview, shared some positive feelings about the adoption:

> *Now she's been adopted – I don't really like it, it would be more better if she was just fostered and that – at least she's got a stable home, hopefully her mind's more at ease and that.* (Birth father, very occasional/minimal one-way indirect contact)

Letters from adopters varied considerably in quality, style and length.

Some were just a few lines reporting factual information in a very formal manner. Others letters proudly shown by birth relatives covered four sheets of A4 paper, full of rich details. Birth family members typically and perhaps not unsurprisingly voiced greater dissatisfaction with the shorter, more formal letters. Many wanted more information on the everyday life of their child, and felt dissatisfied with letters that read like a school report: 'She has started school and she goes to Brownies.' They wanted to know 'What does she eat for breakfast?' 'Does she fight with her brother?' They wanted to know the sorts of things that would bring her personality to life. However, even with more detailed letters, there could be the same problem of a mismatch between what information was wanted and what was received. One grandparent couple were desperate to hear if their granddaughter had been christened. For some reason, despite the apparently open and supportive two-way letterbox contact that had continued for several years, they did not feel able to ask such a direct question in their letters. Many expressed a reluctance to be too demanding and ask directly for specific information. There was a big concern that they might "rock the boat".

For many birth relatives, however, the letters were not as significant as seeing the child for themselves in a photograph. For those who received them, photographs were an immense satisfaction. The direct, clear images of happy and healthy children often took on a much greater importance than anything the birth family had in writing. They thought that photographs were more real and honest. Some spoke of how it was hard to look at them, but the preference was very much to have them rather than not. Those who did not receive photographs often desperately wanted them:

I can give you letters that say she is a very happy girl, you only believe what they say. I want to see photographs, I want to see her face and see if she is okay. . . photographs don't lie. (Birth father, one-way indirect contact)

In a similar fashion, letters or items produced by the child themselves were valued above the letters from the adoptive parents ('I'm not really bothered on [the adopters letters] but I'd like more from [my daughter]'). A reccurring issue for birth relatives was having to chase missing or late letters. When the letter hadn't arrived, their mind was filled with anxieties;

why hasn't it come? What is wrong with my child? Many of them said that a simple reassurance or a photograph that arrived at the expected time was far more important than a lengthy letter.

Responding to adopters

Much of the indirect contact arrangements had not become established or became very minimal because of birth relatives' failure to reciprocate the letter exchange. Several non-respondents provided an insight into this usually silent side of contact. Adopters were often left to make guesses or assumptions about why they were not replying (also see Chapter 4); in some cases adopters wondered if the birth relatives of their child had "forgotten" about the child now or if they really didn't want to write. However, the reasons given by the birth relatives who shared their stories in this study were a world apart from this imagined picture. Many birth relatives still felt overwhelmed by emotions and feelings for their child:

> *I tried to sit down a couple of times and write a letter to them so it could be put in their file for when they reach of age and I just couldn't do it . . . It hurt too much to put my feelings down on paper. It still does.*
> (Birth mother, one-way letterbox contact)

Other common reasons for not responding referred to a "block" of not knowing what to write or how to begin to express their story or feelings in words. The position of being a birth relative writing to an adopted child typically felt bizarre. Where do you start writing a letter to a child who is adopted? There is no blueprint for that. One birth mother ritually wrote birthday cards and Christmas cards to her two boys but placed them in a box never sending them on. She explained this as follows:

> *I just can't* [write a letter back]. *I don't know what to put in it, I don't know what words to write. What can you say to your kids that you haven't got, you know? I'm really sorry, but I couldn't cope, but I love you, you know, it sounds so . . . it's hard . . . and then to tell them that you've got another child that you've managed to keep with you, that's not been taken away . . .* (Birth mother, one-way letterbox contact)

Many were concerned that they did not know how their words would be received. They feared that they might confuse or upset the child or offend adopters. Guidance given over matters such as this was usually lacking: *I don't know whether I'm supposed to put that I love them, whether I'm supposed to put that . . . you know, do I mention that I wish they were here or that I love them so much that it hurts, you know what I mean . . . I just haven't got a clue.* (Birth mother, one-way letterbox contact)

Other interviewees seemed to feel that their response was neither wanted nor needed. They had not considered writing back as they could not understand how it could be good or helpful for the child or the adopters. In contrast, there was also a sense from one or two birth relatives that being able to exert control in the contact system was important to them. Having been so out of control and helpless in the process of their child being adopted, this was one area where they could finally exert control by refusing to comply with contact arrangements.

Some birth relatives did not seem to know that writing back was possible. A few individuals had a vague memory of being given information on the procedures to send information to the agency at a time when they were not in a position to consider it. One birth father recalled being told about the letterbox system when his child was placed for adoption at 18 months old. At that stage he saw no point in writing to his daughter, as she herself would not be able to read his letters. However, at the time of the interview, his birth daughter was nine years old and he was beginning to think he would like to write to her but could not remember what to do or how he was supposed to write. A birth mother had always wanted to write to her child but had been told she could not: *I wanted to send her birthday cards, Christmas cards to know that I'm still, you know, even though she's there I'm still thinking about her and they said 'no' . . . I don't want her to think that I haven't bothered.* (Birth mother, one-way letterbox contact)

Many birth relatives who did respond greatly valued the opportunity that letterbox contact gave them to show love to the child and to show that they had not been forgotten. It seemed to be immensely important for virtually all interviewees that the child would know they had not been rejected. However, these interviewees who had reciprocated the contact often still felt the immense burden of not knowing what to write. Individuals often already possessing limited skills and struggling with personal difficulties had to cope with a completely alien practice, with little or no support. Many spoke of their sense of sending something into the unknown, not knowing what was going to happen. They felt that they were writing to a stranger and did not know what their child knew about them or their adoption. Some were not clear what should they reveal about themselves and their lives, or even how they should sign their name:

[Writing to the adopters is] *really weird and . . . thinking well I am writing to my own son but I have got to write it to a different . . . lady sort of thing. There are times when I want to put to 'Jonathan, love from your mum', but I think no I can't do that. I daren't. 'Cause I don't know how he would react.* (Birth mum, two-way indirect contact with adoptive parents)

Some interviewees saw agency rules regarding how, when and what things can be sent or received as petty, awkward or inflexible. Interviewees typically tried hard to understand the rules from the agency's or adoptive family's point of view, but often felt frustrated and pushed aside by the inflexibility of the system. One grandparent couple felt there had been no exploration of how their desire to offer something to their granddaughter could be met:

Grandmother: *I did phone up and I said would it be alright, I had got this teddy bear and would it be alright if I sent it for C's birthday?, and, she just said 'no, it wouldn't really be right', so . . . I was really quite hurt.*

Grandfather: *They could have accepted it but not told her who it was from.* (Grandparents, two-way letterbox contact, no photos)

Many people referred to the whole experience of becoming part of an agency mediated letterbox system as frustrating, restrictive or even demeaning. A birth grandmother who found it difficult to send anything more than a simple birthday card to her birth grandchildren expressed how having to write personal letters that would be opened and possibly censored was immensely stigmatising. She felt that she was being treated as a prisoner. Others commented:

> *I thought best not to* [send a birthday card]*, because I know every time I go down there they don't send it the day they're supposed to, it's a couple of days late, and I thought well I'm not really going to bother now and sometimes they don't tell me if they've sent it off.* (Birth mother, two-way indirect contact)

> *It seems such a secretive way of going about things . . . There didn't seem much point putting some stuff in if they were only going to pass on what they . . . you know . . . they were going to censor it or edit it . . . [our grandson] could be thinking 'these are a bit offhand' when we are not thinking that way at all.* (Birth grandfather, two-way indirect contact)

Most of the birth relatives that we interviewed felt that they had very little choice over contact arrangements: their experience was of being told what contact they would be allowed, and feeling grateful that this was something, as opposed to nothing. Almost all birth relatives having letterbox contact said they would like more contact; either more information, greater frequency or more direct exchanges, or in some cases face-to-face contact. Very few people having indirect contact had been offered the option of face-to-face contact. Most people had very strong wishes about contact but would not do anything about their wishes because they were scared to rock the boat, were too upset, or they just accepted what they were told. One set of grandparents possessing just one photo of their granddaughter as a small baby never considered asking for a photo despite the annual two-way contact they had been having with their child's adopters for six years.

> *I haven't* [asked for a photo] *because I've . . . don't know . . . I mean I would like one . . . I haven't asked. I just thought, well, if they wanted to send me one they could, do you see . . . I never thought it was possible* [to meet the adopters]*, I don't think I could impose to meet them or anything like that . . . I agreed to what they said . . . because all I wanted was the best thing for her, for the child . . .* (Grandparents with yearly letterbox contact, no photos)

Some were afraid of the consequences of asking adoptive parents if they could increase or change the contact, or worried about the effects increased contact would have on the child. For example, the following birth mother wanted to include a separate letter for the child but had been afraid to ask the adopters if she could do this:

> No, in case she says, 'no you can't do that', I just don't want the disappointment, I feel I will just leave it as it is . . . (Birth mum, two-way indirect contact)

One grandparent couple from our face-to-face contact group had initially been offered indirect contact by the agency but through a chance conversation heard about the possibility of face-to-face contact and subsequently (and successfully) fought for a change to face-to-face contact. This stance of actively taking control to change the contact plan suggested was an exception among our interviewees. Overall, it seemed that many birth relatives with indirect contact would have preferred face-to-face contact. However, there were those who saw benefits with the indirect arrangement:

> I think I would find [face-to-face contact] hard because it would hurt. So [indirect contact] is like kind of removed from that. It is less personal and you can take your time and think about a lot and say that, or not write, it allows you to be in control so it is all less personal. It is easier, it is easier. (Birth mother, two-way indirect contact)

In summary, as we found from the perspective of adoptive parents (also see Chapter 4), maintaining indirect contact can be an immensely complicated experience. Many birth relatives felt confused or frustrated by letterbox systems, and few were given access to any support. While birth relatives were very grateful to receive information about their child's welfare, few were able to write back at all, or in any detail, about their own life.

Findings: face-to-face contact

For those birth relatives who experienced face-to-face contact, a range of satisfactions was expressed. Many expressed feeling very privileged to be able see the child for themselves, to be able to see their personalities, and observe them develop and change over the years. Another important aspect of face-to-face contact was that they were able to show their love to the child, and show him or her that they were not forgotten or rejected. The worry of future post-18 meetings was removed ('. . . when he's old enough and he wants to see [our daughter, his birth mum] . . . the nice thing is he will be able to meet her here with us and we can break the ice'). Many interviewees – both parents and non-parents – also expressed a great deal of warmth towards, and had very good relationships with, the adopters ('It's just like my family now'. 'They are really good friends to me . . . A really good family. I couldn't have hoped for a better one').

In most cases the contact had begun tentatively and followed strict procedures, but as the parties increased their knowledge of each other and trust had developed, the contact became more frequent and open (also see Chapter 5). Birth relatives typically showed gratitude towards the adopters and respected the adopters' positive gestures to include them further in their child's life.

Grandparents made up a large proportion of the relatives in this face-to-face group and arrangements that had developed in these cases often took on a different tone to that with birth parents. Their contact seemed to be very natural and, if distance allowed, frequent (several times a year). Quite often they were included as an equal third set of grandparents in the child's life. Many grandparents felt immensely privileged that they were allowed a continuation of their pre-adoption role, something they had thought they would have to relinquish. Grandparent interviewees spoke readily of their joy and relief that they could continue to see their grandchild:

We've had some fun with him. We've watched him grow up. Not on a photograph. We've felt him grow up. We've tapped him on the head. I've stood next to him now where he is almost up to my shoulder and he's been looking at me and said, 'it won't be long till I'm taller than you'. And I thought no, and I can still see you doing that. (Grandmother, regular face-to-face contact)

In contrast to the dynamics in some birth parent contact where adopters often took on a role of supporting birth parents in their meetings, some birth grandparents became a source of support and strength to adopters. One couple attended family therapy sessions to help their grandchildren come to terms with their early history. Others were available at the end of a phone to deal with little questions and other issues as and when they occurred. Many grandparents' comments about the importance of contact and the benefits it was bringing/would bring to the child often strikingly echoed remarks made by adopters in their interviews. For some grandparents it was very important that they could keep good memories alive for their child and present a positive side to the child's birth history. One grandparent couple, who successfully fought to maintain face-to-face contact, felt it was vital that their grandson did not feel that all people in his life have at some point walked away from him. They wanted him to know that they had always been there for him from the start; that they were the "constant" in the child's life:

> We've kept a stability there from the transition from [birth mum], foster into adoption. We are the main steady line that has always been there . . . We've always been there and we always will be. You know, which I think all children need, they need at least somebody that's gonna follow through from day one. (Grandparents, regular face-to-face contact)

Grandparents also spoke positively of being able to gain extra "family" members through the adoptive parents and/or other children in the adoptive family. In virtually all cases where there was another child in the adoptive family who was not their own birth relation, grandparents also took them on as their own "grandchild"; they were sent birthday cards, given presents, etc, on an equal footing. Not all grandparents felt that they integrated comfortably into the adoptive family network. A minority felt they were in some sense "outsiders", and felt that the relationship felt unnatural or forced. The following couple had never met the adoptive parents on their own without the children and felt they did not really know each other:

> You've got to watch what you say, because obviously the children, you don't know what they understand, you know . . . they're the parents legally now . . . and so you've got to think, you know, it might not be appropriate to go up and do that. You just feel, you know, you should

be that side and stay that side. It's . . . you can't explain it, although you sort of think, 'oh, I'd love to hug her' . . . you can't, you don't feel you can . . . Because it was a court order – you don't know what the lady's feelings were on it: 'Oh I'm going to agree to this, because I want these kids'. Do you know what I mean? You don't know what the other party is thinking. (Birth grandparent, twice-yearly face-to-face contact)

Face-to-face contact was not without problems for all types of birth relatives. A few birth mothers found the travel costs high. For some people, chaotic lives or personal problems could mean that having to be places at a set time was hugely difficult for them. A minority of people made negative remarks about the fact that contact had to be limited or surrounded by rules or restrictions. Some felt unsure of how to interact with the child or felt that they were being constantly "watched". This was particularly the case when contact was supervised:

I hated it when I had to do it through the social workers, absolutely hated it. Being in this room, and all the time being watched and people watching you – you couldn't be yourself and you couldn't do what you wanted really . . . [the child] used to be so nervous he didn't used to talk to us for nearly half an hour, and we were only there for an hour . . . No, I didn't enjoy the visit, I thought, well, I saw him and that was it . . . But then if [the adoptive parents] felt more comfortable doing it in the social place then I would, I would have done it for them. (Birth relative, frequent face-to-face contact)

Such problems were rarely big issues; for the vast majority they were overshadowed by the positive benefits contact brought – they felt it would be far worse not to see the child at all. However, for one birth mother, discomfort with the adopters during contact and feelings of anger towards them led her to withdraw from her own contact plan. Another birth mother felt very mixed about contact and "dreaded" meetings with her daughter, mainly continuing because her husband, the birth father, was so positive about it. However, she felt that to not have contact would be difficult also:

I would have wondered what she looked like, and wondered what she was doing and that. (Birth mother, frequent face-to-face contact)

People often showed a great capacity and motivation to keep very strictly to rules and abided by the adopter's wishes. As with letterbox contact, people were scared that they could lose the contact that meant so much to them ('It's not really long enough I don't think, but I mean I wouldn't like to rock the boat and say we need to come for longer'). Some even imposed extra rules upon themselves, as in the case of a grandmother who refused to take photographs of identifying information such as adopters' car registration plates when they met together in case temptation would lead her to impose more than she should do. Not wanting to upset, impose or harm their privilege was uppermost in the minds of many:

> I am allowed to take them like from the beach on my own . . . If they say be back at a certain time, then I will make sure I am back five minutes before, you know 'cause if I don't do that then they won't trust me to do it again. (Birth mother, yearly face-to-face contact)

Most relatives said they would always wait for adopters to make each initial move regarding a contact visit – the adopters would phone and suggest the meeting first. However, taking this backseat approach meant that, as with letterbox contact, unexplained gaps in the contact meetings could be very distressing:

> If it is the children that are getting upset, if she'd said to me, I would have said, 'Alright we'll leave it', you know, and it's just not knowing why it stopped, you know, that's the thing, because I don't know why. (Grandparent, previously twice-yearly face-to-face contact)

Another unfortunate consequence of birth relatives wanting not to upset anyone by asking for more contact, or not taking a more active role during meetings, was that sometimes adoptive parents interpreted this hesitance as a lack of interest in the child.

Conclusions and implications

It is clear from these interviews that post-adoption contact is very much valued by birth relatives. Without fail all birth relatives spoke of how contact was very important to them. Many also expressed how they felt lucky to have it and would not do anything to upset the level of contact they had been granted. Despite the adoption having been very much against the wishes of this group of birth relatives, most seemed to have moved on from feelings of anger, or at least were not directing the anger towards the adoptive family in their contact letters or meetings. Most birth relatives also showed that they were thinking about the child's welfare and wanted to make a positive contribution. There were many examples of both kinds of contact providing a great source of comfort and satisfaction for these birth relatives of young adopted children. However, the interviews revealed that indirect contact could be challenging both practically and emotionally. It was particularly difficult for those individuals who had considerable problems generally in writing, reading or expressing themselves in words – a common characteristic of parents of children adopted through care proceedings. Participating in the alien and immensely difficult practice of writing letters as a birth relative to an adopted child, while having little or no knowledge of the child's situation or state of mind, was often an impossible task. There were also many instances of worry and concern caused by missing or late information and by simple wishes for particular information being unmet, and much scope for misunderstandings between parties.

There is clearly a need for support and guidance for birth relatives, especially to help them with the task of responding in both types of contact. This may need to come from an independent agency. None of the interviewees had been offered a review to discuss the contact plan with the agency or the adopters of the child, yet it was clear that in many cases this could have been helpful and desirable. In particular, reviews could allow adopters and the agency to take into consideration the changed psychological position of many birth relatives, and for birth relatives to take into account changes in the adoptive family. Reviews could ensure that all parties are still clear about the rules and systems for letterbox contact and that they are working effectively and taking changes into account. A neutral confidant could help to clear up misunderstandings or communicate wishes and concerns to the other party. Agency systems could sometimes be unclear or disabling and could add to the difficulties of establishing smooth and open communication. It could be questioned whether rules and restrictions are necessary in all cases – it may be that these should be decided on a case-by-case basis rather than an agency having a blanket rule. Such rules are unhelpful if they alienate birth relatives who are no threat, or stifle contact unnecessarily.

The difficulties picked up by the Brief Symptom Inventory (BSI), and shown to be prevalent in the birth parents of our sample, are the kind of difficulties that are likely, at least in some cases, to impede birth parents maintaining useful contact. The BSI data could be taken to indicate that grandparents may be more psychologically robust and therefore may be more able than some birth parents to establish positive and sustained contact. Grandparent contact may also be more easily or naturally incorporated into the adoptive family network. It is surprising, therefore, that agencies do not involve grandparents more in contact arrangements. It could be said that grandparents may be an underused resource, having strengths to offer that should not be overlooked, either as an alternative to birth parents or in addition to birth parents. It may also be that grandparents can be an important support to birth parents in some cases, helping them write back or attend contact meetings.

A key theme from our interviews with birth relatives was their sense of powerlessness in contact arrangements. People felt they had little say over the nature of contact, and many people were afraid to ask for any change in the contact they had been granted for fear of losing what they already had. This powerlessness seemed to have both positive and negative effects. On the positive side, birth relatives were highly anxious not to upset the adoptive parents. This, combined with a genuine desire not to do anything that could be bad for the child, meant they were motivated to stick to the rules. On the negative side, a desire not to overstep boundaries often meant that birth relatives were very passive. Our interviews with adoptive parents revealed that, while adopters valued the fact that birth relatives respected rules, in many cases a more active stance by birth relatives would have been welcomed: passivity could be interpreted as disinterest.

Summary

Three main aims
- To examine the experiences of post-adoption contact from the perspectives of birth relatives of children adopted from care.

- To elucidate the difficulties and challenges involved in birth relative participation in contact arrangements.
- To explore the practice factors associated with birth relatives' perspectives.

Three main findings

- Contact between adoptive families and birth relatives can be a great source of comfort and satisfaction for birth relatives, the main benefit being reassurance about the child's welfare.
- Birth relatives who have neither requested nor desired adoption can, when it comes to contact, often have the child's best interests in mind and do not want to disturb the placement or upset the contact arrangement.
- Both letterbox and face-to-face contact arrangements can work well; however, indirect contact can be particular challenging. It can be extremely difficult for this group of birth relatives to respond fully to indirect contact.

Three main implications

- Ongoing support and guidance is vital to enable birth relatives to participate positively in contact arrangements.
- Regular reviews should be built in to ensure contact is continuing to meet needs and work through any issues.
- The level of openness and the rules and restrictions applied should be decided on a case-by-case basis.

References

Derogatis, L. R. (1993) *BSI: Brief Symptom Inventory: Administration, scoring and procedures manual*, Minneapolis: National Computer Systems, Inc.

Festinger, T. (1986) *Necessary Risk: A study of adoptions and disrupted adoptive placements*, Washington: The Child Welfare League of America.

Lowe, N., Murch, M., Borkowski, M., Weaver, A., Beckford, V. and Thomas, C. (1999) *Supporting Adoption: Reframing the approach*, London: BAAF.

Neil, E. (2000) 'The reasons why young children are placed for adoption: findings from a recently placed sample and implications for future identity issues', *Child and Family Social Work*, 4(6), pp. 303–316.

Neil, E. (2003) 'Accepting the reality of adoption: birth relative's experiences of face-to-face contact', *Adoption & Fostering*, 27(2), pp. 32–43.

Smith, C. and Logan, J. (2004) *After adoption: Direct contact and relationships*, London: Routledge.

7 Direct post-adoption contact: Experiences of birth and adoptive families

Janette Logan and Carole Smith

This chapter reports the findings of our research study which took place between September 1997 and April 1999 and focussed on direct (face-to-face) contact after adoption. The study was designed to include a sample of adoptive and birth families where it had been agreed that direct contact would continue after adoption. The specific aims of the research were:

- to understand the significance of adoption for those people most closely affected by this form of legal arrangement;
- to identify the advantages and disadvantages of direct post-adoption contact from the perspectives of adoptive parents, adopted children and birth family members having contact;
- to identify what kinds of factors influence the extent to which direct post-adoption contact is experienced as beneficial or otherwise for those most closely involved;
- to understand the impact of direct post-adoption contact on the lives of adoptive families, children and birth family members;
- to learn lessons for policy and practice about circumstances that indicate that direct post-adoption contact is likely to be beneficial for children and those that suggest direct contact should be avoided.

Four agencies identified all adoptive families who had agreed to contact arrangements. The resulting overall sample of 96 children placed with 61 adoptive families therefore includes a broad age range of children who had been adopted for varying lengths of time. Most children had "special needs" in the sense that they required adoption placements with siblings, they had experienced neglect and/or abuse, and they had moved between several placements before joining their adoptive families. A small number (nine) also had physical or learning disabilities. The vast majority had been subject to care orders under section 31 of the Children Act 1989.

Forty-three children in the sample were boys and 53 were girls. Ninety-two per cent were white British and the remainder were of mixed parentage. All the white children were placed in white families, as were three of the children of mixed parentage. The remaining five children of mixed parentage were placed in racially matched families. Thirty-nine children were placed singly, thirty-six in sibling groups of two and twenty-one in sibling groups of three. At the time of the research, the youngest child in the study was two years old and the oldest was 18. Eight children were aged between eight and ten, 21 were aged between 11 and 13 and the remaining six were 14 or over. The majority of children (74 per cent) were under the age of five when they were placed with their adoptive families, and 25 per cent were under the age of two. At the time of the study, the majority (85 per cent) of children had been placed with their adoptive families for three years or more.

Agencies provided us with background information about the children and their families and semi-structured interviews were carried out by the researchers with adoptive parents, birth relatives and children wherever possible. We were able to talk to 60 adoptive mothers, 50 adoptive fathers, 51 adopted children, six birth mothers, two birth fathers, 18 birth grandparents, five birth aunts, one uncle, and 11 siblings who were either "looked after" by the local authorities or living independently. We had hoped to interview, wherever possible, birth family members and adoptive parents and their children who were experiencing the same contact arrangements. However, gaining access to birth family members proved difficult for varying reasons. (For a full discussion of methodology see Smith and Logan, 2004.) The findings reported in this chapter are from these interviews.

Contact arrangements

Our study revealed a highly variable and complex range of direct contact arrangements. Of the 96 children in the whole sample, one-third were having direct contact with birth siblings, but not with any adult birth relatives. The remaining two-thirds were seeing one or more adult birth relative (birth mothers and grandparents being the relatives most usually involved), and some of these children were also having sibling contact. Most children (71 per cent) met their birth relatives between one and four times a year and 13 per cent met them between six and 12 times a year. Some children (16 per cent) were seeing different relatives on different occasions, resulting in numerous contacts each year. For example, contact was agreed for one child with his birth mother three times a year, his birth mother and grandmother together three times a year, his grandmother an additional three times a year and siblings six times annually or more frequently.

Preparation and planning for direct contact

Parker (1999) highlights the importance of early planning for direct contact and the need to integrate planning for contact with the assessment and preparation of prospective adopters. During the process of preparation, practitioners are in a powerful position and can play an important role in helping prospective adopters to understand the additional challenges that come with adoption and in anticipating and responding to their anxieties or misapprehensions. Practitioners' values and attitudes can significantly influence the views of prospective adopters, as can the formal and informal messages they receive during the process of assessment and preparation (Grotevant and McRoy, 1998; Neil, 2002a). A combination of positive attitudes towards birth families, education and the provision of emotional support is more likely to encourage prospective adopters to think about contact as being potentially beneficial for themselves and their children (Baumann, 1999; Silverstein and Kaplan Roszia, 1999).

We asked adoptive parents at what point in their work with the agency they had been introduced to the idea of contact and what kind of preparation they had received. We were particularly interested in how far they experienced their preparation as helpful and whether, as a consequence, they felt adequately prepared for direct contact. We were also interested in the process of planning for contact, how adoptive parents recalled the plan's introduction and the extent to which they had been involved in decisions about contact arrangements.

In general, adopters were introduced to the idea of contact at the stage of training and preparation prior to approval, and agencies were conveying the message that they should expect their children to have some form of post-adoption contact. Contact was one of the many themes included in their general preparation for adoption. Helpful preparation included the opportunity to meet adopters who had first-hand experience of contact and discussions with adopted people who shared their stories of a life without contact. Adopters found it useful to hear about relevant research and some had seen informative videos from New Zealand. Meeting birth relatives was considered particularly helpful, and was influential in shaping their attitudes towards birth relatives.

We did have one occasion where we actually had some birth mothers come in and talk to us about how they felt and it makes you feel really humble and you feel very sorry for them. You're certainly made aware through the training of what it must be like for those people.

Studies have demonstrated that contact cannot be achieved simply by emphasising children's needs or insisting that adoptive parents should comply with contact plans as a condition of approval and placement (Kedward *et al*, 1999; Neil, 2002a and 2002b). In order for adoptive parents to feel comfortable about contact, they need help to understand why contact is now included in most adoptions and why it is likely to be beneficial for themselves and their children. They also need to appreciate the purpose of particular contact arrangements in relation to children's experiences and relationships with members of their birth families. Additionally, prospective adopters should be encouraged to express their concerns and worries so these do not become future obstacles to facilitating contact or sources of resentment and suspicion. Responses from adoptive parents in our study, however, suggested that these areas were not consistently covered and agency preparation was sometimes viewed as inadequate for helping them to cope with the realities of direct contact. Preparation tended to concentrate exclusively on children's needs for contact and insufficient attention was directed at helping adopters to anticipate their own feelings towards birth families and their responses to the kinds of management issues that might arise after adoption.

We were prepared for the mechanics of it, but how it affects you emotionally and how it affects your relationships with the children is something that isn't very well covered.

Aspects of preparation group work that were unhelpful included being told horror stories about difficult contact arrangements and being told they would not be approved if they did not agree to contact. This merely served to silence them and would only store up potential problems in the future.

We were told basically in a nutshell, that if you didn't go for contact there would be less chance of getting a child. You will say anything and do anything at that stage.

Adoptive parents were all expecting that some form of contact would be required for their children, but were aware that they could exercise some choice about accepting particular children and could negotiate the type of contact they felt able to live with. It was clear from their responses, however, that when they were presented with a possible placement, contact plans were incorporated as "part of the package". This hindered their willingness and ability to hesitate or to object to contact since they risked having to wait for an alternative match:

No, not really, there was no choice. Well, the way it was worded, I knew there would be some form of contact and that would be part of the deal. We didn't have an option. If we'd said no, then I don't think we'd have got him.

Adopters were largely presented with information about children for whom contact planning was already under way, although detailed arrangements had not always been resolved. We wanted to know how far adopters felt they had been involved in the process of planning detailed contact arrangements. Their responses fell into four categories: First, in thirty-three families (54 per cent), adopters reported that the agency had proposed a plan for contact with which they were prepared to agree. Their experiences differed, however, in the extent to which they were involved in discussing detailed arrangements. Some were presented with the agency's intention that direct contact should continue, but were invited to discuss and agree decisions about frequency, location, supervision and ways of arranging meetings.

We had meetings with everybody's social worker, we all got together and decided how contact was going to be worked out. We had quite a big say in what went on. There were issues we brought up they hadn't thought about. We were totally involved right from start to finish. To a certain extent we had quite a lot of say in what went on.

Others, however, were left to negotiate the details of contact arrangements with little or no professional help. Most of these involved contact with siblings who were living with other adoptive families and the adopters reached a mutual agreement about the frequency and venue for contact. While most adopters were happy to sort things out themselves, social workers should nevertheless be aware that some adopters may need their help and at least offer them their support and assistance. Adopters valued having been involved in negotiations about detailed arrangements for direct contact. They felt that the views of all parties were taken into consideration and that this enabled everyone to accept and to be clear about contact arrangements from the beginning.

Second, adoptive parents in 12 families were presented with a plan for contact but were not involved in negotiating detailed arrangements. Most of these situations involved children who had been in foster care, contact arrangements were already well established and working well, and adopters were happy to continue with the arrangements.

We were treated with respect but we didn't have a contribution. We just said fair enough, we'll accept whatever's been happening. It seemed fair enough.

However, in a minority of cases (3), plans for contact had not been finalised before the children moved into their adoptive homes. Adopters in these situations had felt disadvantaged because they were not agreeing to plans which were already tried and tested and shown to be working well. These adopters expressed more ambivalence about contact, but felt they had little choice about whether to accept the plans:

It was put to us that it was important to the child so we accepted it. It was a necessary evil.

In all these situations, adopters were anxious about meeting the birth relatives. Once contact was established, however, it continued to work satisfactorily and the adopters were happy for it to continue.

Third, adoptive parents in ten families reported that contact planning was either agency led, driven by recommendations from the child's guardian, or promoted by arguments from birth relatives' solicitors. Adoptive parents had been unhappy with the plan for contact, and, although they accepted it, they remained hostile to its implementation. In all these cases, adopters felt they had not been involved in the planning process and some had been forced into accepting a greater frequency of contact than they had originally anticipated.

Sean's adoptive parents had been unhappy with the level of contact that was imposed upon them. He had originally been placed with them for long-term fostering and had frequent contact with his birth mother, grandparents and siblings. Over four years later, they finally adopted him, and while they agreed that contact should continue, they anticipated a reduction in its frequency. However, the guardian *ad litem* took a different view and they were left with monthly contact, which they thought would be difficult to sustain in the long term. At the time of the research, these arrangements had continued for eight years but they had not been unproblematic. The adoptive father said:

> We were stitched up by the guardian. He made the recommendation to court. Both social services and ourselves were stitched up, but they didn't argue the case either. But that was the social worker. She was frightened to death.

Sally is severely disabled and was placed with her adoptive parents at birth. They had stated in their assessment that they did not want a child placed with them for whom direct contact was the plan and the placement was made on this understanding. However, shortly before the adoption hearing, the social worker had phoned to say the birth parents would not agree to the adoption unless they could see Sally once a year. By this time, Sally had been placed with them for seven months and they were frightened of losing her if they refused to comply with the plan for contact. Sally's adoptive mother said:

We were emotionally blackmailed into it. I feel very resentful because of the way they did it. We have seen them three times now and it's a real blight on my life. In fact it's ruined my life.

It is perhaps unsurprising that, at the time of the research, adopters described most of these contact arrangements as problematic, and contact was terminated at the adoption hearing in two cases which fell into this category.

Lastly, in six families, adopters had initiated the process and pushed social workers to sort out plans for contact. In all but one of these families the adopters were experienced foster carers who adopted their foster children and were keen for them to continue existing contact arrangements.

Advantages of direct contact: perceptions of adoptive parents and birth families

Adoptive parents, birth relatives and adopted children all contribute to how far direct contact is experienced as beneficial and how far it successfully develops to meet participants' needs as these change over time. There is evidence from our study and other research (Grotevant *et al*, 1999) that adult interaction and relationships bearing on the management of contact are likely to affect children's well-being. We thus concentrate here on the perceptions of adoptive parents and birth relatives in our sample. One of the factors which motivates adopters to maintain direct post-adoption contact is that they think there are advantages in doing so. Adoptive parents in our sample were able to identify advantages for participants from at least one side of the adoption triangle. Adoptive parents of 56 children in 35 families (57 per cent) identified advantages for themselves, their children and birth family members. In 20 families with 27 children, adopters thought that although they gained little from contact, it had advantages for their children and birth relatives. Parents in only three adoptive families with six children felt that contact had no advantages other than for birth relatives.

When identifying advantages for themselves, adopters discussed the importance of access to information about their children's histories, keeping knowledge about birth families up to date and actively participating in conversations about their children's past. They did not want their children to blame them for excluding birth relatives from their lives and some felt they would be better prepared if children wanted to trace other members of their birth families when they grew up. Adopters explained, for example:

I think with his Mum, he also knows he can talk about her with us. I mean – he doesn't much but we'll occasionally say the name of someone and he'll say 'oh, we knew somebody called that when I was with Linda' [birth mother]. *Or he'll occasionally say incidents that happened like his sister got a fork down her throat when he was with Linda. He feels totally free to be able to talk about it.* (Adoptive mother: direct contact with maternal grandmother, birth mother and adopted siblings)

It's about knowing what makes Dave tick. We didn't find that out from the paperwork but we can get what makes him tick from his mother – not from information but from the feel of the whole family. Because Dave is so complicated you have to get to know as much as you can to get inside his head. (Adoptive mother: direct contact with birth mother, siblings, maternal grandmother and aunt)

Adopters described the advantages for their children associated with contact. These largely related to adopters' feelings that children need to maintain links with their "roots". Children had direct access to information and when they grew up there would be no shocks or any unexpected discovery of "skeletons in the cupboard". While these aspects of contact were largely identified as advantageous for children, it was clear they also gave adopters some peace of mind about their children's future well-being. An adoptive mother explains:

She's always known her own family. If she has any questions they are there for her to talk to. She doesn't have to go through us or when she is 18 she doesn't have to start the process of finding out about her background because they've always been there to have contact with. (Adoptive mother: direct contact with birth father and paternal grandmother)

Adoptive parents seemed to recognise something special about separated siblings' needs for contact with each other. Their views were based, not so much on the importance of access to information or identity issues, but on the recognition of an emotional closeness that grows out of shared histories and mutually supportive relationships. Many adopters intuitively grasped messages from research about the particular quality of sibling relationships (Borland *et al*, 1998; Morrow, 1998) and the sense of loss experienced by separated siblings (Whitaker *et al*, 1984; Harrison, 1999). For example:

> The emphasis and importance he places on his sisters is very, very important. There is an extremely strong bond with his sisters, which we recognise. He always speaks very fondly of them . . . he hugs and kisses them . . . they pick him up. There's just a very strong bond there. They still like to see their little brother and to a certain extent the older sister mothered him and brought him up. (Adoptive father: direct contact with two sisters living with maternal grandmother and one with maternal aunt)

We should not paint too rosy a picture of sibling contact. While adoptive parents in our sample could identify advantages for their children in maintaining sibling contact, two particular issues tended to present themselves as disadvantages for adopters. First, adopters were aware that their children worried about siblings, particularly if they were not settled with a family. This sometimes led adoptive parents to shoulder the worry on behalf of their children and to emphasise the advantages of contact for birth relatives (siblings) rather than for their adopted children. Second, sibling contact was sometimes experienced as difficult by adoptive parents even when they perceived it as advantageous for their children. As compared to contact with birth parents, for example, sibling contact is not necessarily an easy option. This is particularly so when siblings are in the care system and adopters worry about the effects of their bad language, sexual knowledge and experience, rough and excitable behaviour and attention-seeking demands. Permanent carers in Rushton *et al*'s study (2001, p. 41) expressed similar concerns. All the adopters could identify advantages of direct contact for birth relatives even when this was not matched by perceived advantages for themselves or their children.

For birth relatives, the most commonly articulated advantage of contact was their ability to see the children growing up and to gain reassurance that they were well and happy. All the birth mothers and fathers gave this as the only or most important advantage of direct contact. The four birth mothers who were initially opposed to adoption also felt that contact made their children happy and served to confirm their continuing emotional significance for the children. The two relinquishing birth mothers of children with Down's Syndrome were unsure about whether their children benefited from contact. Fifteen of the 18 grandparents also emphasised the importance of seeing how their grandchildren were getting on while the others simply said they wanted contact because they loved the children. Having first-hand evidence of the children's well-being was also important for aunts and an uncle, while this was identified by six of the 11 birth siblings as the major advantage of contact. They said, for example:

It helps me in the sense that I know he's all right and I like to know who he looks like in the family and who he's taking after and about his school. And every time you see him, they change, don't they, as they grow older, and it's marvellous, the change, you know, you watch them each step. I like to know he's all right. (Birth mother initially opposed to adoption but who eventually gave her consent)

Birth relatives were most likely to describe advantages for the children in terms of their relationship and the children's pleasure in seeing them. Seventeen (45 per cent) of the 38 birth relatives who responded to this question went further than this. They explained that they thought contact helped the children by providing access to family histories and information, contributing to their sense of identity and confirming that their birth families still loved and cared about them.

While all birth relatives could identify advantages for themselves and nearly half thought contact had specific benefits for the children, only six mentioned any gains for adoptive parents. Although some birth relatives identified contact as benefiting children in specific ways, it was evident that their own needs for reassurance, family continuity and emotional gratification were uppermost in their minds. These motivational factors coincided in most cases with children's needs and wishes and with adopters' perceptions of the advantages that flowed from contact. In a small number of cases, however, birth relatives appeared to be so caught up with their own needs that this caused discomfort for the children and/ or adoptive parents. This serves as a reminder that birth families also require help to deal with their feelings about adoption, separation and loss. They, as much as adopters, need preparation and support for managing contact visits and understanding and accepting the purpose of direct contact.

Satisfaction and comfort with direct contact

Although adoptive parents and birth relatives identified advantages of direct contact, this does not mean contact was always unproblematic. We were impressed by the way in which the majority of adopters and birth family members worked at achieving common ground in terms of their expectations and ability to manage relationships that had only grown out of their shared interest in the children. In order to assess how adopters and birth relatives *experienced* contact, we discussed their feelings of satisfaction and comfort. For adoptive parents, we distinguished personal comfort and parental comfort, although the two are closely related. Personal comfort may be undermined, for example, if birth relatives cannot give permission for adopters to assume a parenting role or if they act in other ways to diminish adopters' sense of confidence, security or self-worth. Parental comfort becomes eroded if adopters feel their children are unsettled or distressed by contact. In these circumstances adopters became upset for their children and wanted to do something to protect them. Feelings of satisfaction with contact refer to how far adopters assessed it as being beneficial for their children in relation to its frequency and children's needs for information, reassurance, genealogical continuity and so on.

Some adoptive parents experienced personal discomfort during contact but persevered because they were satisfied it had advantages for their children and was in their best interests. A degree of parental discomfort may be endured if adopters are satisfied that the long-term advantages of contact outweigh the short-term disadvantages for children. The maintenance of direct contact is problematic in those cases where *parental discomfort is high and satisfaction is low*. Adopters have to negotiate a balance in their attitudes to contact based on their experience of personal and parental comfort and satisfaction with short-term disadvantages versus long-term advantages. It is a complicated and sometimes emotionally challenging equation. Adopters frequently felt they had been inadequately prepared by agencies to deal with these issues.

It is encouraging to report that 67 per cent of adoptive families were comfortable and satisfied with contact. A further 11 adoptive families (19 per cent) experienced discomfort, but remained satisfied that contact was in their children's best interests. Two examples may illustrate this relationship. Adoptive parents in one family experienced personal discomfort but felt that the potential advantages afforded by contact made it worth continuing. Initially, contact with maternal grandfather and birth mother had been held at a social services centre and was supervised by a social worker. Meetings subsequently moved to neutral territory and were unsupervised. The adopters reported that the birth mother disliked meeting in communal places so they agreed to meet at the grandfather's home. Visits were described as "chaotic" with the children's birth mother wrapping up presents for them as they arrived, shouting and taking the children into the bedroom for private conversations. The adoptive mother described her feelings about this situation:

I'm not saying she would do any harm to them but you're out of that, you've no control over what's happening, you can't hear what she's saying to them, you can't interrupt, you can't alter the situation. And you wriggle and you squirm and my husband will look at me and I'll look at him and I know he's getting himself into a state. And we have granddad sitting there and he loves seeing the children, but he finds her hard to cope with at the best of times and there's all this going on – this undercurrent, you know, and we're trying to keep an aura of normality.

In another family, adopters experienced personal and parental discomfort but again felt satisfied that contact with her older siblings would benefit their daughter in the long term. The adoptive mother explained:

She'd actually say and she'd tell everyone I was a naughty mummy – I took her back [to visit her birth parents] *and I shouldn't have taken her back. She'd come back and cling more to Andy* [adoptive father] *because she said I'd taken her and I was horrible. She used to face me*

– you're a naughty mummy. You shouldn't have taken me. We tried to explain but she wouldn't have it and she sulked for a week. In future I hope that they [social workers] *are right and that she will forget all those bad times and bad experiences and having the stress and that she will only remember the continuance of contact. And out of it I suppose I see a positive side for her – that she will get more of the truth and will be able to discuss, particularly with Charlie* [oldest sibling] *about what really happened and they could probably support each other through that.*

In nine families (13 per cent) adopters identified feelings of personal and/or parental discomfort and thought that contact was either harmful or had no benefits for their children. These were the contact arrangements that were in trouble and in three families contact had stopped. The reasons for these difficulties are complex but significant problems arose where birth mothers had opposed adoption and/or where contact was so frequent (every month) that adopters felt they had little social and emotional space in which to construct family relationships.

For birth relatives we assessed their experience of personal comfort, role comfort and satisfaction with contact. Role comfort refers to birth relatives' ability and willingness to accommodate children's new (adoptive) family relationships and their feelings about the social and emotional space that they had come to occupy in the children's lives. Neil (2002b, p. 15) points out that 'a key psychological issue for birth relatives after adoption is to adjust to their changed role in the child's life, the reality that their child is also part of another family'. This reality is likely to be acutely experienced during direct contact when birth relatives are visitors to the adoptive home, when they witness parent–child relationships acted out between children and their adoptive parents and when children talk about their (adoptive) extended families and their everyday activities. Birth relatives only get an occasional glimpse of the children's new and very different lives.

As we noted earlier, all birth relatives were satisfied with contact insofar as they identified advantages for themselves and the children. However, the vast majority of birth relatives also expressed a high degree of personal and role comfort. Grandparents, aunts and siblings did not experience role discomfort, feeling that the children still related to them in ways that confirmed their (birth) familial status and emotional significance. They said things like:

When they come here, it's just as if it's never stopped. You'd have to see the boys when they come here. Immediately they grab hold of you, they kiss you, they hug you, this is the way they are. And everyone's quite easy. When we pick the boys up they fly to you straight away. There's no fresh contact, it's just as though it's ongoing. Put it this way, it's not a matter of access – we are just out and out grandparents, that's all it is. (Maternal grandfather)

They don't remember mum and dad but they do remember me and our brother. It's mainly me they remember most because when they were little I used to look after them a lot and they remember me as their big brother who was really nice to them and that's how they still see me. (Sibling)

Role comfort was problematic for three birth mothers: two of them had opposed adoption and one had agreed at the "eleventh hour". They confirmed that they still considered themselves to be the children's mothers and had difficulty accommodating the adopters' parenting role. Four related birth siblings expressed role discomfort because they had no prior relationship with their adopted sibling and struggled to know how they should relate to him. Only one grandmother and one birth sibling expressed personal and role discomfort.

Conclusion: implications for practice

Our interviews with adoptive parents and birth relatives suggest that the majority of direct contact arrangements were working well, several years after they had initially been agreed. However, where this was the case it appeared largely due to adopters' willingness to keep their promises about contact and their ability to see long-term benefits for their children. Birth relatives appreciated that adoption had turned out to be best for the children, even where some of them had initially opposed it, and they expressed enormous satisfaction about being able to see the children grow up. There are several ways in which agencies might have contributed more effectively to these outcomes and helped families when they ran into trouble:

- A high proportion of adoptive families who were excluded from discussions about contact and/or who felt they had been forced to accept problematic arrangements, were facing difficulties in managing contact at the time of our study. Social workers need to include prospective adopters as *partners* in negotiating contact as early as possible.

- Preparation for adoption and direct contact needs to move beyond persuading prospective adopters about the benefits of contact for their children. Social workers need to anticipate issues and prepare new parents for the social and emotional challenges that they will face in "sharing" their children with birth families over time.

- Preparing birth relatives for ongoing direct contact requires attention to their expectations and understanding of the kind of role they can expect to play in the children's lives. This is particularly important for birth mothers, who may find it difficult to relinquish their parental status and role to adoptive parents.

- It is a mistake to think that sibling contact is relatively unproblematic. While the vast majority of adoptive parents in our study were satisfied that sibling contact was in their children's best interests, its impact on their children frequently caused them concern.

- It is also a mistake to think that birth mothers' agreement to adoption automatically bodes well for direct post-adoption contact. Some birth mothers in our study finally agreed to adoption because they were worn out with resisting, rather than because they were ready to relinquish care of their children to adopters. In a small number of cases, these mothers caused their children distress during contact visits and exacerbated adopters' worries about continuing contact.

- Our study suggests that social workers were much concerned with negotiating contact arrangements at the time of placement but that after adoption they left adopters and birth relatives to work things out as best they could. Support, consultation and mediation needs to be available to adoptive parents and birth relatives as and when they need it. Arrangements for direct contact cannot be approached as a one-off event. Participants' feelings and expectations about contact develop over time and arrangements that social workers make prior to adoption will have changing and challenging consequences for many years.

- Social workers should think carefully about the purpose of direct contact, since this will inform its frequency and management. Similarly, agreeing visits at Christmas and children's birthdays was experienced as intrusive by many adopters and introduced unnecessary tensions into their relationships with birth families.

Summary

This chapter is based on a study of face-to-face contact after adoption, and uses data from interviews with adoptive parents and birth relatives.

Three main aims of the research

- To identify the advantages and disadvantages of face-to-face contact from the point of view of all three parties (adopters, children and birth relatives).
- To identify the factors that influence whether face-to-face contact is experienced as beneficial or detrimental by those involved.
- To learn lessons for policy and practice about when direct contact is indicated.

Three main findings

- Contact worked best where adoptive parents and birth relatives were well prepared and were involved in *detailed* planning for contact arrangements.
- The majority of both adoptive parents and birth relatives identified advantages of face-to-face contact for at least one party and were able to articulate its value for adopted children.
- Although face-to-face contact was sometimes complicated or difficult, participants were still able to experience it as beneficial. Adoptive parents could tolerate personal discomfort if they felt contact was in children's long-term best interests. Birth relatives' satisfaction with contact was associated with role comfort, where they had been able to acknowledge and adapt to their changed role in the children's lives.

Three main implications for practice

- Ensuring direct contact will work well requires actively working with and supporting both birth relatives and adoptive parents from the very beginning of the planning process. Contact arrangements should reflect the purpose of contact.

- Simple assumptions about factors that indicate relatively easy or problematic contact are unhelpful. It is important to take a case sensitive approach, which considers individual participants' expectations, experiences, needs and attitudes in the context of relationships and contact.

- Support, consultation and mediation need to be available to all parties in the long term. Arranging contact is not a one-off event but the beginning of a process that involves complex work, negotiation and relationship-building over time.

References

Baumann, C. (1999) 'Adoptive fathers and birth fathers: a study of attitudes', *Child and Adolescent Social Work Journal*, 16(5), pp. 373–391.

Borland, M., Layborn, A., Hill, M. and Brown, J. (1998) *Middle Childhood: The perspectives of children and parents*, London: Jessica Kingsley.

Grotevant, H. D. and McRoy, R. G. (1998) *Openness in Adoption: Exploring family connections*, London: Sage.

Grotevant, H. D., Ross, N. M., Marchel, M. and McRoy, R. G. (1999) 'Adaptive behaviour in adopted children: predictors from early risk, collaboration in relationships within the adoptive kinship network and openness arrangements', *Journal of Adolescent Research*, 14(2), pp. 231–247.

Harrison, C. (1999) 'Children being looked after and their sibling relationships: the experiences of children in the working partnership with "lost" parents research project', in A. Mullender (ed.) *We Are Family: Sibling relationships in placement and beyond*, London: BAAF.

Kedward, C., Luckward, B. and Lawson, H. (1999) 'Mediation and post-adoption contact: the early experience of the Post-Adoption Center contact mediation service', *Adoption & Fostering*, 23(3), pp. 16–26.

Morrow, V. (1998) *Understanding Families: Children's perspectives*, London: National Children's Bureau.

Neil, E. (2002a) 'Contact after adoption: the role of agencies in making and supporting plans', *Adoption & Fostering*, 26(1), pp. 25–38.

Neil, E. (2002b) 'Managing face-to-face contact for young adopted children', in H. Argent (ed.) *Staying Connected: Managing contact arrangements in adoption*, London: BAAF.

Parker, R. (1999) *Adoption Now: Messages from research*, Chichester: John Wiley and Sons.

Rushton, A., Dance, C., Quinton, D. and Mayes, D. (2001) *Siblings in Late Permanent Placements*, London: BAAF.

Silverstein, D. and Kaplan Roszia, S. (1999) 'Openness: a critical component of special needs adoption', *Child Welfare*, 78(5), pp. 637–651.

Smith, C. and Logan, J. (2004) *After Adoption: Direct contact and relationships*, London: Routledge.

Whitaker, D., Cook, J., Dunne, C. and Rocliffe, S. (1984) *The Experience of Residential Care from the Perspectives of Children, Parents and Care-Givers*, University of York: Department of Social Policy and Social Work.

8 Promoting security and managing risk: Contact in long-term foster care

Mary Beek and Gillian Schofield

Late placed children in long-term foster care commonly have divided loyalties between their foster carers, who are their current source of care and protection, and their birth families, for whom they may have strong but ambivalent feelings of love and anxiety. They must find ways to think through and accept the membership of two families (Fahlberg, 1994; Thoburn, 1996), whilst also managing their personal histories in ways that do not involve excessive anxiety or blame. Contact is the point at which the two families overlap in the child's life and mind and is therefore a delicate and complex area. It holds the potential to assist children in managing their dual identities and to develop or sustain positive relationships with their relatives, built on realistic understandings and appreciation of their strengths and difficulties. However, contact can involve difficult transitions, the arousal of painful memories and feelings and the exploration of relationships that have been destructive in the past. It can also have a positive or negative impact on the child's sense of permanence in the foster family.

Every contact arrangement therefore requires careful thought and management to ensure that the child is protected from anxiety and supported to cope with the dilemmas and uncertainties that may arise. Children at different ages and stages in their development may need different types of contact and different types of support in managing it.

This chapter examines the contact experiences of a group of children placed in long-term foster care. It considers the extent to which the potential risks of the contact were managed and balanced in ways that enabled the children to feel secure, comfortable, supported and free from anxiety when they connected with their birth families.

The Growing up in Foster Care study

Growing up in Foster Care is a longitudinal study, following the progress of a group of children and young people who are living in foster families on a planned, long-term basis. The broad objective of the study is to explore how far the various and complex needs of the children can be identified and met in long-term foster care. An important aspect of this is to consider the relationships between the children and their birth relatives and the ways in which contact arrangements may promote or undermine the children's well-being and placement stability.

The sample of children in new, planned long-term foster placements was first identified in 1997–8 (Phase 1) and followed up in 2000–2001 (Phase 2). At Phase 1, the group consisted of 58 children aged 4–12 (mean age ten), from four shire counties, three unitary authorities and one London borough. At Phase 2 of the study (2001), 52 of the original group of children, then aged 7–15 years, were followed up. (For full details of the project see Schofield *et al*, 2000; Beek and Schofield, 2004).

Three of the children were of minority ethnic origin, the remainder were white, English. The majority had been placed in their long-term families in middle childhood and many had spent at least the first five years of life in their birth families. Significantly for contact, more than half (59 per cent) had birth siblings still living in the birth family. Learning difficulties affected 25 per cent of the children and in four cases, these were severe. Levels of abuse and neglect were high, with 81 per cent of the children having experienced three or more forms of maltreatment. It was not surprising, in these grave circumstances, that the emotional and behavioural development of the group gave cause for concern and social workers judged that 93 per cent of the children had difficulties in this area. The Strengths and Difficulties Questionnaire (Goodman, 1997) showed almost half scoring in the abnormal range and a further 17 per cent were borderline.

The birth parents of the children were also in the main a troubled group, with 76 per cent having difficulties in two or more of the following areas: abuse in childhood, physical and mental health problems, learning difficulties, and drug and alcohol misuse. Patterns of caregiving in the birth family were secure and reliable in one or two cases, but for the most part unpredictable and uncertain, hostile and rejecting, or frightening and out of control (Schofield *et al*, 2000).

The foster carers were all white and all except one were English. There were 38 couples and seven single carers. Motivation to foster on a long-term basis was varied. Some carers were seeking to establish or increase their young families through fostering, while others were experienced foster, adoptive or birth parents for whom the long-term fostered child or children represented a second family, later in life. A small number were recruited and paid as professional carers with the expectation that they were caring for children with high levels of need.

Both phases of the study used a combination of qualitative and quantitative research methods. This enabled the baseline data and the changes and outcomes for the children to be described in statistical terms (within the limitations of the sample size) but it also provided deeper understandings of the children's relationships both within and outside the foster home. Research tools included questionnaires for social workers, interviews with children, foster carers, birth families and social workers, and the Strengths and Difficulties Questionnaire (Goodman, 1997). Information regarding contact was obtained at both phases and from all possible sources.

Contact frequency and arrangements

At Phase 1, there were high levels of face-to-face contact in the sample. As many as 90 per cent had some form of face-to-face contact with an adult birth relative and 64 per cent also had some form of indirect contact. Frequency of contact varied, but 70 per cent saw an adult birth relative at least once a month. Meetings could take place in foster homes, on neutral ground or in birth family homes. Some visits were supervised by social services staff, some by the carers and some not at all.

At Phase 2, the overall picture was one of fluidity. Frequencies of meetings had increased or decreased depending on circumstances, supervision had become more or less intense or ceased altogether and different venues had been tried. As the children grew older, they were tending to meet their relatives independently and make their own decisions about frequency and venue. In no cases, however, had face-to-face contact ceased.

Promoting security and managing risk

In each case, it was possible to discern something of the nature, role and meaning of contact for the child. The experience of contact would influence the child's capacity to resolve painful issues and manage the membership of two families. This would be positively or negatively mediated by a range of variables, such as the practical arrangements and the sensitivity of the foster carers. Concepts of "security" and "risk" and the way in which these two elements were balanced, helped us to classify the children's experiences. Contact was described as promoting a sense of security when children appeared to feel physically and emotionally safe before, during and after their contact meetings. Contact was seen as risky when it was associated with unacceptably high levels of anxiety, uncertainty or, in some cases, fear for the children. Our model allowed for the fact that even the most "straightforward" of contact arrangements could potentially involve a degree of "risk" for the child (for example, confusion, the awakening of feelings of loss, etc). However, what was important was the extent to which this risk was acknowledged and successfully managed by all parties.

Security and risk around contact were built on and connected to the quality of both foster family relationships and birth family relationships, but were also affected by social work practice. The planning, organisation and monitoring of contact was crucially important. The most sensitive, available carer would find it difficult to compensate for a young child being taken to an unknown venue, by an unknown supervisor to meet an unpredictable number of birth relatives, one or more of whom had previously abused her – and this happened. The extent to which security was promoted and risk managed depended on interplay between factors in the child, the foster family, the birth relatives and the agency policy and practice. Thus the model representing this interplay is highly inter-active (Figure 1).

Degrees of security and risk occurred on a continuum, but the sample could be divided into three broad groups as follows:

- Contact promoting security/risks managed;
- Contact raising some anxiety/risks partially managed;
- Contact actively harmful/risks poorly managed.

Figure 1
Contact in long-term foster care

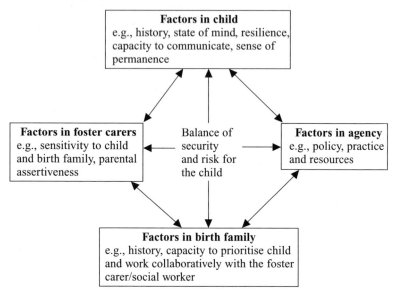

In this chapter, each of these three variations of contact is examined in turn and, using anonymised case material, the characteristic features of each group is explored.

Contact promoting security/risks managed

In these situations, children appeared to feel secure and at ease when seeing their relatives and were not unduly anxious or stressed before or afterwards. A degree of anxiety might be expected in most cases, but potential difficulties and complex feelings were anticipated, acknowledged and dealt with as they arose.

Secure and comfortable contact was more likely to be achieved when foster carers were able to endorse a sense of both foster and birth family membership. The child was seen, unequivocally, as a fully included and equal member of the foster family and could be assured of practical and emotional support throughout life. At the same time, however, this need not preclude birth family membership. Confident of their own centrality in the child's life, sensitive carers could think and talk openly about birth family members and acknowledge their strengths and difficulties. They could convey to the child that they understood and accepted both positive and negative feelings about birth family members. Definitions of "mother" and "father" were not exclusive and it was possible to be "mum at home" as one carer put it, while at the same time, acknowledging the significance of another mother.

As close relationships developed with the child, foster carers felt increasingly central to their child's development and well-being and children began to trust in their carer's physical and psychological availability. Carers had come to represent a "secure base" from which the children could explore the outside world, safe in the knowledge that they could return in times of anxiety. Contact was likely to involve complex feelings and so the most comfortable arrangements were those in which the child had ready access to their secure base, if needed. This might be achieved by carers being present during contact, or delivering and collecting the child and making time to talk with the birth relatives at each end to ensure a smooth transition. Occasionally, such arrangements had led to close relationships developing between foster carers and birth relatives. Joshua, for instance, had the most frequent contact in the sample, spending part of most weekends with his birth father. The arrangement was flexible, and could be altered by agreement if the foster family had a commitment or the birth father had to work longer hours. However, this comfortable arrangement did not mean that there were no complications. Joshua's loyalties could feel torn but his carers accepted this and encouraged him to talk through his complex feelings. Using his secure base in this way, Joshua was able to reach a compromise regarding Christmas arrangements.

He now finds it difficult at Christmas time. His Dad'll say, you know, 'I'll take him at Christmas' and Joshua's, like, 'Oh, but I wanna be here Christmas and I wouldn't mind going there Boxing Day'. You know he finds it hard. He says, 'I wanna be in both places'. In the end he says, 'I think I should be here Christmas Day and then I'll go to my dad's Boxing Day' something like that. He says, 'I feel as if I should be here just part of the family at Christmas'.

In some situations, the physical presence of the carer during the contact meetings was an explicit reminder of the availability of the secure base and could be of great reassurance to the child.

Samantha (14) had become highly stressed by her birth mother's erratic attendance at contact meetings hosted and supervised by social services. Her foster mother decided to change the arrangements so that she could supervise them herself and the birth mother could choose a venue in which she felt comfortable. When Samantha had easy access to her secure base in this way, she was able to relax and enjoy her contact and also to manage her loyalties to both families.

If we keep it like it is now and it's successful and Samantha's not unhappy, she looks forward to it and it's made pleasant. And then afterwards we chat about it and it's still all nice and she doesn't wet the bed that night and she doesn't have a tantrum before we go and she doesn't keep saying, 'What time is it, what time is it?' And that sort of thing like we used to have, you know, then I think well, we've got the right formula don't you know, because it's Samantha's needs not [birth mother's] needs that I'm supposed to be fulfilling.

When it was felt to be unsuitable for the carer to be present, it was important that the experience of the contact was in some way communicated to the foster carer so that complex feelings might be known and understood. One arrangement involved a known and trusted social worker providing the transport to and from the contact and taking time to talk with the carer and child together both before and after the meetings, thus offering security and continuity. Even the contact meetings taking place in an environment that was known and familiar to both the child and the carers (e.g., a family centre) might help the child to hold the carer in mind during the meeting and provide a route into sharing the experience afterwards.

Contact could raise deep and painful issues at times, and these could remain hidden, particularly in children who struggled to express their true thoughts and feelings.

Linda (14), for instance, had recently been troubled by the memory that, as a young child, she was left alone at home to care for her four younger siblings. She used a meeting to share this memory with her birth mother who immediately told her that it was not true. This was extremely difficult for Linda, a child whose sense of self and reality was fragile and fragmented. It might also have raised questions about whether other memories of sexual and physical abuse would be denied. The foster father's presence at the contact meeting at least ensured that Linda was not struggling alone with this denial of her experiences and he could offer reassurance afterwards. Accurate information about children's early experiences is important if carers are to offer sensitive support to contact.

When carers had first-hand or reliably reported knowledge of the birth relatives, more realistic understandings of their difficulties and dilemmas were likely to develop. For instance, one foster mother could see that the process of claiming bus fares from social services was complicated and humiliating for a birth mother. She proposed a system where she reimbursed the birth mother herself and then claimed the money back through her allowances. Putting this into action required the child's social worker and the family placement worker to understand the significance of this gesture and attend to the practicalities but such co-operation had helped to build trust between the carer and the birth mother, and this was of great benefit to the child.

For such trusting relationships to be established, however, it was helpful if firm foundations had been laid from the outset and agency practice was important in this respect. Familiarity with the carers through a prior introduction that did not involve the children was greatly appreciated by birth relatives. This provided opportunities for gestures of friendship or indications of empathy from the foster carers which were deeply significant, as this birth mother reported.

I began talking to her [the foster mother] on the phone first of all, and then she said, 'why don't you come round for coffee while he's at school?' So I did. And it sort of grew from there really.

Equally important was the capacity of the birth relatives to reflect at some level on the reasons why they could not care for the children. This did not preclude feelings of sadness, anger, guilt or a sense of injustice, but a level of acceptance in the birth relatives enabled them to hold in mind the needs of the child and give some degree of explicit or implicit support to the placement. This was often coupled with admiration and gratitude, as these birth parents of a child with severe disabilities describe.

I visit sometimes and I think they look knackered and I think I have put that burden on them and feel sad. But then I just think, I couldn't do it like them.

With this level of acceptance, foster carers responded readily and were often proactive and creative in removing barriers and enhancing the quality of the meetings with the child. However, the promotion of birth family membership and empathy on the part of the carers did not mean that contact was pursued at all costs. Where carers were focussed on the needs of the children and could see that contact was harmful at a particular time, they would take steps to reduce or suspend it, while not losing sight of the potential for positive links to be sustained.

Liam's birth mother repeatedly failed to come to contact meetings and the foster mother described his "humiliation", when sharing the disappointment with the other children in the foster family. The foster mother found this unacceptable and, at the time of the research interview, was about to propose steps to make the contact more attractive to the birth mother but also to set limits that prevented Liam (8) from being let down. The support of the child's social worker was essential to this plan and the foster carer was confident that this would be forthcoming.

Young children needed this level of protection, since they could not make sense of their parents' difficulties and could be overwhelmed by feelings of rejection, anger and guilt. For some of the older teenagers, however, the situation was rather different. They usually wanted to pursue relationships with their parents more independently and therefore could not be protected from all potential risks. However, if they had established a strong sense of a secure base in the foster family and if they were beginning to understand and contextualise their parents' difficulties, their foster carers tended to feel that it was time to "let go" and allow them to explore the relationships more independently. At the same time, they would know that the foster family base was ready and waiting to support them, if needed.

Amanda had only had sporadic contact with her parents since the age of three, partly because of their prison sentences for drug-related offences. As a 15-year-old, she went to meet her birth mother in the local shopping centre, but her mother did not appear. Immediately, Amanda telephoned her foster father and he was readily available.

I said to Amanda, 'Come home if she don't turn up', and she's upset now. 'Alright', I said, 'Stop there. I'll come and get you.' So I brought her home.

Although this was troubling for Amanda, contact was not stopped and there were subsequent successful meetings where mother and daughter went swimming or shopping together. There were also some more missed meetings. But Amanda made contingency plans and if her mother did not come, she would phone home and go shopping with friends instead. These experiences helped Amanda to let go of her rather idealised view of her mother and left her with a more balanced view, which had helped her to move on in terms of her commitment to the foster family.

Other children had also gained some clarity around their two families as a result of well-supported risk-taking by foster parents that empowered the children but also protected them.

Zoë (13) had always had a very emotionally entangled relationship with her mother that in part contributed to a previous placement breakdown. Her next foster mother understood Zoë's needs to explore her connections to her birth family. With the support of the social worker, she agreed to Zoë's persistent requests to sleep over at her mother's home, twice a month. Over time, this arrangement proved too much for the birth mother to cope with and it was reduced to once a month, which seemed manageable. As a result of this freedom within safe limits, Zoë lost her sense of urgency regarding contact and instead, was able to find a comfortable "niche" in her mother's household when she visited. As her foster mother put it:

I think if you put a block on something that someone wants to do they want to do it even more. I think it is important for Zoë to feel part of the [birth] *family you know, to get her niche with her sisters and brother... and I think she has, yes, she has. I know she has.*

Zoë herself talked of the shift in her allegiance to the foster family, which had occurred in the context of that contact experience.

When I was with Pam [previous foster carer] *I always wanted my mother, but now I'm here I'm much happier. I'm not always wanting to live with my mum. It's better off for me here than with my mum.*

The shift was not caused by the contact, but understanding Zoë's needs regarding contact was part of the way in which the foster carer managed to provide a sense of balance and security.

Contact raising some anxiety/risks partially managed

In a number of cases, contact arrangements were seen by social work staff as progressing fairly smoothly, but the children continued to experience them as rather stressful and anxiety-provoking. This might be because they were unsure of whether their birth relatives would attend, or because the meetings themselves could be fraught and confusing. It was perhaps, symptomatic of the problem that less information could be gleaned from the interviews in these cases. Our major informants were the foster carers and they often had very little sense of what actually happened during contact. Children, too, were less open in talking about their birth relatives where contact was unsettling and disconnected from their foster families.

The foster carers associated with these situations often tried to be sensitive to their children's needs and were keen to promote the child's sense of belonging in both families, but they could not help feeling uncertain and sometimes anxious about the contact. It emerged that they often felt unable to query or challenge arrangements since they had a sense that contact had to be endured, regardless of the impact. One key to the uncertainty surrounding the contact arrangements was the lack of physical or psychological overlap between the two families, often as a result of organisational factors. Not only were foster carers absent from the meetings, they also lacked the possibility of using the supervising social worker as a "bridge" and in some cases they had never or rarely had a face-to-face meeting with the contact relative. So absolute was the divide between the foster family and the birth relatives that there was virtually no shared ground from which the carers might discuss the contact with the child or from which the child might feel his or her experiences were known and understood.

For younger children, the most common arrangement was to be taken by someone who was not well known to them (sometimes a taxi driver) to a "neutral" or social services venue where the supervised meeting would be planned to take place. The reported risks in these situations were that the birth parents might not attend, that inappropriate things might be said to the child or that the child would be in the presence of a previously abusive adult. Although these risks were managed in the sense that the contact was supervised, the supervisors did not know the children well and would be unlikely to pick up the more subtle signals of distress or confusion. On return home, the carers may or may not be given basic information about the contact, but the child's experiences were an unknown quantity to them. As day-to-day parents of the children, who had knowledge of and responsibility for every aspect and detail of their lives, this gap in their common experience was extraordinary.

Other arrangements that fell into this rather stressful and anxiety-provoking category were those in which young children were left for lengthy periods with relatives who were felt to be basically reliable (often grandparents). There were associated risks in that these relatives sometimes gave confusing messages of both loving and rejecting the child, or allowed other relatives who were not so trustworthy to visit when the child was there. They could also give accounts of the child's early experiences that conflicted with the accounts the child received from the foster carers or the social workers. It was difficult for the foster carers to know how to influence these apparently uncontentious arrangements or to protect the child.

Ben (7) was regularly taken by the foster mother to visit his grandparents for the day, but within an hour or two he would be on the telephone asking to come home. He was a very fragile child who was unsettled by the tension surrounding the difficult 13-year-old grandson that lived in the household and the grandparents seemed unable to manage the situation. Feeling that she ought to support the contact plan, the foster mother would try to persuade Ben to stay longer, but felt uneasy in doing so. In such circumstances, the child had to bear feelings of disappointment, rejection or confusion without having access to the person in whom he had come to rely on to recognise his signals of anxiety and provide comfort and support.

There was not necessarily evidence that birth relatives were deliberately wishing to disturb their children's lives (though some talked to researchers of actively wanting to get the child back) and yet the lack of opportunity for them to build relationships with the carers led to feelings of distrust in both directions.

Carrie's foster mother had only met her birth mother on one occasion, at a review when a difficult decision had to be made about Carrie's long-term future. In this highly stressful situation, the birth mother had shouted and been abusive to the foster carer, in Carrie's presence. There had not been an opportunity to repair this damage and the foster mother was understandably uneasy about the child's subsequent contact meetings. After this incident, the birth mother started to send packets of biscuits home with the child, for the whole family to share. The foster mother recognised this as a positive gesture and knew that Carrie (10) was delighted that her mother was showing this sign of acceptance of the foster family. However, there had been no social work intervention to set up further meetings to explore the possibility of building trust and thus making the contact more comfortable for the child.

These rather tense situations were frustrating for the researchers to hear about, since there was often a good deal of social work staff time and resources expended on the contact arrangements and yet they remained unsatisfactory. In some cases, it seemed that a piece of short-term mediation work might have resolved some of the difficulties and paved the way for an arrangement which involved more overlap between the foster carers and the birth relatives. If contact was seen as making a positive contribution to the child's life, then it would seem illogical that those in the day-to-day parenting role should be excluded from it.

Such cases were particularly problematic when there was no allocated social worker who could listen to the views of all parties, understand the child's perspective and formulate a more comfortable contact plan. At Phase 2, this was the situation for 25 of the 52 children and often allocated workers were not given the time to follow up cases, since they were seen as stable and therefore the lowest priority. Carers in this group tended to feel that although entrusted with the child's welfare, they were powerless to change things. Higher risk contact persisted because of various interacting factors, including children's early maltreatment, contact with multiple birth family members, lack of social work involvement and committed but less assertive foster carers.

Contact potentially harmful/risks inadequately managed

In a smaller number of cases, the elements of risk in the contact arrangements were extreme and had not been well managed at all. Children were exposed to situations that provoked great insecurity, anxiety and even fear.

In each of these situations, the contact was unsupervised and the children were directly exposed to relationships that were manifestly causing them stress or potential harm.

Natalie (13), for instance, appeared emotionally drained and cognitively confused by the contact with her mother. Phone calls and unsupervised days out in the mother's home town perpetuated the relationship in which there had been a role reversal, with the mother requiring her daughter's support for her health problems, criminal convictions and depression. This pattern of dependency, which had contributed to Natalie being looked after in the first place, was apparent at Phase 1 of the research and at Phase 2 little seemed to have changed. The carers described mother and daughter now competing over who would end a telephone conversation and who loved who more.

Lisa [birth mother] *says, ' Oh, you put the phone down first' and Natalie says, 'No, you put the phone down first' . . . Then Lisa says, 'I love you' and Natalie says, 'I love you' and Lisa says, 'I love you more than you love me.' 'No you don't, I love you more.'*

In another, rather similar case, there had been a long history of an entangled relationship in which a grandmother gave confusing messages of love and rejection. For many years there had been a recurring pattern of the grandmother wanting Stuart to visit and then sending him back because he was unmanageable.

As Stuart matured through his teens, he became increasingly anxious about his grandmother's reported health problems and said that he felt guilty for not being there to look after her. Eventually, at 15, he left the foster family to go to his grandmother but after only a few weeks, she said that he could not stay. Regrettably, in an agency where foster placements for teenagers were desperately needed, Stuart's place in the foster home was not kept open and he did not return. He then slipped into a "downward spiral" of temporary accommodation and failing to attend school. The combination of his contact history and the foreboding of his foster mother might have been enough to suggest that the arrangement was unlikely to last. As a 15-year-old who was not the subject of a Care Order, Stuart could just walk out, but the door needed to be firmly left open for his return.

Although the importance of some degree of overlap and collaboration between the foster family and the birth family has been highlighted as a key aspect of comfortable and secure contact, there were occasions when the nature of this collaboration could leave the child isolated and further rejected.

Rachel (15) had been singled out for profound rejection by her mother from birth, although she remained in her care for nine years. The foster carers formed a close and collusive relationship with the birth mother and stepfather, with everyone agreeing that Rachel's stubborn and difficult personality lay at the root of her problems. At this stage, Rachel began to feel worthless in both families. The placement subsequently broke down, Rachel returned home and within a short time was rejected again. She, too, went into a downward spiral and at Phase 2 of the research was not attending school and was lodging, temporarily, on the sofa of a friend.

Finally, there was one case in which a child who had been physically abused by his father was exposed to his father's violent temper towards his partner during contact.

At Phase 1 of the research, Patrick's carers were extremely anxious about this and noted that he was often in a "trance-like state" when they collected him from his father's home. It seemed that the traumatising effect of the fear and dread that he had experienced in his father's care were repeated during contact. Again, as an accommodated child, the local authority felt that there was little they could do. In spite of exceptionally committed, loving and sensitive carers, Patrick's anti-social and violent behaviour escalated and the local authority moved him into a residential facility, where his behaviour was continuing to deteriorate. It seemed that Patrick (13) had, in his foster family, a window of opportunity to heal some of his early damage, but his carers had no way of protecting him from his father.

Careful supervision, legal advice and rigorous reviewing might identify such situations at an early stage. However, it is also essential to listen to the carers who are attuned to the child's responses and to pay close attention to children's behaviour as well as their words, as it is here that the deeper effects of risk and trauma are evident.

Implications for practice

Various messages for practice emerge from the accounts in each group. The study has generated inspiring models of collaboration and well managed and beneficial contact in circumstances of high risk. However, contact is rarely straightforward and will always require a careful balancing of risk and protective factors which are unique in each case. At any point in time the benefits for the child will be a consequence of the needs, strengths and difficulties of the child, the foster carers and the birth families interacting with each other and mediated by social work planning, intervention and support.

Some implications for practice are:

- Foster carers who are most likely to promote positive contact are those who are sensitive to the thinking and feeling of both the child and the birth parents.
- The capacity to provide a sense of foster family membership while at the same time accommodating the child's sense of birth family membership is important.
- The complexities of contact for children should never be underestimated. They need opportunities to think and talk about their relationships with their birth relatives and to express their mixed and often confused feelings about them.

▶

- When planning contact arrangements, the aim should be to reduce anxiety and promote security for the child. This aim should be reflected in the frequency and duration of the contact, the supervision and the venue that is chosen.
- Anxiety is likely to be reduced when there is a degree of overlap or continuity between the foster family who have come to represent a "secure base" for the child and the birth family. This can be achieved by the foster carer being present during part or all of the meetings, or by a known and trusted adult providing a bridge between the two.
- When face-to-face contact is planned for the child, every effort should be made to facilitate a positive working relationship between the birth relatives and the foster carers. If this can be established, children are likely to feel more able to talk about their complex feelings and carers are in a better position to be physically and/or emotionally available to the child during contact.
- When assessing children's responses to contact, it is important to take into account both their words and their behaviour. When behaviour indicates that contact is reawakening the feelings associated with earlier trauma, the benefit of the contact must be seriously questioned.
- Carers who are sensitive to a child's thinking and feeling are likely to have a good sense of the impact of contact and whether or not arrangements should be adjusted to provide greater security for the child. It is important, therefore, to listen and respond to the views of sensitively attuned foster carers.
- In long-term fostering placements, it is important that contact arrangements are monitored and reviewed over time. It is unlikely that arrangements made in the early days of placement will remain suitable as children grow older, placements become more or less settled and birth family circumstances change.
- When making decisions about contact in long-term fostering placements, the question of the positive developmental *benefit* to children is important. The key question would appear to be: 'What are the proposed benefits of the contact and how do they link with the arrangements that have been made?' The presumption of contact, the

unquestioning acceptance that children need to see and know their birth family, and practical arrangements that revolve around *preventing significant harm* are not appropriate in situations where foster carers are providing the child with a full sense of security and permanence in their families.

Conclusion

When children have been placed in long-term foster care, it is the intention and hope that they will find their primary source of security within their foster families. For many, this can be achieved alongside carefully planned but flexible links with a range of birth family members. All such links involve a degree of stress to the child but this can usually be reduced and managed through contact arrangements that are sensitive to the critical factors in the child, the foster family and the birth family and geared to promoting the child's feelings of security and comfort. When the stress is such that it cannot be successfully managed, the wisdom of ongoing face-to-face contact should be carefully questioned.

Summary

Three main aims of the research with regard to contact

- To understand the experience of face-to-face birth family contact for a group of children in long term foster care and its impact on their security and sense of permanence.
- To examine the role of foster carers in these contact arrangements.
- To examine social work planning and practice in promoting security / managing risk in making contact arrangements.

Three main findings of the research with regard to contact

- The children appeared more relaxed, positive and at ease with their contact when the arrangements involved a degree of overlap or continuity between their foster families (who had come to represent a "secure base") and their birth families.
- Foster carers who were sensitive to the thinking and feeling of both the foster child and the birth relatives were able to judge the impact of

141

contact, to propose and support beneficial arrangements and to help children make sense of their feelings.

- The most comfortable contact arrangements were those in which the social workers took into account the child's needs for a primary sense of security and belonging in the foster family and made arrangements that respected this alongside an appropriate acknowledgement of the child's membership of the birth family.

Three main implications for practice

- When planning contact arrangements, the aim should be to reduce anxiety, promote security for the child and keep in mind the impact of contact at different stages of the child's development. These aims should be reflected in the frequency and duration of the contact, the supervision, the venue that is chosen and the support for the child.
- Anxiety is likely to be reduced when there is a degree of overlap or continuity between the foster family who have come to represent a "secure base" for the child and the birth family. This can be achieved by the foster carer being present during part or all of the meetings, by the foster carers having regular communication with birth relatives, or by a known and trusted adult providing a bridge between the two families.
- When face-to-face contact is planned for the child, every effort should be made to facilitate a positive working relationship between the birth relatives and the foster carers. If this can be established, children are likely to feel more able to talk about their complex feelings and carers are in a better position to help the child feel comfortable about belonging to two families.

References

Beek, M. and Schofield, G. (2004) *Providing a Secure Base in Long-term Foster Care*, London: BAAF.

Fahlberg, V. (1994) *A Child's Journey Through Placement*, London: BAAF.

Goodman, R. (1997) 'The Strengths and Difficulties Questionnaire: a research note', *Journal of Child Psychology and Psychiatry*, 38(5), pp. 581–586.

Schofield, G., Beek, M., Sargent, K. with Thoburn, J. (2000) *Growing Up in Foster Care*, London: BAAF.

Thoburn, J. (1996) 'Psychological parenting and child placement', in D. Howe (ed.) *Attachment and Loss in Child and Family Social Work*, Aldershot: Avebury.

9 Placing older children in new families: Changing patterns of contact

Julie Selwyn

This chapter reports on the findings from a Department of Health funded study (Selwyn *et al*, 2003). The study had three main aims:
- to examine why some children were more easily adopted than others;
- to estimate the unit costs for adoption; and
- to consider the support needs of those adopting older, more challenging children.

The study did not specifically set out to answer questions about contact, but to discover what had happened to 130 children who were aged 3– 11 years (mean age 5.7 yrs) when the adoption plan (the "best interest decision") was agreed between 1991–1995. Unlike many previous adoption studies, the sample was complete and no children were excluded. By choosing the time of the adoption best interest decision, we were able to portray the "success" of adoption more accurately as the pathways of all the children could be charted, rather than, as is more usual, examining outcomes of children already in adoptive families.

All the children's case files were read and information was gathered from files on the children's birth families, delays, placements, contact arrangements, costs, decision-making and psycho-social outcomes. We also interviewed adoptive parents and long-term foster carers and a number of standardised measures were used. Maintaining or stopping contact was an issue at every stage of the children's care careers and consequently we had rich data from files and interviews about the impact of contact on children's and carers' lives. Before discussing the frequency and management of contact in the children's permanent placements, it is important to give a brief picture of their birth families and patterns of contact when the children first became looked after.

The children's birth families

The 130 children were born into families with multiple problems who were in the main well known to social services departments (SSDs). Previous children had already been removed in 32 per cent of the children's families due to abuse and neglect and were either currently looked after or already adopted. Sixty-three per cent of the mothers had been in care themselves; most had spent long periods in residential care as a consequence of abuse. Very few mothers had any educational qualifications and 27 per cent were described as having moderate to severe learning difficulties. It was not surprising, given their histories, that 59 per cent of the mothers had a diagnosed mental health problem. Their partners had similar difficult personal histories and patterns of mental illness, and consequently parental relationships were rarely stable, with high levels of domestic violence, conflict and instability.

Women often had very dependent relationships with their partners and were so pre-occupied that they were unable to provide care and protection for their children. Thirty-one per cent of the children were living in a house where a person convicted of a sexual offence was living or was frequently visiting and these men were often attached to a household where the mother had learning difficulties. Alcohol and drug misuse were frequent, with parents going out on drinking binges and leaving their infants alone. Sixty-six per cent of the children lived in houses where the families had significant debts. At times, there was no heat or lighting in their homes, as all services were disconnected. Living conditions were often sparse, with descriptions of bare rooms with little furniture and no toys. Homes were said to be dirty with the smell of stale urine pervading all the rooms, and dogs and cats being given the run of the house. Some of the children had no bed and slept on the floor. Children often found themselves in adult roles looking after their parents and some children, as young as five, were found begging for food or cooking for their parents.

Not all the children were neglected through general impoverishment. Some (38 per cent) were actively rejected and abandoned on several occasions at bus stops, at SSDs and at health centres. These children were the *only* child in their family to face such treatment. They were rarely spoken to and were locked up for long periods. These rejected children were not only neglected and physically abused but often subjected to sadistic maltreatment.

Just under half of all the children had physical injuries that involved broken bones, head injuries, bite marks or burns. Sexual abuse was confirmed for 15 per cent of the children and suspected for a further 20 per cent. Sexual abuse occurred when the children were very young, the average age being three years old. Nearly all the children had experienced at least one form of abuse and 68% had experienced multiple forms of abuse.

During the time they were receiving family support, the children moved in and out of care, around relatives and had frequent changes of address, but eventually concerns grew to such an extent that they became looked after for longer periods and care orders were sought. At the point of entry to long-term care, the children were aged on average three years old (range between one and ten years old).

Case summary

Tom was the second child of three boys, born while his mother's partner was in prison for sexual offences and violence. Tom's mother was an alcoholic and had also been in prison for violent behaviour. She had been, and still was, sexually abused by her own father and Tom was a result of this abuse. The family moved around the UK when her partner was released, moving through bed and breakfast accommodation and in and out of refuges. Tom was hated by his stepfather and suffered numerous injuries from beatings. Other sexual offenders visited the home and his mother's mental health deteriorated culminating in a serious suicide attempt. When Tom was four, an Emergency Protection Order was taken after his mother came home drunk and attacked him.

The children's lives in care

The great majority of the children (81 per cent) had some form of contact with their birth families when they first became looked after. Three-quarters of all contact took place in the foster carers' or the birth family home with the remaining contact supervised in a contact centre. Children's visits home were often made to parents whose circumstances had changed:

new siblings had been born, families had moved and mothers had new partners. Some circumstances did not change, however, and sexual offenders continued to be present in 32 per cent of the children's homes, and violence and problems of addiction continued to present a risk to the children.

Sometimes contact arrangements were complex and set at unrealistic levels, which birth parents and foster carers found impossible to stick to or manage. Other parents refused all contact and seemed glad to have got rid of the child they did not want. Disclosures by children also precipitated the end of contact. For example, after one girl disclosed that her mother's partner had sexually abused her, she received without warning in the post every letter, card and present she had ever sent to her mother with a note not to contact the family ever again.

It was more usual to find recording of contact that was not going well, than contact that was going smoothly. There were reports of parents disappointing children and failing to turn up, of children arriving at their birth parent's home knocking on the door only to be refused entry, of birth parents arriving too drunk/high to hold any kind of conversation. Twelve per cent of the children were physically abused during unsuper-vised contact, returning with unexplained bite marks or burns on their bodies. A further six per cent continued to be sexually abused by their mother's partner. It was also suspected that a further 11 per cent of children experienced physical or sexual abuse during unsupervised contact but there was a lack of evidence to support social workers'/foster carers' suspicions. The same contact arrangements were made for siblings, irrespective of their individual needs or family dynamics. For example, a mother lavished praise and presents on the eldest sibling while the youngest one was relegated to a corner where she received no presents and only criticism from her mother.

Frequency of contact often determined which pathway children should follow. It seemed to be assumed by social workers that if there were high levels of contact, long-term fostering should be the placement plan, while those with less frequent contact were generally approved for adoption much quicker. Few files contained any assessment of the *quality* of the contact, what it was for, and how it would be managed. In many cases there was an assumption that all contact was good for the child. There

147

were attempts to re-establish contact for rejected children and for those who had been sexually abused by many family members. It was often only when events occurred, such as further incidents of abuse, that plans were changed.

Although social workers worked hard at maintaining links with birth mothers, fathers seemed to be less considered, both when relationships were reasonable as well as when they were not. It may have been this lack of attention to relationships in the triad of father, mother and child that left some children vulnerable to further abuse. It also led to some fathers, who had expressed love and concern for their children, disappearing from children's lives.

Parental contact visits diminished over time. The numbers of children whose parents refused any form of contact with them grew from 10 per cent when the children first entered care to 34 per cent at the point of the best interest decision. Most of these children had been rejected by their birth parents. Contact was also stopped by SSDs in a further 14 per cent of cases because the parent's behaviour was unreasonable and abusive. By the time the children were being considered by the adoption panel, just under half of the 130 children had no contact with their birth parents.

Plans changed and eventually all 130 children had an adoption best interest decision but not all were placed with an adoptive family. There is not the scope within this chapter to outline why this was so, but in relation to their placement outcomes in 2001–2, 80 children were living with adoptive families, 34 were in long-term foster care and 16 children had led very unhappy and unstable lives with no placement lasting for very long.

Adoptive families and birth family contact

Ninety-six children had been placed for adoption and 80 children were still with their adoptive families at the time of follow-up, which was on average seven years after placement. Sixty-four children's families (80 per cent) agreed to be interviewed and they were asked about contact in the first year that the child came to live with them and also about contact at the time of the interview in 2001–2.

Face-to-face contact in the first year of the placement

Twenty children (31 per cent) had face-to-face contact with a birth parent in the first year, half unsupervised by social workers. Fourteen per cent of children were having face-to-face contact with only their birth mother, 12 per cent with both of their birth parents and 5 per cent were seeing only their birth father. A much larger number (90 per cent) had face-to-face contact with birth siblings, most (75 per cent) supervised just by the adopters. A third of the children (34 per cent) were also having direct contact with their grandparents or another birth relative during the first year, again mostly (75 per cent) unsupervised.

More of the children (54 per cent) placed into established families (i.e., adopters who were already parenting children) were having contact with their birth parents than either children adopted by their foster carers (36 per cent) or those placed with childless adopters (22 per cent). Though striking, these differences did not quite reach statistical significance and were not echoed in the levels of sibling or birth relative contact. Children placed in established families were older and it may have been that contact patterns were more firmly established or there may have been more support for contact from these families.

At the start of the placement, some adopters thought that they had been misled to believe that contact arrangements were non-negotiable and it was only after discussions with other adopters or with solicitors that they discovered they could alter arrangements. Others thought that birth parents were trying to buy affection or provide evidence of their parenting capacity for the courts by bringing extravagant presents to contact visits:

He would go to dad with a list in his pocket of things we wouldn't let him have and his dad would buy it. It would cause a lot of problems. Social services just said that dad could spend what he liked. He could spend £50 if he liked and we had to accept it, as he was the parent. Never mind the effect it was having on us.

Most adopters (60 per cent) stated they were on the whole supportive of contact, with adoptive mothers being more positive in their responses than adoptive fathers (59 per cent v 36 per cent):

Him and his mum had the same conversation every time, they talked

149

about the past, about times when things had been good in the family . . . after contact he was relaxed. He had satisfied himself that they were still there and he could get on with his life.

Of the ten supervised contact visits, two adoptive families reported that the children became very distressed during contact. More adopters reported that children were distressed before and after contact:

When there was a threat of Pauline being abducted we got the police involved. We had to arrange escape routes for all the children. I was terrified to be alone in the house and didn't know what I would do if the stepfather turned up. It was terrible for the children, terrible for us and especially for Pauline . . . it was devastating for the whole family, and it marked the first year.

The first couple of times she wet herself beforehand and as we were going down there in the car she'd be saying 'Oh, you're not leaving me are you, you're not leaving me are you?' We had to have sort of a bribe to get her to stay there, like we'll go to Wimpy when it's over, or something.

Adopters reported that 45 per cent of the children were more "wound up" and anxious in the weeks preceding contact with birth parents. This would show itself in more wet beds, bad dreams and generally more difficult behaviour. There were also knock-on effects in the weeks after contact, with some families (30 per cent) reporting that the children took several weeks to settle down again:

Roger frequently got into trouble at school after a contact; it unsettled him. We began to prepare ourselves for difficulties afterwards and in the end we moved it to the school holidays.

Only 10 per cent of adopters were happy with the guidance and support they received from their social workers about managing contact arrangements. The vast majority (90 per cent) had received no guidance at all, but during the first year many adopters reduced or changed the contact arrangements.

Birth sibling contact was, on the whole, well received by the adopters (67 per cent):

When he saw him they'd just have a great time playing, they were like two peas in a pod, it was lovely to see.

Adopters reported that 22 per cent of children showed distress as a consequence of contact with siblings. Sometimes this was as a consequence of separation but also guilt, fear and sorrow for siblings left at home or in foster care without an adoptive family of their own:

He'd always be very quiet and withdrawn for a couple of days after the contact because of the disappointment at not being with his brother.

[Home] . . . *is a very dangerous place to be* (child's comment after seeing baby still living with the birth parents).

Adopters (90 per cent) generally believed that the children should maintain links with their birth siblings, but some found that doing this could in reality be quite an undertaking, especially if children lived a long way apart or if their parents or carers were not supportive of contact:

I'm totally for contact, but it is quite exhausting because there is a lot to do, all the arranging and then dealing with the aftermath in his emotions and then worrying about the emblem on his school jumper and all sorts of things that make it quite complicated.

Adopters (76 per cent) were also largely positive about contact with other birth relatives. The majority of the children were reported to thoroughly enjoy these contact visits:

They [the grandparents] *are very nice people. They obviously cared a lot about Carrie and always gave us a nice lunch and we reciprocated.*

Children (44 per cent) did show distress before and after these visits. Adopters thought this was due to unhappiness about separation, reminders of the past and for a few (3) children there were concerns that grandparents were exposing the children to abusive situations:

He saw his gran about once every three weeks, she used to come and take him out . . . but we found out that she was taking him to a house so the social worker stopped that. He did seem distressed when he came back, he would have nightmares.

In this case, organised sexual abuse was thought to have been continuing during contact visits.

By the end of the first year, most (75 per cent) of the face-to-face contact with birth parents occurred once or twice a year. Three children were still seeing their birth parent(s) three or four times a year and two children continued to see their mothers fortnightly.

Letterbox contact during the first year

Just over half of the children (56 per cent) had letterbox contact with one or more members of their birth family during the first year. Some children were distressed by the content of letters they received:

His mother sent him a letter and a sweet shop as a present and the social worker just came around and gave it to him. I was quite cross about that because it was quite disturbing as it said stuff like his mum wanted him back. He was just getting settled . . . but he just said 'Rubbish, rubbish, my mummy loved me, rubbish,' and 'I don't want to go back'.

Other children became upset if they didn't receive an expected card or letter, especially from their birth parents:

Birthdays are still a very painful time for him. It's painful if he does get something from them and painful if they don't send anything . . . I don't see the point. It's like keeping a wound open all the time, isn't it?

Indeed, very few adopters spoke positively about early letterbox contact with birth parents, although such contact with siblings was generally welcome. Adopters could resent the intrusion into their new family life and several commented that the children were often reluctant to write letters. Most (67 per cent) complained that they had received very little guidance about how to handle letterbox contact and said that deciding what constituted identifying information in letters that were sent out, and what was and wasn't appropriate for the children to receive, could also prove stressful:

There were vague plans to exchange cards with their sisters once or twice a year. In principle we were supportive of this, although there was something of the fear of the unknown. Our main concern was that we didn't want every birthday and Christmas to become traumatic because of it.

It was always a struggle to get him [child] to engage in the process of sending out cards. There was often a lack of interest and he didn't seem to recognise who we were doing it for. . .

Adoptive families and birth family contact at follow-up

There had been a great deal of change in the patterns of contact since the first year of placement. By the time of the follow-up in 2001–2, some young people themselves or their adopters had ended birth family contact that was perceived as very difficult or too distressing for the child:

. . . [Father's] wife had just had a new baby and I knew Alfie wouldn't want to go to their home. It was throwing it in his face and he wouldn't go. When I tried to arrange the next contact he said, 'I can't be bothered. I don't want to see him any more'.

Birth family contact had stopped for five children/young people.

Face-to-face contact at follow-up

Eleven children (17 per cent) had had face-to-face contact with a birth parent in 2001–2. Seven children had seen their birth mother and three of these were also in contact with their birth father. A further four children had face-to-face contact only with their birth father. Seven of these children had had regular face-to-face contact with their birth parents over the years. Contact that had continued over the years was perceived by the adopters as beneficial for the children. This was not to say that the visits were always easy or that the children did not show distress, but that there was a purpose and quality that had ensured contact continued.

Adopters (in four cases) also reported "new contact": contact that had occurred because children had asked to see their birth parents. These meetings were frequently emotional but adopters thought that, on the whole, they had been a positive experience for the children. It was not possible to know how much re-established contact was likely to continue:

Last year he started doing very odd things at school, throwing himself at cars . . . but he wouldn't say what was wrong and the teachers were very concerned. I didn't know what to do . . . and so I phoned his social worker . . . his social worker did some more life story work with him . . . and then one day after it, he said to me that he'd like to meet his mum. I'd always said I'd let him, so his social worker came and did lots of background work with him before it. He was quite excited about it; he'd been counting the days to it. He wasn't anxious or frightened, he'd been very well prepared . . . and his parents were very good and we had quite a pleasant afternoon really and it was actually really good for him. He's been completely OK since. All the problems at school stopped and he's quite happy in himself now. He said he just needed to know what they were like. He wasn't disappointed in them at all.

Another adopter reported:

We've had a lot of problems since the meeting with his birth parents. His mother wasn't keen to do it and she'd made no effort. She was very lacklustre about it and it was very sad and Simon picked up on it. He said, 'She didn't make any effort did she mum? And who is she? She's just a woman who came. I don't know her.'

In contrast to the few children still seeing their birth parents, 55 per cent of adopted children had seen their siblings in the last year. This was generally perceived by the adopters as positive or 'just part of the normal routine'. Although fewer children were seeing their siblings, often the contact had not formally ceased. It had just "not happened" in the year we were interviewing. Once children became teenagers, they were more likely to make arrangements themselves via email or mobile phones. Again, adopters reported that although contact had difficulties, children (91 per cent) were generally positive about sibling contact:

We see them now most weeks, more during the summer holidays. They argue and fight now like all other siblings do; it's a perfect relationship.

Ten children (16 per cent) were also still having contact with other birth relatives by the time of the follow-up. For half of the children these visits were wholly positive, a fifth had mixed emotions following the contact and the remainder showed no reaction.

Letterbox contact at follow-up

Over the years, two-thirds of the children adopted by strangers and all of the children adopted by foster carers maintained letterbox contact with their birth family. The number of letters had decreased and for a handful, letterbox was a continued reminder of a painful past. For others, the passing of time had lessened the impact and it was just part of normal routine. For a few children, adopters thought the letters had been funda-mental to an evolving understanding of their history:

> *Quite recently I* [adopter] *met his birth father's wife and we both talked about how we could help the father and son to have a better relation-ship. Then I wrote his father a letter, which was very truthful, saying how he was fundamental to Alan, but how angry Alan had been and asking if he wanted to write back. It took him a while, but he wrote back saying how he'd tried his best, but couldn't work it out with his mum and couldn't manage Alan on his own and that helped Alan very much because it was obvious he cared.*

Not all the children in our sample had been adopted. Thirty-four children were placed with long-term foster carers while the remaining 16 children were mainly in secure accommodation, having never found a placement that could contain their difficult and often violent behaviour. Two of the children had been returned home as no placement could be found for them. We were able to compare their contact patterns with the children who were adopted and there are some interesting findings.

Long-term foster carers and birth family contact

The long-term foster carers of 23 of the children agreed to be interviewed and were asked about contact during the first year that the placement had been approved as permanent and how that compared with contact arrange-ments during 2001–2. In the first year after placement, only two of the children were not in contact with parents or kin. By the follow-up, this had risen to 11 (48 per cent) of the young people with no birth parent/kin contact. At the beginning of the placement, there was frequent (twice a month or more) face-to-face contact with birth parents, the majority of which was supervised. Consequently there was little letterbox and phone activity. Carers were present at most of the contact meetings and reported that children's reactions to parental contact were fairly evenly split with 50 per cent having a favourable response and 50 per cent expressing negative emotions.

Both male and female carers were more supportive of sibling and extended family contact but there were some concerns about parental contact. Foster fathers were more negative about contact with birth parents than were foster mothers. Concerns centred on the impact on, and distress caused to, children:

> Contact with birth mother was supervised by the social worker. She would slag off social workers during the visit, one time she even slapped the social worker... the kids were really frightened... I used to dread it. It was terrible to put two children through it.

More than half the carers reported receiving little or inadequate guidance from social workers about how to manage contact and 19 per cent of foster carers thought that it had a negative impact on the child's ability to form attachments within the foster family.

By follow-up, contact arrangements had changed as the children grew older and had become more vocal about their own wishes and more independent. Face-to-face contact had reduced with both birth parents, as had levels of supervised contact. Of the face-to-face contact that was occurring with birth mothers, 87 per cent was regular contact that had endured over the years. The majority (88 per cent) of foster carers were supportive of the arrangements that had continued because they recognised the importance of the relationship to the young person. These meetings could still be fraught and young people were often extremely difficult before and after the visit. Satisfaction with the level of guidance given by social workers had increased to 75 per cent and this might reflect social workers' increasing awareness and knowledge of the issues:

> No matter what their parents are like the kids still want to see them... sometimes dad would be drunk, Alex would be hyper... couldn't sleep, was he going to turn up or not? I wasn't sure who was parenting who... whose needs were being met. When I saw them, they were affectionate together. As a professional carer it is easy to think 'What is the point?' but when you see them together you can see the point.

A few carers felt that they were forced by the social worker to continue contact:

It always ends in tears . . . he is always in a terrible state when he comes home . . . undoubtedly she loves him and has a tremendous amount of guilt . . . but she just sabotages everything else that happens for him . . . mum has been able to undermine any progress we have made . . . some really decisive decisions need to have been made much earlier by [social services].

Nearly half the children were no longer in contact or had never had contact with birth parents. Some carers (25 per cent) complained that they felt under pressure from social workers to re-establish contact even when young people stated they did not want this. Some complained that lack of contact was raised at every review and one social worker wrote in the case notes that the young person's refusal to see her mother was 'an affront against the doctrine of the Children Act'. These carers felt they had very little influence on social work decision-making, even though they had cared for the young person for many years.

Where contact (13 per cent) had been re-established after many years due to the efforts of the social worker, there was no support for contact plans from foster carers:

The social worker is determined to arrange contact with his birth mother. She has been stoned out of her head the last time it was organised and didn't turn up. Her [the social worker's] *idea was to take the mother and Tony to a café and leave them to get on with it!*

Foster carers complained that social workers did not understand that, although the young people were adolescent and some nearly adults, they were still very vulnerable and might need support or protection during contact visits. They couldn't just be left to get on with it.

The unstable care career group and birth family contact

This group of children had spent their care careers in numerous foster and residential placements and in 2001–2 were mainly being cared for in secure accommodation. Poor planning and delays had blighted their care careers. The children were from families with the highest incidence of serious maternal mental health problems and had suffered the severest forms of multiple abuse. The lack of active social work planning was reflected in the poor management of contact. Contact was unrestricted and unregulated, with social workers leaving the carers to manage arrangements. This worked well when parents and carers could have a reasonable relationship, but this was mainly not the case. Unrestricted contact led to parents bombarding carers with phone calls throughout the day and night or threatening the adoptive/foster family.

Contact plans were often ill thought out. For example, in two cases there was twice-weekly contact with birth parents, as the child was moved into an adoptive family. In another case, a child was reintroduced to his birth father eight days before moving into an adoptive placement. Some of these children went through numerous placements with the same parental behaviours disrupting the placement, until eventually the children were moved into out-of-area residential placements. Disruptions during their care careers had occurred primarily because of the children's challenging behaviour and the lack of permanency and contact planning.

Overall patterns of contact

If we look at the whole interview sample, contact with birth parents began to reduce from the time children's status in the care system became long-term. Abuse during unsupervised contact visits (21 per cent of cases), children's disclosure of previous abuse, parental rejection, and the realisation that the children would not be returning home all contributed to contact with birth parents diminishing. Where information was available at follow-up, 61 per cent of the children had had no contact at all with a birth parent in the previous 12 months and 26 per cent had no kind of contact with anyone during that time from their family or previous carers. Table 1 (on the following page) shows the changing patterns of contact over time among the three placement outcome groups.

There had been a reduction in face-to-face contact with birth parents for all the children. As the follow-up for this study was on average seven years after the children had been placed, most of the children were adolescent and their own wishes in relation to contact were becoming more prominent. It is interesting that for those adopted or in long-term foster care, indirect contact with others outside the nuclear family increased over time. The young people's lives were also very busy so that, although they had had less face-to-face contact, parents/carers stated this was because young people preferred to text or talk by phone. Sadly, the children who had had unstable care careers had the least contact of all the groups. This group had high planned levels of contact at the time of the best interest

Table 1

Comparison of recommended contact patterns at the time of the adoption "best interest" decision and actual contact at follow up in 2001–2

	Successfully adopted		Long-term foster care		Unstable care career	
	BI decision n = 64	Follow up n = 64	BI decision n = 23	Follow up n = 23	BI decision n = 16	Follow up n = 16
Face-to-face with mother	20%	11%	50%	30%	38%	13%*
Letterbox or phone with mother	17%	19%	6%	26%	19%	0%
Face-to-face with father	16%	11%	35%	17%	13%	13%
Letterbox or phone with father	11%	9%	3%	9%	6%	0%
Face-to-face with siblings	53%	34%	71%	69%	56%	31%
Letterbox or phone with siblings	11%	36%	6%	52%	0%	0%
Face-to-face contact with others (kin, previous foster carers)	23%	26%	35%	30%	6%	6%
Phone or letterbox with others (kin, previous carers)	13%	23%	12%	21%	25	0%

*Two children placed at home

decision, but as their behaviour became more concerning and their placements became more specialised and distant from their birth families, contact with everyone diminished. These children may also have had less access to mobile phones and less autonomy about whom they contacted.

Implications for practice

Good-quality assessments are essential for the development of contact plans. Too often contact plans for the children in this study were made without any assessment of the risks to the child, of the relationships within the family and of the ability of the non-abusing family member to protect. There seemed to be an assumption by social workers that in the long run contact would be good for the child. Many of the birth mothers in this study were subject to domestic violence and were not able to protect themselves or their children. In making an assessment, social workers need to bear in mind the power and control that is exerted over women by violent partners. There also seemed a reluctance to accept that some mothers could inflict severe cruelty on and/or sexually abuse their children. Although the children were in the care system, 21 per cent were known to have suffered further physical/sexual abuse during unsupervised contact visits. There were expectations that once in care they would be safe, but this was not the case for too many of the children.

The role of male partners was also given insufficient attention and, as a consequence, some birth fathers whose relationship with their children seemed good, dropped out of children's lives when contact could have maintained the relationship. The "blind spot" that affected work with birth fathers was also apparent in the lack of work with adoptive and foster fathers. Substitute fathers were less engaged in discussions about contact and were less likely to be supportive of the arrangements than their partners.

Adopters and foster carers need far more help in managing contact. They need help thinking through how their child is likely to respond to contact, taking into account what is known about their history and personal characteristics. Particular attention needs to be paid to the possible impact on the child's behaviour in school and contact visits might need to be arranged in school holidays. Contact is a very individual experience and consequently children placed as a sibling group need to be treated as individuals. Each child will have a different experience of relationships within the birth family; they will have different roles, be of different levels of maturity, and have different experiences of abuse. Contact plans need to take account of this and ensure that damaging and abusive patterns of behaviour are not repeated during contact visits.

For contact to continue, all parties need to agree that it has a purpose and it needs to be manageable. A balance has to be struck between the adopters' wish to "claim" the child, the child's need to feel they belong in a new family and the need to keep meaningful relationships with birth families open. Poorly managed contact causes a great deal of distress for all parties. The frequency of contact has got to fit with this balance.

Adoptive parents/carers need help not just with face-to-face contact but also with the writing and receiving of letters. Many struggled with just what they should write, how the person receiving the letter might view it, and what was appropriate to receive. Children were reluctant to write letters and adopters found themselves getting into arguments with children over their responsibility to write. The letterbox system can be used well (as was evident by some of the responses in this study) but too often it became a chore.

Different authorities had very different practices in managing their letterbox systems. For example, in one authority every letter was read by a social worker, while in another, only letters from the adopter to the birth parent were read by an administrative staff member looking for anything that might identify the whereabouts of the child. In the authorities that read every letter, concerns were growing that letterbox was not a "risk-free" activity and there was some evidence of continued grooming by paedophiles. All types of contact need the same careful assessment and planning.

There has been very little practice guidance on working with young people and adoptive/foster families where contact has been re-established after many years. Adopters and foster carers thought that current practice expected young people to display far greater maturity and emotional stability than was reasonable to expect. Re-established contact needs careful planning and work with the parents/carers to ensure that they are supportive of the plan and are prepared for any consequences.

The average age of children in this study was 14 at the time of the follow-up and they were increasingly taking over their own contact arrangements. Young people preferred to text and use mobile phones. Technology gave them power to choose whom they had contact with. This did not always please adopters/carers or social workers. Some were using the opportunity to persecute their birth family and demand money and gifts, some refused all contact, while others expressed curiosity about family members not seen in years. Adolescence often brings with it concerns about identity and from previous research we know this can be a particularly difficult time for adopted children. We are only just becoming aware of the particular issues around contact during this time, as the children affected by the shift in policy to more open adoptions reach adolescence.

Contact by itself is not going to promote good outcomes for children. Contact is a process through which relationships can be repaired, maintained or ended temporarily or permanently. It is dynamic, changing across time as individual circumstances change. Contact is the means through which all parties can work at relationships and relationships are not easy or simple. The role of the social worker, once a thorough assessment has been completed and concluded that contact should continue, is to facilitate this work by ensuring that arrangements are made which are feasible, safe and supported by all parties. This requires experience, skill and time. We now need to move beyond generalisations of whether contact is harmful or beneficial, and to consider for *which children*, in which circumstances and by which means, contact should be promoted or ended.

Summary

This study tracked a complete sample of 130 older children who had an adoption best interest decision. The children's characteristics and family backgrounds were typical of children whom agencies are trying to place today.

The study had three main aims

- to examine why some children were more easily adopted than others;
- to estimate the unit costs for adoption;
- and to consider the support needs of those adopting older more challenging children.

The key findings from the study with regard to contact were that:

- Contact was not always a positive experience for children. Contact plans were rarely based on an assessment of the child's relationships within their birth families, especially the ability of the non-abusing parent to protect. Whilst they were in the care system and in adoptive/ long-term foster placements, 21 per cent of the children were physically and/or sexually abused during unsupervised contact. Letterbox arrangements were not a "risk-free" activity and needed to be assessed and managed with as much care as other forms of contact.
- Adopters and foster carers were sometimes insufficiently involved and supported in contact plans. Adoptive and foster fathers were often less involved in the making of contact plans and less supportive of the plans than their partners. Adopters and long-term foster carers received very little guidance in managing contact at the start of the placement.
- Contact arrangements often changed over time. At follow-up (average seven years after placement) there was little face-to-face contact continuing but there was more indirect contact. Young people's preferred method of communication was texting and using mobile phones.

The three main implications for practice with regard to contact are

- Good quality: assessments that take into account the quality and safety of contact are essential.
- Ongoing support for all parties needs to be available, including when contact is by "letterbox".
- The role of male partners in both the birth and the adoptive/foster families requires more attention.

References

Selwyn J., Sturgess W., Quinton D. and Baxter C. (2003) *Costs and Outcomes of Non-Infant Adoptions*, Hadley Centre for Adoption and Foster Care Studies, School for Policy Studies, University of Bristol.

10 Contact in foster care:
Some dilemmas and opportunities

Kate Wilson and Ian Sinclair

After about a year, it didn't really bother me about my mum. Even right now, it doesn't bother me. It's like I don't really need her. Sometimes I do think, I don't really need her. Because she hasn't been there for the last five years, and I've coped without her. If she came back, I wouldn't really need any help . . . Do you know what? I was thinking what a big family! I've got my dad's side. I don't get on with them, my mum's side, I don't talk to them at all. I've got his dad's side – mum and dad – they love me. And then I've got [my foster carer's] whole side – her sisters' and her husband's side. So I've got like families everywhere. That's what I feel like – I've sort of got families and families and families, and I've got my own family now. Even my leaving care worker, I've met his wife and kids in town, and that, so we have a good relationship. (Tara, young care leaver in study)

And it was really strange – she used to start reminiscing about the past – you know how you chat about the past with the children. And she used to start saying things like, I did this with my Mum. My Mum took me out in a car. And I'd say, no – your mother can't drive, Carole. And she said, yes, she did, she drove me to Southsea. And I'd say, no, that was Jo (my ex). So she was like replacing the memories she had with Jo in that mother/daughter relationship. And taking Jo's head off and putting her mother's head on. (Foster carer in study)

This chapter is about foster care and the contact between foster children, their birth parents, their siblings and other relatives. Fostering involves some kind of break with a previous family as well as a temporary sojourn with a new one. As these quotations from a young person and a carer interviewed for our study of foster care show, the relationships of foster children with birth family and with foster family are inevitably inter-twined, as the children and adults variously view these relationships as compatible, possibly compatible, or mutually exclusive. Arguably, too, it is only if the relationships with foster family are secure that it is possible to take a cool look at those with the birth family. Contact takes place within the context of these variable and complex relationships. To isolate it from its context or to see it as a simple variable with invariable effects is to misunderstand it.

In this chapter, we draw on evidence from our longitudinal study of foster placements. The principal aims of this part of the study were to see whether, and if so in what circumstances, contact benefits children who are in foster care. Specifically, we were concerned to explore the views and experiences of the children and young people about contact with their birth families; to see whether contact helped families get back together or occurred simply because of its connection with other factors e.g. the relationship between parent and child; and to see whether there were circumstances in which contact could be said to have a positive or deleterious effect. We describe some of the specific findings of the study concerning the characteristics and impact of contact and argue that contact needs to be seen as a complex and dynamic network of relationships. We then use material from our case studies to draw out some of the practice implications of our study.

Our evidence comes from three linked studies of foster care, which were carried out between 1997 and 2001 in seven English local authorities: two London boroughs, a metropolitan district council, two shire counties and two unitary authorities. The studies focused on the experience of foster carers and their needs for support; foster placements and their outcomes; and the "careers" of foster children and young people* – what happened to them over a period of three years. The studies were based on a cross-sectional sample of 596 foster children of all ages placed with the foster families. Comparisons with other studies and national statistics suggested that the sample was representative, except that relative carers were under-represented. The authorities had almost exactly the national proportion of children looked after per 10,000 population and the national proportion of those looked after in children's homes or adopted. Our

---

*For ease, we shall refer to them in the chapter as children, although our sample included children and young people of all ages.

information was mainly achieved through a postal survey in 1998 to foster carers, social workers and family placement social workers, and a follow-up survey 14 months later to the same sources. In addition we had 150 questionnaires from foster children describing their experience and carried out 24 case studies of placements (12 "successes" and 12 "less successful"). For our third study, we looked at the destinations and outcomes of the original sample of foster children after three years, by means of questionnaires and face-to-face interviews with a sub-sample of 30 cases.

We should note at the outset that the findings do not cover all the issues which are relevant to contact. We have, for example, no evidence on the views of parents or on the impact of contact on their parenting skills. Second, it makes a difference that our information comes from a sample of children and young people in placement at a particular point in time. As far as we can tell, they are typical of the foster children one would find in England as a whole, if one were to get information on those in placement on a given date. For example, the ages of the foster children, the proportions of them on care orders and the lengths of time they have been fostered match almost exactly the proportions for the rest of England; the proportion of children from minority ethnic backgrounds is comparable to that in other large studies of foster care (e.g., Rowe *et al*, 1989). They are not, however, typical of foster children who enter foster care over a year, most of whom return home quite quickly. It seems highly likely that the relationship between outcomes and contact in the two groups will be different – for example, the birth parents of children in foster care where the plan is for a short-term assessment may well have an intensive parenting programme with their looked after child, in order to improve the prospects of the child being able to return home, in contrast to the possibly more limited contact arrangements for the child placed "for permanence".

In such longer term placements, contact takes places in a context where children have differing views about the degree of involvement they want with their own families on the one hand and their foster families on the other. Most children want more involvement with their families. Asked to give two wishes for their future, just over a quarter of the children completing our questionnaires gave a wish that involved seeing more of

167

or getting back together with their birth family. 'I wish my mum and dad had some nice friends so I could go back home.' Even children who were apparently happy in the placement could wish they were home. 'I like it [here] but I don't really want to be here. I want to be with my parents, but I like everyone here.' Nevertheless not all children take this view. Some do not want to return to their families but do want continuing contact. 'I think all children should see lots of their natural family, even if they are in care.' Others wanted to see some members of their family but not others and were discriminating in setting out their wishes: 'Let me see Richard and Jean (step-mother). I would like to see Gran and Grandad (mum's side) or speak on the phone with any family' (Sinclair *et al*, 2001). A common wish was to have the "best of both worlds" – either to remain with foster carers but see much of their birth parents or to return to parents while remaining in close touch with foster carers.

The importance given to contact by children in our study is supported by other studies.research prior to the Children Act 1989 reported a desire on the part of children for more contact, difficulties in providing it, and an association between contact and return home. The requirement to promote contact is enshrined in the Children Act. A body of literature has argued the case for it, and its positive impact on outcomes (Berridge and Cleaver, 1987; Hess and Proch, 1988; Fratter *et al*, 1991; Wedge and Mantel, 1991; Sanchiro and Jablonka, 2000). A review following the Children Act showed an increase in contact (Department of Health, 1994). However, although the arguments for the benefits of contact are persuasive, they are not conclusive. Researchers have not invariably found positive associations between contact and good outcomes and the evidence is more equivocal than has sometimes been acknowledged. For example, the generally better attachments which are found between children who have frequent contact and their parents could be explained in other ways – they might precede the placement and produce more frequent visiting rather than be the result of it. The association between contact and returning home may reflect the connection of both with other factors – for example, the wish for it on both sides, and the social workers' plans for return home. So while the moral case for contact remains unimpaired there may now be some doubt that it produces the outcomes claimed for it.

Against this background, the qualitative material from children, foster carers and social workers in our studies suggests that contact between foster children and their birth families is a major issue in foster care. It does not suggest that the issue can be resolved by simple rules of thumb, for example, to the effect that "contact is always good". What evidence relevant to the debate can be drawn from our quantitative, statistical and qualitative material?

The purpose of contact and its role in return home

Our first question concerns the purpose of contact and the placement plans, as given by the social workers in their questionnaires on each placement. If the plan for the placement was return home, then it would be reasonable to suppose that a major reason for contact would be to promote this. In fact, in less than a fifth of the cases (18 per cent) were the social workers planning for a return home. Where there was some contact between child and family, we asked the social workers what they themselves saw as its purpose, providing them with a fixed list of possible reasons together with an "other" category. The most striking result of this exercise was that in only eleven per cent of the cases where there was contact did they indicate that its purpose was to "prepare for return home". The most common reason given was to "maintain relationships" (81 per cent) followed by "to meet child's wishes" (47 per cent) and "to meet parents' wishes" (34 per cent). These results emphasise the moral or emotional imperative behind the visits. They do not suggest that with this group the key role of contact was to promote return home.

However, although reunification was not the immediate reason for contact, visiting might arguably be said to promote it. One of the propositions put forward in the most influential study of contact, that carried out by Milham and his colleagues in 1986, was that the care system operated in such a way as to reduce the likelihood that children would return home by eroding over time their contact with their families. Conversely, it might be expected that maintaining a pattern of visiting would increase the probability of return home. In fact, 44 per cent of the children saw a relative at least once a week, and of these, 20 per cent were at home when we followed them up. Only six per cent of the others (i.e., those with infrequent or no contact) had returned home by this time. This association does not, however, necessarily imply cause and effect. Thus, parents almost invariably had weekly contact with the child when return home was planned. In such cases, 86 per cent of the children had weekly contact as opposed to 37 per cent of the remainder. So was it frequent contact that led to return home? Or was the key variable the social worker's plans? Or did both plans and contact reflect other variables, for example, what child and parent(s) wanted?

It certainly seemed to be the case that where there were no plans for return home, weekly contact had little influence – five per cent returned where there was no weekly contact and six per cent where there was. Arguably, then, weekly contact is more important where plans existed but does not on its own make return more likely. The visits themselves are associated with return home. It is not at all clear that they cause it.

The experience of contact

Other arguments for promoting contact have been that it prevents unhelpful idealisation, helps the child to settle in the placement and, arguably, therefore reduces the risk of disruption (Atherton *et al*, 1986; Smith, 1999). Our second question, therefore, concerns the effect of contact on the placements – whether contact reduces distress on the part of the children and seems to promote successful placements.

As one might expect, the foster carers reported a wide range of experiences in relation to contact, both in relation to how satisfied they themselves were with the arrangements for contact and how stressful or enjoyable they found the visits and in relation to the children's reactions to the visits.

Some of the diversity revealed in their open-ended comments in the questionnaires related to who visited and how important their visits seemed to be. Grandparents and siblings could play a key role as well as birth parents.

> *Anna's maternal grandad and his partner who do not live locally ring about once per week and send letters. They try to see her every month and take her out. Her mother has given up and does not want much contact. Anna is upset about her mother . . . She loves visits from her grandfather.*

Mixed feelings when mum does not turn up but loves going to see his brother and sister.

As implied above, the visits also varied in their impact. On the positive side, some children were said to welcome the experience:

Very pleased for child. Child looks forward to contact.

From the very beginning we set out to have a good relationship with the birth family. It hasn't been easy but we have learnt to see their (especially mum's) side of things. We have built up a strong relationship to the extent that mum goes on holiday with us occasionally and we socialise with the maternal grandma. Because of how we have reacted to the family the child has responded positively.

Sometimes things were more problematic and mixed:

The child's maternal grandma is an excellent support both to us and her grandchild. Her positive loving attitude has helped us all. The father has visited the house drunk and uninvited, insisting he sees his children and has never hurt them.

The main problems appeared to relate to the children's behaviour after the visit. Foster carers reported that some children were rude, some regressed to more childish behaviour, some tried to play them off against the birth parents, some had nightmares and others were generally confused and distressed:

Sometimes she comes back upset and that upsets all the family. She plays me up a lot when she has to leave dad and gets me uncomfortable and doesn't like us much.

We have to pick up the pieces when John's mother promises him impossible things. He now uses her for material gain.

The child is often very distressed after contact with mother. His behaviour at school and at home improves significantly when he does not have regular contact with mum and he is much happier and more relaxed.

In the foster carers' eyes, the reasons for upset were varied. Some children wanted more contact with parents than parents were willing to provide. Others felt that they were being pressured into contact which they did not want. Others were upset by the way the parents treated their children – promising the impossible, or saying the foster carers did not love them, or failing to keep appointments, or shouting and getting them over-excited, or keeping the children up late and generally accustoming them to a disordered way of life. Some carers said that the birth parents tried to set the foster children against them:

The contact with the children is going well, but lately one of her sons does not want to go for the contact because the birth mother calls me names and speaks against me to them.

These comments were in keeping with the statistical evidence, which showed that while some children were said to experience no distress, nearly six out of ten (57 per cent) did. The children's distress was reflected, perhaps understandably, in the extent to which the carers themselves found the visits stressful. Foster carers commonly had mixed reactions to contacts and in a minority of cases found them highly stressful.

Contact and breakdowns

So far, the picture we are putting together about the impact of contact suggests, perhaps unsurprisingly, that its effects vary – that for some children it is a welcome experience, while for others it is distressing, and may make the placement more problematic. The discussion has focussed on the impact of ongoing contact arrangements. We now turn to the question of the kinds of arrangements, specifically forbidding contact, which might make a difference – in other words, since it is likely that the effects of contact vary according to the relationships between child and birth family, whether it is possible to identify circumstances in which contact might have a "good effect" and others where it might have a negative or nil effect. To consider this, we looked at whether there was a discernible link between characteristics of the child's background, contact arrangements, and outcomes (in this case, whether or not the placement disrupted).

We first examined the relationship between forbidding contact and "disruption" when the child had not, on the evidence of the social worker, been abused. There was little difference. Sixteen per cent disrupted when there had been no restrictions on contact and 19 per cent when there had. The situation was very different when the child had been abused. Nearly a third (31 per cent) disrupted when there was no prohibition and by contrast only 12 per cent disrupted when contact had been restricted – a highly significant difference. The difference remained when we allowed for age and/or time in placement. It was also significant when we allowed for the child's level of disturbance, and when we took account of the foster carers' characteristics (which included social worker ratings of parenting qualities and a measure of child-centredness) (Sinclair and Wilson, 2003).

The association between forbidding contact and lack of disruption held true for all categories of abuse. It was very rare for contact not to be forbidden to someone when there was strong evidence of sexual abuse so our numbers are small. However, no case in which there was such evidence, and also embargoes on contact, disrupted. By contrast, three of those where there was no prohibition did disrupt (a significant difference). In the case of the other three categories of abuse, the percentage disrupting was consistently around two and a half times as great when no one was forbidden contact. Taking all categories of abuse together, cases on which we had a social worker questionnaire where there was strong evidence of abuse, and an embargo on contact, were much less likely to disrupt. Placement breakdown was three times more likely where there was no prohibition than in cases where there was.

The fact that someone was forbidden contact did not mean that the child had no contact with members of the birth family at all, although visits were less common. Taken as a whole, therefore, the results suggest that forbidding contact between the child and particular individuals can in certain circumstances have a good effect on outcomes.

This is clearly an important finding, particularly perhaps for practitioners trying to find the most helpful solutions for children whose contact arrangements are fraught or unsatisfactory. Although we can only guess at the mechanisms which underlie the finding, it seems likely that sustaining a difficult or conflicted relationship through visits may not only be upsetting to the child, but may make it harder to settle down, commit to and thrive in the placement, and that conflicts may be perpetuated and exacerbated. (Another of our findings, about the importance for success of the child's motivation to be in the placement, also seems relevant here.) Three of our case examples, quoted below, provide further illustration of these dynamics: in two, firm action in terminating contact which had appeared to be prolonging the children's uncertainties seemed to enable both to begin to settle in the placement. In the third, the failure to resolve the painful uncertainties over Carole's relationship with her mother seemed to have contributed to the downward spiral and ultimate breakdown of the placement.

In our third study, where we followed up the children after three years, we looked at whether similar relationships between disruption and evidence of abuse held. We also broadened our enquiry, to see whether there was any association between contact and children being abused again. Some of our cases had by this time been "tried at home" so our results take this into account.

The results were similar. Where there was strong evidence of abuse, re-abuse was significantly more likely if no one was forbidden contact. Breakdown over three years was also significantly more likely. Trial at home was similarly associated with evidence of subsequent re-abuse, as was weekly contact with a relative over the time the child was fostered. The explanation is probably that contact exposed the child to the risk of being abused again, and is also associated with return home. The latter in turn increases the risk of abuse.

A model of successful foster care

Some of the issues which we have been discussing can be illustrated by the accounts in our case studies. In the second of our three linked studies, we developed a model of successful foster care, which is based on the quantitative and qualitative material and case studies in the research. The model involves a specification of the relevant factors and the way in which they operate to bring about a given outcome.

The model identifies two key components which are seen as relevant to successful placements. The first of these is a quality which we describe as *responsive parenting* and refers to the way in which the carer deals with the child and which we see as an essential ingredient in a successful placement. The second component we suggest are *conditions* which, although not necessary or sufficient for success, make it more, or less, likely that the carer will be able to parent responsively. These conditions include: first, the characteristics of the child, the carer, and the compatibility between them; and second, relevant for our discussion about contact, factors which impinge on the placement from its wider context, which include relationships with the birth family as well as the response from school, social workers and the carers' own family members. Thus placements are more likely to go easily where:

- members of the birth family are not seeking to disturb placement;
- relationships between the birth family and the carers are managed sensitively;
- the carer's family is committed to the placement;
- there are not clashes between child and particular members of the family;
- social services support the carer's preferred view of placement's purpose;
- the child's social world (school, friends, etc) supports the placement expectations.

Many of the cases lend support to some of the findings from the questionnaires, and additionally suggest ways in which skilled and sensitive handling of contact by foster carers and social workers can help placements succeed. For example, in the following case involving the placement with an experienced foster carer of a nine-year-old boy with learning difficulties (which we have written up in more detail elsewhere, see Wilson *et al*, 2003), in addition to the termination of contact with the foster child's abusive parent, the foster carer, Mrs Stanton, differentiates between the relationships with grandmother and mother.

She supports James' attachment to his grandmother, seeing this as something which was highly significant to James in his earlier childhood ('*she was his lifeline*'). She accepts contact with his mother, although she thinks that as he grows older it is likely that he will recognise that it offers him little. However, she sees this as James's choice, and is untroubled by the mother's visits to their house.

Personally, I don't think the contact with mum has any significance whatsoever. I think in everybody's interest it would just be better if she would take a back seat, because she can antagonise the situation through his Nana. But I'll wait until it's James' choice. And I'm just waiting for James to sort of think, is it worthwhile? And the more he's becoming involved in our family, I do feel the more he will sort of switch off. As he gets older, and he identifies that there's nothing out of it, either materially or emotionally, for him, I think he'll learn. And it'll be his choice.

Mrs Stanton accepted James' initial wariness when the placement began, allowing him to remain more distant but was receptive to and encouraged a developing attachment to her on his part. She helped this by being flexible, and indeed supporting, of his relationship with his grandmother, and tolerant of his relationship with his birth mother, so that he has not experienced tensions around having to choose between his foster family and his other relationships. The placement therefore offers containment, security, but a permeable boundary, in the sense that outside relationships are accepted without difficulty or a sense of competitiveness or threat.

This willingness on the part of the foster carer to be open to, and indeed to value, the child's relationships with birth family members is illustrated by another of the cases which we identified on our criteria as "successful".

Robert, now aged 12, had, when we interviewed his foster carer, been in the placement for nearly four years. Again, contact with one relative suspected of having sexually abused him had been terminated, but contact with other relatives had been maintained on a regular basis. Along with their commitment to him, and his to them, the foster carers accept Robert's attachment to his birth family: '*When you foster, you know that you're fostering someone else's child. You don't actually want the child for yourself*'. Robert has asked whether the Walkers would adopt him, but Mrs Walker feels that his relationship with his birth family is too strong: '*For all their faults, they love him. And deep down inside, he loves them. There is that bond there. And I think it's something that should be encouraged. And when Robert's older, it's up to him what he does*'.

In the following placement, also judged as successful on our criteria, the birth mother's pattern of periodically seeking custody is difficult for her ten-year-old daughter, Sophie, to handle and her behaviour becomes more and more problematic as her anxiety and uncertainty about the outcome increase. Her foster carer comments:

She settled down beautifully. We could see a real improvement. We felt we were really getting somewhere. But now over the last three months, we've just seen this awful deterioration again. Her mother's gone to court to try and get her back, and ever since she's found out, her behaviour's deteriorated. She's confused about what she wants. I think she likes the idea of living with her Mum again, but I think deep down she knows it wouldn't work.

In this case, the foster carer's ability to remain tolerant and accepting (while making it clear how much she wanted Sophie to stay) seems important in enabling the placement to continue. The psychologist had recently intervened and made a firm recommendation that Sophie should remain in foster care and that contact with her mother should be curtailed. The social worker, commenting that Sophie seemed now to be accepting the psychologist's recommendation and was settling down in the foster placement, adds:

Barbara's [foster carer] always spoken sympathetically as well about Sophie's Mum. She never said anything sort of condemning or negative. If they had been condemning in any way, I think Sophie would have retaliated against that and been probably more loyal to her Mum.

The ability to work conscientiously and professionally with the child's attachment relationships, even when these seem to be counterproductive, is illustrated in an analogous situation, this time involving a previous adoptive placement which had broken down.

Susan's adoptive parents found it difficult to accept her wholeheartedly (they limited her contact with them to an overnight stay once every two weeks, and were highly critical and negative about her) but could not bring themselves finally to admit failure. Susan was nonetheless set on returning to them, and so was not open to a very close relationship and kept her carers to some extent at arm's length. They were able to accept her without feeling personally rejected, and worked under the instructions of social services to try and help effect Susan's rehabilitation to her adoptive home. The continuing uncertainty had had a deleterious effect on her behaviour. However, some weeks before our interview, Susan's therapist had insisted that her adoptive parents resolved the uncertainly about her return and they had decided that she should not come back. This seemed to have allowed Susan to be more receptive and open to a relationship with her foster mother in particular and her behaviour had begun to improve.

The positive features of these cases have included the foster carers' skill in handling relationships with the child's birth or adoptive family members without feeling threatened either by them or by the child's hesitations in developing new attachments while remaining attached and loyal to earlier attachment figures. They have also been characterised by the helpful involvement of social workers, and in three of the cases, therapists. (For reasons of space we have omitted discussion of the therapist's involvement in the first case.) The contribution of social work help was not always (in our study) easy to unravel. However, in these cases the decision to be decisive about the children's future rather than allowing this to drift, the readiness of the social workers to address concerns with the child over contact, and the provision of support where the foster carers were themselves working with the child over significant relationship issues, all seemed to be important in allowing the central relationships between foster carer and child to prosper and in facilitating the foster carer's *responsive parenting*. Our final case, quoted at the beginning of this chapter, which had by the time of interview disrupted, illustrates the way in which this aspect of the *conditions* of our model can vitiate the success of the placement.

Carole, who was 12 years old at the time of interview, had remained in the placement for seven years until she left earlier in the year to go to a succession of different foster carers. Her foster carer, Mr. Roberts, saw the breakdown of the placement as stemming from her unquenchable yearning to return to her mother, and to the lack of social work support at critical moments when these feelings, and Carole's resulting efforts to sabotage the placement so that she could return to live with her mother, emerged most strongly. He bitterly regrets accepting the advice of social services to seek a residence order for Carole (which he considers was motivated in part by pressure from the department to reduce fostering costs). He considers that it did not change Carole's feelings of belonging or security in the placement (the grounds on which he was persuaded) but removed social work support at a critical period. The social workers who are now involved again with Carole accept that there was a lack of proper involvement, partly reflecting restructuring in the authority at the time.

Carole's wish for contact with her mother was continual, and Mr Roberts finally forbade her to telephone her mother, because her mother was so unreliable and unresponsive, insisting instead that her mother took the initiative (which she rarely, if ever, did). Carole's feelings, in Mr Roberts' view, were never reciprocated but her fantasies about her mother grew ever stronger. However, he seems to have been unequal to the task of helping Carole with her ambivalent attachment towards her mother, perhaps being unable to remain sufficiently open to it and accepting of the latter (of whom he candidly acknowledges his dislike – *'I don't like the mother – that is evident. We don't like each other at all'*). Carole's birth mother was evidently unsupportive of the placement, consistently undermining the foster carer's attempts at discipline, and holding out promises to Carole (about contact and about a future life together) which were or could not be kept. Crucially, because of the residence order, little social work involvement was available to prevent the downward spiral of relationships as Carole struggled to try and get placed back with her mother. The placement broke down when Carole refused to come home one weekend and the emergency duty team, in what Mr Roberts saw as a crucial moment, supported her instead of insisting that she return.

Conclusion

This chapter has drawn material from a larger longitudinal study of foster placements. We have used both quantitative and qualitative approaches. Each considers similar issues in relation to contact. Insofar as these come up with similar messages, we may have more confidence in the two in combination than in either on its own. We have also used our case studies to provide concrete examples of some of the practice issues and skills involved in working with the relationships involved in contact.

As we have seen, birth families were very important to the children in our study. That does not mean necessarily that they wished to return to them. Neither did they necessarily wish to see all of them. Nor did they necessarily wish to have the same kind of contact with each member. However, other things being equal, the children, the social workers and the foster carers mostly seemed to want contact. Social workers and foster carers were more satisfied with contacts when these were frequent.

The study highlights the diverse reasons for which social workers supported contacts with birth families, and the stress these sometimes involved for carers and children. Visits were commonly seen by foster carers as causing distress for the children. Their replies suggested various reasons for this – it could arise because the children missed their family, because they felt unsafe with them, because the birth family set them against the foster carer, because the contact was unreliable, or because of the complete contrast between how they were expected to behave at home and in the foster placement. Distress, of course, may be at times inevitable and is not always to be avoided. Nevertheless, it was more common when there was strong evidence of sexual and/or emotional abuse, suggesting perhaps that there were inherent problems in the relationship. Distress on contact where the child has experienced abuse, and the potentially negative consequences of these upsets, lends plausibility to our other important finding: contrary to what some might expect, the placements of abused children were more likely to be successful if someone was forbidden access to them.

In general then, on the evidence of this study, the moral and ethical case for contact remains unimpaired: most foster children want it, and in most cases it is to be encouraged. However, the study also raises doubts as to whether contact produces the benefits which have been argued for it and highlights circumstances where contact may be distressing and lead to poorer outcomes. Overall, it requires a high degree of professional skill rather than rules of thumb which can be applied across the board. These skills are likely to require, on the foster carers' part, avoiding confrontations with children over their views of their parents and avoiding conflicts of loyalty over parents. For their part, social workers should encourage contact in a way which differentiates between family members when planning it; pays attention to the differing views of children concerning contact and return home; and ensures that children are not put at risk during contact. They should be willing, on occasion, to forbid contact and be ready to engage with carers and children on the kinds of support needed over managing the relationships between foster child, foster family and the birth family. This may require more active involvement when contact takes place than sometimes occurs.

In short, as we explained in our introduction, the main aims of this part of our study were to explore whether:
- contact helps families get back together or is it simply associated with return home;
- children wanted more contact and did not find it distressing;
- there were any barriers to contact – in particular whether prohibition of contact with specific family members might in certain circumstances affect outcomes.

To summarise our main findings:
- Social workers do not generally see the purpose of contact as being to promote return home. Contact is more likely to be associated with return rather than causing it.
- Although most children wanted contact, and often more contact and more differentiated contact than they were getting, nearly six out of ten children were reported as finding contact distressing, and foster carers also found contact at times stressful, sometimes highly so.
- Where there was strong evidence of prior abuse forbidding contact to at least one family member was associated with a significantly higher level of success.

The implications of these findings are, we suggest, as follows:
- A high degree of professional skill and judgement is required in planning contact rather than rules of thumb which can be applied in all circumstances; social workers and foster carers need to engage with children and their birth families in handling contact to avoid confrontations and, as far as possible, distress.

- There is a need to pay attention to the views of children concerning contact, many of whom wanted a differentiated approach to contact with individual members of their family.
- Social workers need to distinguish between individual members in planning contact and recognize that contact with the family member may be beneficial to the placement while that with another may be harmful. They should be prepared to forbid contact in certain circumstances.

References

Atherton, C., Kelly, G., Ryan, M., Brabbs, C., Burch, M. and Kearns, B. (1986) *Promoting Links: Keeping children and families in touch*, London: Family Rights Group.

BAAF (1999) *Contact in Permanent Placement: Guidance for local authorities in England & Wales and Scotland*, London: BAAF.

Berridge, D. and Cleaver, H. (1987) *Foster Home Breakdown*, Oxford: Blackwell.

Department of Health (1994) *The Children Act 1989: Contact orders study*, London: HMSO.

Fratter, J., Rowe, J., Sapsford, D. and Thoburn, J. (1991) *Permanent Family Placement: A decade of experience*, London: BAAF.

Hess, P. and Proch, K. (1988) *Family Visiting in Out-of-home Care*, Washington DC: Child Welfare League of America.

Rowe, J., Hundleby, M. and Garnett, L. (1989) *Child Care Now: A survey of placement patterns*, London: BAAF.

Sanchirico, A. and Jablonka, K. (2000) 'Keeping foster children connected to their biological parents: the impact of foster parent training and support', *Child and Adolescent Social Work Journal*, 17(3), pp. 185–203.

Sinclair, I., Gibbs, I. and Wilson, K. (2001) 'A life more ordinary', *Adoption & Fostering*, 25(2), pp. 17–26.

Sinclair, I. and Wilson, K. (2003) 'Matches and mismatches: the contribution of carers and children to the success of foster placements', *British Journal of Social Work*, 33, pp. 871–884.

Smith, S. (1999) *Learning from Disruption*, London: BAAF.

Wedge, P. and Mantle, G. (1991) *Sibling Groups and Social Work*, Aldershot: Avebury.

Wilson, K., Sinclair, I. and Petrie, S. (2003) 'A kind of loving', *British Journal of Social Work*, 33(8), pp. 991–1004.

11 Post-placement contact between birth parents and older children: the evidence from a longitudinal study of minority ethnic children

June Thoburn

Introduction

This chapter is based on a longitudinal study of 297 children of minority ethnic origin placed from care with permanent substitute families not previously known to them (71 per cent for adoption and 29 per cent as permanent foster children). The children were mostly over the age of three at the time of placement in the early 1980s and were a sub-sample of a cohort of 1,165 children. Data on the full cohort were obtained from schedules completed retrospectively by the agency workers or researchers between three and five years after placement (Fratter *et al*, 1991).

More detailed quantitative and qualitative data on the sub-sample of minority ethnic children were obtained from a file search conducted by the researchers between 10 and 15 years after placement when the young people were aged between 14 and 30 (Charles *et al*, 1992). Compared with children currently being placed for adoption, more of them were in the older age ranges. Only just over a third were under five at the time of placement, a quarter were aged between five and eight and the largest group (39 per cent) were aged between nine and 17 when they joined their new families. One or both of the adoptive or foster parents of 51 of these young people was interviewed, as were 28 of the young people themselves. One of the issues covered in these interviews was contact with birth family members (Thoburn *et al*, 2000; Moffatt and Thoburn, 2001). For the original cohort of 1,165 and the sub-sample of 297, whether or not the placement lasted or disrupted was the only outcome measure, though data were also available on whether there was any face-to-face birth family contact after placement.

For the small sample of 51, a range of outcome measures was used, including standardised measures of well-being, employment and education status, ethnic and adoptive identity and overall satisfaction of the parents and young people. When these young people were placed, often after several years in care, it was most usual for all contact with birth parents and adult relatives to have already petered out, or for it to be formally terminated before the children were introduced to their adoptive parents. Only 20 had moderately frequent contact during the months leading up to placement, a very different picture from today when decisions about placement for adoption are made more quickly after a child starts to be looked after, and more strenuous efforts are made to facilitate contact in the early stages after leaving home (Cleaver, 2000). Eighty-nine (34 per cent) had at least some direct contact after placement with a birth parent and in most cases also with siblings and/or adult relatives; 74 (41 per cent) had contact with an adult relative or sibling placed elsewhere but not a birth parent; and for 134 (a quarter) no contact was planned with any member of the birth family until the child reached adulthood.

There was more likely to be continuing contact with birth parents for the 29 per cent of the sample who were placed with foster carers. It was part of the plan for 59 per cent of those joining "permanent" foster families but for only seven per cent of those who were placed for adoption.

Data were rarely provided in the records about the nature and frequency of contact for any analysis other than using a dichotomous variable of "any contact with a birth parent" after placement and "no contact". For the full cohort of 1,165 children, those whose birth parents were both of minority ethnic origin were significantly more likely to have post-placement contact with a birth parent than were white children or those of mixed ethnicity.

For the full cohort, 21 per cent of placements were known to have broken down and for the sub-sample of minority ethnic children 24 per cent had disrupted (over a longer period of time). When key variables including age at placement and evidence of behavioural or emotional disturbance at the time of placement were held constant, for the full cohort of 1,165 children, those who had at least some contact with a birth parent after placement were less likely to experience placement breakdown than was the case for those who had no contact. That was also the case for those placed with a sibling, or having post-placement contact with a sibling or adult relative but not a birth parent. For the smaller sample of 297, there was no statistically significant association between contact and either disruption or the continuation of the placement. These quantitative findings (of contact as either a "protective" or a "neutral" variable) are consistent with those from other studies of adoption or foster care stability that have included large enough numbers to control for a range of variables (Borland et al, 1990; Barth and Berry, 1988).

Having briefly described the quantitative aspects of the study, this chapter then concentrates on the qualitative data about the patterns of contact and how it was experienced by the adopters/foster carers and young people for the 51 intensive sample cases.

Patterns of contact

From a detailed analysis of patterns of contact emerging from the 51 cases and from others of the 297 when sufficient details were available on the files, five broad patterns of contact were identified, and these will be illustrated with the words of the young people and their adoptive parents or foster carers. Contact arrangements, or the lack of them, were to some extent determined by the age and wishes of the child, in that older children were more likely than those placed as infants to have ongoing contact, particularly if they expressed a view that this is what they wanted or, as in some cases, refused to accept placement with an alternative family if that meant cutting links with the first family (Thoburn, 1996).

If they had said mum couldn't come to the house it would have bothered me. (Young woman placed in a permanent foster family at 12 with siblings aged nine and three, quoted in Thoburn et al, 2000, p. 101)

The wishes of the birth parents appeared to have little impact on the decisions. Information in respect of the birth parents' wishes on future contact was not recorded in respect of 46 per cent of the mothers and 78 per cent of the fathers. Where it was recorded, two-thirds of the mothers expressed a wish to maintain contact after placement, as did 64 per cent of the 63 fathers about whom this information was recorded. Contact arrangements did not appear to be associated with prior events such as maltreatment, nor with any particular problems of the child or parents. As Neil (2000) found in her study of placements made more recently, it did appear to be associated with the practice and philosophy of the placement agency, the attitudes of individual social workers, and the attitudes of the new parents. With respect to the new parents, the main difference was that children joining black or Asian families were more likely than those joining white or mixed partnership families to have continuing direct contact. As will be seen from the quotes below, this was in part related to the motivation to become parents or to enlarge their families through adoption or long-term foster care. At the time of the research interviews, a majority of those for whom no contact had been planned had re-established links with at least some birth family members. For those who had not, the research interviews with both the adopters and the young people required considerable sensitivity in approaching the question of contact.

The no contact group (contact with birth parents and adult birth relatives ended before the child was introduced to the new parents, and there had been no renewal of contact at the time of the research interview)

Most of the new parents in this group were broadly empathic towards the birth parents and in most cases they had met both or one parent (usually the mother) after being introduced to the child but before the placement. According to both groups, the main reason for no contact was that it had not been discussed as a possibility, although with the foster children it was more likely that contact had been allowed to lapse some time before permanent placement was discussed and the question of restarting it did not appear to have been raised (see the research on similar cases by Masson *et al*, 1997). The adopters of babies and young children tended to combine empathy for the birth parents with gratitude to them for allowing their child to be placed.

Particularly complex emotions were expressed by this South Asian woman who had adopted two toddlers:

I tried to understand that this was a young Asian mother new to this country, who was very unsupported and that perhaps her husband hadn't been that reasonable in his attitude towards keeping the family together. . . I liked her from the start. I liked her enormously. I was just so sad for her. She was so isolated and did not have the capacity to be a parent. I remember thanking her for giving us two such lovely children, you know, her loss was our gain (Thoburn *et al*, 2000, p. 90–91).

In these cases it seems likely that, had the social worker suggested continuing contact, it could have been incorporated into the placement planning. We learned from some that they had actually sought to find birth parents as the child grew up.

We would really want to find her and our son (placed at four) went through a period of wanting to find her when he was about eight. The social worker had left and the mother kept changing her name. Assuming the children would like to, we think that it is not only best for the children but it is also best for us because you are dealing with not a fantasy but also flesh and blood, and that has got to be better for the child. We don't have that. Once the social worker had left, that was it (Thoburn *et al*, 2000, p. 94).

In a smaller number of these "no contact" cases, it seems likely that, had contact been suggested, the adopters would have been reluctant to facilitate it.

I actually don't feel anything in particular towards the birth mother . . . and when I do there is a feeling of dislike because I feel she did not protect her daughter. The feelings are of negative indifference rather than anything else (Thoburn *et al*, 2000, p. 92).

The most usual response from this group of parents was that, at the time of placement, they would probably have been wary if contact had been suggested, but in retrospect they could see that it might have had a positive impact.

We met the mother. It was very difficult. She was crying and didn't want her daughter to go. She had been in care for four years so we didn't think we were taking her away from her mother. They didn't offer any contact or ask us about it. They said they thought it would be disruptive for her but she had this rosy picture of her mother. In retrospect I think it's helpful for children to see their birth parents. At the time, I thought it would take her longer to bond, but in retrospect it would have helped us (Thoburn *et al*, 2000, p. 138).

The views of the young adults in this group are similarly varied. Some, like this teenager, could still remember their distress at separation and, had they been given the choice, would have been likely to request continuing contact. When specifically asked, none of the young people who talked to us about these earlier feelings of sadness or curiosity said that they had talked about them with their new parents. Those under 18, and some of their parents, thought that they could do nothing about re-establishing links until they reached adulthood.

Personally I'm not too bothered about finding my birth mum because I'm happy now. Years ago when I was younger I used to cry for her. But now it's more curiosity than anything. She might accept me. She might not accept me. I do love her because I've got memories of her. But I don't know her (Thoburn *et al*, 2000, p. 94).

In this as in the other groups, most of the children were doing at least "well enough" in their families, but some placements had not worked out. There were some cases in the group where there had originally been "letterbox" contact but in all cases this had petered out, often with feelings of sadness or anger on the part of the children.

No contact during childhood (contact with birth parents ended before the child was introduced to the new parents but the young person had had some contact as an adult)

This group was very similar to the first, except that they were older when we interviewed them and had therefore had time to re-establish links. The role of siblings placed elsewhere was sometimes important in facilitating meetings with birth parents and in other cases the birth parents contacted the adopters, sometimes through the adoption agency.

The mum was pestering us to meet her, and she got in touch with social services. This was last year when Nicola was 18. So we said to her, 'Look, your mum has written to the adoption agency looking for you and would you like to meet her?' and she said no, not until she meets her dad. When she met her dad, she was even more angry with her mum because she found out that she's always been in touch with her dad, although she had previously said that she never knew where he was. But meeting her mum was good because she got to see what she looked like, and learned about her life history and where she came from . . . She still sees us as family. We have left her to deal with her own mother, and we hope in time she will get a more realistic picture of her (Thoburn *et al*, 2000, p. 96).

This case introduces the important dimension, especially for children of mixed ethnicity placed with white families, of contact with a part of their heritage that they had already been cut off from before they joined their new families.

Contact re-established during childhood (contact ended prior to placement but resumed after a gap of several years in response to the needs and/or wishes of the young person and with the assistance of the adopters and/or placement agency)

It has already been noted that some adoptive parents in the "no contact" group had, over time, come to the conclusion that contact with the birth parents might have been helpful to themselves and their child. A small number contacted the agency for assistance, or set about re-establishing links themselves. Some of the children in this group had been perplexed about why siblings had remained at home and they had been adopted. Some of these had been, as Rushton *et al* (2001) put it, 'singled out for rejection' but others had been removed because of maltreatment from parents who opposed placement. This teenager of Indian heritage, adopted by a single Asian woman, was, when interviewed, working hard at integrating her two family identities. Both she and her adoptive mother, who felt that the resumed contact, including unsupervised visits to the family home, had been helpful said:

I think she feels better about herself than she did before, although this is a more difficult time because she is in the teenage phase. Sometimes she will say 'I wish I was with my family'. But she says that when she has chores to do (Thoburn *et al*, 2000, p. 98).

Her daughter spoke of her love for her adoptive mother and her birth parents and siblings. She attributed the long wait before she could see her parents to being adopted rather than fostered:

[Birth] *Mum has already told me. She said they fought for me. I don't think my parents had a choice about placing me for adoption. They* [social services] *thought they could do anything they liked with me. So they picked me up and shoved me somewhere. That's what it feels like at the moment . . . Adoption is more for life, and you have to be prepared for it. With fostering, at least you would get to see your parents. I mean, with adoption, you do get to see your parents, but it's usually after a long gap. With me, it was like when I was about nine or ten when I saw them, so that is five years. That's quite a lot to be away from your parents . . . I know I'll never return. I know that this is a full-time thing.* [Adoptive] *Mum's explained to me that I will be here until I am 18. By the time I'm 18 I'm not going to move back and live with mum and dad. I'll probably move out by then, do my own thing* (Thoburn *et al*, 2000, p. 98–9).

Even with the openness of attitude on the part of the adoptive mother, her daughter was not entirely comfortable about talking through her feelings with her adoptive mother:

I really don't want to go to my [adoptive] *mum and say, 'Hey, why did you adopt me?' They tried to explain when I was a child but I was only five years old and was I meant to understand? . . . Apparently it was because I was unhappy, but I get unhappy now and I'm not taken away from my mum. She says, 'You were unhappy and your mum couldn't cope' and it's like it's all my fault – you know – I wasn't happy – mum couldn't cope with me because I was being a pain* (Thoburn *et al*, 2000, p. 95).

"Bursting-out" to resume contact (contact ended prior to placement but young person sought out a birth parent in adolescence, often against the wishes of the adopters and often without telling them they intended to do so)

Although still infrequent, it was more common than the last "pattern" and the young people in this group were the most troubled of all those

191

interviewed. This young man's behaviour became extremely violent and his adoptive parents had spent a great deal of time and money trying to support him, with almost no help from the social services department who had placed him, in a range of independent living situations. Despite her attempts to detach herself emotionally, his adoptive mother was still very concerned about his future.

It was obviously very painful for me because you have given 13 years of your life and you loved this kid and he is suddenly going off and finding another family. His family now are none of my business. He has to sort out his family. You know, I don't have to worry about them. He is now living with them (Thoburn *et al*, 2000, p. 100).

Some had never really settled, but those placed when younger had appeared to settle well and their behaviour and attitudes toward their adoptive families had appeared to change in early adolescence. This adoptive parent of a boy placed at six and whose placement disrupted when he was 12 described how he started to spend long hours away from home riding around on his bike. She later came to realise that he was (literally) trying to find his mother in the general area in which he knew she lived.

He was moving away from us. Deep down I think he wanted to find his real mother, which he did (Thoburn *et al*, 2000, p. 97).

Some adoptive parents were still grappling with a sense of bewilderment that the children who had been so central to their lives could choose to live with parents whose lifestyles, in their own eyes and probably object-ively, were so much less conducive to a positive future.

Mostly we only had the views of the adopters and we were not able to interview any of the young people currently living with their birth parents. However, for two of those interviewed and one whose adopter we inter-viewed, this was a necessary but temporary stage before moving on to independent living. One 22-year-old had resumed contact with her adoptive mother when she become pregnant, following a period of years of ambivalent but mainly hostile communications from her. In some cases, the adopters described extreme concern for the physical safety and emotional well-being of their children when they went to live with parents whose lives involved poor living circumstances, drugs and criminal activity.

Contact maintained (there was direct contact between birth parent/s and child after placement and usually, although the details of the arrangements changed, there was some contact throughout childhood)

Most of these children were aged three or over at placement, although one mixed heritage teenager was placed as an infant with white adoptive parents and had regular contact with her white birth mother (which involved going on her own to visit her mother's home as she got older). This (from the accounts of mother and daughter) highly successful placement had more in common with the infant placements described in Chapter 2. Although she was not in contact with her African-Caribbean birth father, she told the interviewer that she could gain all the information about him which, to date, she felt she needed through her birth mother and was weighing up if and when she wanted to seek contact with him.

Although some in this group, as in the other groups, disrupted, none of the adoptive or foster parents or young people regretted that contact had continued or attributed the ending of the placement to continuing birth family contact. This young man had a realistic picture of why he could not live with his mother:

> *I feel angry at my birth mother. You see if you make one mistake with one child, that's OK but with a second one you could say OK again, but if you make the same mistake with the third or fourth one, then that's rubbish really, isn't it? You ain't no good, mother. Simple as that. But you can't choose your parents, you can't choose your relatives and what you're stuck with you're stuck with* (Thoburn et al, 2000, p. 101).

However, he would only move from his children's home if contact could continue:

> *It would have made a difference if I hadn't seen my birth mother because I knew that I wanted to see her* (Thoburn et al, 2000, p. 101).

Neither he nor his foster mother attributed the breakdown of the placement after two years to contact. He rejoined his mother because that was an available option when the placement was no longer viable, but quickly moved into independent living and retained some contact with his foster mother.

Some described contact as having been an easy process. For most of those placed when older it had had its ups and downs, its moments of shared pleasure, as when members of both families joined in wedding preparations and celebrations, and its moments of sadness, boredom, frustration and anger. The majority in this group were African-Caribbean parents (some foster carers and some adopters), a part of whose motivation was to provide a service to black families who were doing less well than themselves. Often membership of a faith group was an important part of their lives. Some were mixed partnership families in which at least one partner had worked in the caring professions. (Some of the white parents who facilitated contact had also worked in social work, nursing or teaching.) These parents had an inclusive attitude to family life, and the elements of altruism in their motivation led them to the conclusion that it would be wrong to cut off links between parents and children (see Rashid, 2000, on the strengths of black families). Some "parented" the birth parents and took pleasure in seeing them as well as their children make progress.

With this group the more traditional task of adopters of "telling" about the reasons for adoption was replaced by the new parents and birth parents repeating the information given at the time of placement in an age-appropriate way.

We have always been positive about her mother. We don't see it as our job to rubbish her mother (Thoburn *et al*, 2000, p. 91).

Sometimes, but not always, the birth parents and the new parents told the same or a similar story, and sometimes the child would have preferred them to tell a different story. Despite her daughter, who had already been in therapy when placed at the age of four, being at times distressed by contact, this African-Caribbean adoptive mother refused to accept the advice of social workers that it should be discontinued:

She found it difficult to cope with. As a child, she needed us to be enemies and couldn't cope with us as friends . . . As she grew up her mum was very much an idealised figure. She used to miss her mother a lot and this was something I had to talk to somebody about. She still feels this way now because there is a role for her mum. There are things she likes to ring her mum up about and talk about (Thoburn *et al*, 2000, p. 102).

Her daughter, now a mother herself, and emotionally still very close to her adoptive mother, but also with a sense of belonging within her birth extended family said:

The contact with my mum has helped me to see what she is really like. She used to be nice in the beginning, but she is not nice any more. If I hadn't seen my mum and dad I would have been wondering what they were like . . . I used to take out my anger and how I used to feel with my mum on aunt [adoptive mother]. *I think I still do that now sometimes. I can't seem to bring myself to tell my mum how I feel. We don't get on very well. I know that if I hadn't left my mum I'd be dead by now because she used to batter me . . . When I was younger I used to like them* [birth mum and dad]. *I didn't know much then. I was living in a fantasy world* (Thoburn *et al*, 2000, p. 102).

It had taken her longer than some of the others to reach an understanding of why she could not live with her birth parents. Most in this group had "cut their losses" on their first families before joining their new families or shortly after.

I don't hate my mum. I suppose I love her because she is my mum. We used to get on sometimes, and sometimes we never used to. I'm glad that we didn't stay with her (Thoburn *et al*, 2000, p. 102).

Although in some of these cases the social workers had a part to play in the detail of contact in the early stages, within a short period of time the foster carers or adoptive parents took charge of the arrangements, and as they moved into the teenage years, the young people made their own decisions, in some cases going for long periods without seeing birth parents but spending more time with siblings or birth relatives. Most often, especially with younger children, contact took place in the home of the adoptive or foster parents, and less frequently it took the form of an outing with both families to a park, leisure centre or other place that suited the two families. Contact was sometimes in the home of the birth parent(s), with the adoptive parent taking the younger children there and remaining with them. This was seen as the obvious way to do things by the African-Caribbean parents, though sometimes it was against the advice of the social workers. The words "casual" and "no big deal" expressed the sorts of arrangements these young people preferred:

> *Mum would just turn up at the house. I think that turned out alright for me but my foster mum would probably have preferred if these visits had been arranged. My foster dad didn't mind. He just sat and watched television. Mum thought it was OK, she got looked after, she got her dinner* (Thoburn *et al*, 2000, p. 101).

Contact maintained or re-started and then stopped

It seems likely that there is a sixth "pattern" in which parental contact that was maintained at the time of placement, or re-established at a later stage, was then ended. Although in our study the how, where and when of contact changed over the years, there were no cases in the interview sample of its totally ending in those cases where there had been some post-placement direct contact. For the larger sample, the data on the detail of contact were too sketchy for us to know if it continued into adulthood. Other researchers have identified this pattern of early contacts being formally ended or just petering out, but few have yet followed up the children into adulthood to see if contacts that were stopped were later resumed.

Discussion and conclusions

The data from these interviews gives some clues about the potential impact of different contact arrangements on the lives of adoptive and long-term foster families.

The evidence from the young people and parents interviewed is that, when contact continues during and after placement, the new family may have a more "bumpy ride". They have to deal from day one with issues around the reasons for placement, the complexities of having two families and often the distress, confusion, and anger of the children as the unreliability and other shortcomings of the birth parents becomes more obvious to them. However, the young adult usually emerges from such arrangements with a sense of belonging to the new family but still having a place, (if they choose to take it up) in the extended first family. As with the majority of children growing up adopted, irrespective of the nature of contact arrangements, he or she will have good social skills, reasonable self-esteem and a generally positive view of having grown up as a member of an adoptive or foster family. However, there is a higher likelihood that those who retain some direct contact with one or both birth parents will emerge with a better understanding of why they could not remain with their birth families.

Although they may have a smoother path in the early years of the placement, some adoptive families with no opportunity to meet up with a birth parents as the child grows up, find that issue around past and possible future relationships go underground, only to emerge in early or late adolescence. This is especially likely with children whose wishes to retain links with the birth family have been unheard or overruled. There is a high risk that these young people will "burst out" of the placement without telling their adopters what they are going to do. They may be highly vulnerable when trying unaided to resume a relationship with parents who are still experiencing the sort of difficulties that led to the need for care.

The easiest path is probably that taken by those adopters whose children were too young at placement to formulate a view and who leave the deeper thinking about their stories and about any future links with their birth families until they are adults. But as Howe and Feast (2000) discovered, an "easy" path for adopters and children in childhood may result in difficulties in resolving complex identity issues as an adult. There was evidence from Thoburn et al's (2000) study that some who had lived with their birth parents for two or three years, were placed when under five and appeared to settle easily and to "forget about" their past, had quietly grieved for weeks or months before "putting their past behind them" (both terms we heard from adopters and young people). Many of the children currently being placed without direct contact with birth parents are in this group. Some will remain puzzled about what exactly has happened to the birth parents, or will worry about them. They may wonder (anxiously or in hope) whether, as was the case in earlier placements before they joined their new families, their birth parents will just one day turn up. They may worry, as some of those we spoke to did, whether new brothers and sisters are being maltreated as they were. Very few will raise these questions or concerns with their adoptive or foster parents, and most will brush their parents aside if they try to do so. In part, this is because they sense that this is emotionally dangerous territory, but for some, past experience will have taught them that their wishes are of no consequence so there is no point in expressing them.

It is unlikely that the contact arrangements in any of these cases contributed in a major way to the placement continuing or disrupting. Success in placement, I conclude from this and other studies, is most strongly associated with the characteristics of the child and of the new parents, and especially with the "fit" between the needs and wishes of the child and the needs, skills, and motivations of the new parents. However, there was much evidence from the interviews with those adopters who successfully facilitated contact from the start, or restarted it, that they had the attributes that others have associated with successful parenting of children placed past infancy who have been harmed by earlier experiences. I would pull out particularly "enjoying a challenge" (a term that appeared frequently when motivations were discussed); a blend of altruism and self-directed motives, with the insight to understand what they hope to get back from the child as well as what the can give; and above all the capacity to empathise with the birth parents as a way into an understanding of the child's history and coping strategies. They took any challenges raised by contact in their stride, as they took in their stride the much more major challenges of parenting a confused and troubled child.

There was some evidence from interviews that contact with birth family members could contribute to a more positive sense of ethnic and cultural identity and pride in belonging to a particular ethnic group. This was especially the case when children were placed with a family of a different ethnic or cultural background. Even for young people of mixed heritage who only had contact with a white birth mother, the ability to ask questions about the other part of their heritage was important. Although not all had taken the step of connecting with (usually) their birth father, the possibility of doing so was more open than for those who had no contact with either parent. Some adopters spoke of meetings with birth family members providing opportunities for issues around "race", ethnicity, culture and heritage to be brought naturally into the conversation either by themselves or their children. Transracial adopters without these opportunities were more easily "brushed off" by their children when they tried to raise these issues.

We have a growing understanding of the psychology of adoption and are moving, with the help of adult adopted people for whom contact decisions made "in their best interest" had a momentous impact on their lives, towards an understanding of the psychology of contact. I want to end on the "human rights" aspects of contact decisions. The UN Convention on the Rights of the Child and the Human Rights Convention, now incorporated into UK law, require the wishes of parents and children to be given due consideration when major decisions are taken. There can be no doubt that the decision to terminate contact or to facilitate it is a major decision in the eyes of all concerned as well as in law.

With respect to the birth parents, their rights to maintain a relationship with their children are appropriately limited by the need to ensure the welfare and safety of the child. But in those cases where contact can be safely achieved, their rights come into play, especially if there is evidence in a given case that the child wants to continue the relationship and could possibly benefit from it. Turning to the child, in law and rhetoric, there is no doubt about children's right to have their wishes respected unless there is clear evidence that to do so would contribute to significant impairment to their development or threaten their safety. In this study, information was recorded about the child's wishes in respect of the placement for only 78 children, yet 165 of them were aged five or over and did not have a severe learning disability. Of these 78, nine did not wish to move from their current placements, 11 wanted to go to live with parents or relatives and six had mixed feelings about moving to a new family. Only 35 were specifically recorded as wanting to move either to an adoptive family or to a new family through either adoption or fostering. There was even less information about their wishes with respect to continuing contact, with 49 recorded as wanting to continue contact with a birth parent and 24 not wishing to do so. There is evidence from case material, court reports and recent studies that it is not unusual for children's wishes about contact to be overruled (see, for example Thomas *et al*, 1999; Timms and Thoburn, 2003). The argument is likely to be made that, in balancing "welfare" considerations, the child's wish for contact is less important than the need for the legal status of adoption. In such circumstances, it is the wishes of the adopters (or the perceived wishes of those who may become adopters) that take precedence.

It was only a small number of older children in the study reported above who were able to assert that they wanted to maintain meaningful links with a parent or adult relative. From the interview data, it seems likely that others would have thrown out hints, left clues to be picked up, but not dared to say what was on their mind in case it was rejected or led to them not being placed. Most wanted a family who would provide stability and the good basic care their parents had not given them, so it is not surprising that, if not specifically offered the chance of continuing birth parental contact, some who wished for it did not ask for it in so many words.

Finally, it would be a mistake to assume that rights and psychology are unrelated. Returning to the psychology of contact, questions should be asked about the impact on children's self-efficacy of having their wishes on such an important issue apparently given little weight or credence. Young people in this and other studies who have spoken to researchers about their wish, or even their longing, for contact (or for more contact than they currently have) often explicitly say that they have not spoken to their adoptive or foster parents about this. The experience of having their wishes unheard or rejected in the past when contact arrangements were being worked out may be part of the explanation.

Summary

This chapter is based on interview data from a longitudinal study of children of minority ethnicity who were permanently placed with either adoptive parents or foster parents. The young people were followed up when they were between the ages of 14 and 30 years old. The three main aims of the study with regard to contact issues were:

- To obtain a long-term perspective on contact arrangements from the point of view of young people and their adoptive/foster parents.
- To identity different patterns of contact over time
- To examine how contact with birth relatives relates to other aspects of young people's adjustment to and satisfaction with their permanent placements.

Three main findings

- Some older children will not allow themselves to be placed with new families if that means they cannot maintain a relationship with a birth parent or adult relative who is important to them. For these children, the continuation of contact has greater relevance than whether it is an adoptive or a foster placement.
- Adoptive and foster parents who are good at facilitating contact are also likely to have many of the other characteristics associated with successfully parenting an older child. Black families appear to be particularly understanding of the importance of maintaining positive birth family links and to be skilled and resourceful in facilitating them.
- Birth family contact can be particularly important when children are placed transracially.

Three implications for practice

- The contact arrangements that accord with the needs and wishes of the child have to be a major element in the matching decision, and must be to the fore when a child is being discussed with a potential new family. In some cases it will be appropriate for prospective adopters who are unsure about whether they will be able to facilitate contact to meet the birth relative/s who will be having contact, before reaching a decision about whether the proposed match should proceed.
- Social workers need skills in helping birth parents, new parents and young people to negotiate and re-negotiate contact arrangements. When adopters are from a different ethnic group from a birth parent, a high degree of cultural competence is required of the social worker and the family, especially at the matching stage and when contact arrangements are being decided on.
- Family placement workers have much to learn from black families about how to facilitate comfortable contact arrangements.

References

Barth, R. and Berry, M. (1988) *Adoption and Disruption: Rates, risks and responses*, New York: Aldine de Gruyter.

Borland, M., Triseliotis, J. and O'Hara, G. (1990) *Permanence Planning for Children in Lothian Region*, Edinburgh: University of Edinburgh.

Charles, M., Rashid, S. and Thoburn, J. (1992) 'The placement of black children with permanent new families', *Adoption & Fostering*, 16(3), pp. 13–19.

Cleaver, H. (2000) *Fostering Family Contact: Studies in evaluating the Children Act 1989*, London: The Stationery Office.

Fratter, J. Rowe, J., Sapsford, D. and Thoburn, J. (1991) *Permanent Family Placement: A decade of experience*, London: BAAF.

Howe, D. and Feast, J. (2000) *Adoption Search and Reunion: The long-term experience of adopted adults*, London: The Children's Society (re-published by BAAF, 2004).

Masson, J., Harrison, C. and Pavlovic, A. (1997) *Working with Children and "Lost" Parents*, York: York Publishing Services.

Moffatt, P. G. and Thoburn, J. (2001) 'Outcomes of permanent family placement for children of minority ethnic origin', in *Child and Family Social Work*, 6, pp. 13–21.

Neil, E. (2000) 'The reasons why young children are placed for adoption: findings from a recently placed sample and a discussion of implications for subsequent identity development', *Child and Family Social Work*, 5, pp. 303–316.

Rashid, S. P. (2000) 'The strengths of black families', *Adoption & Fostering*, 24(1), pp. 15–22.

Rushton, A., Dance, C., Quinton, D. and Mayes, D. (2001) *Siblings in Late Permanent Placements*, London: BAAF.

Thoburn, J. (1996) 'Psychological parenting and child placement', in D. Howe, *Attachment and Loss in Child and Family Social Work*, Aldershot: Avebury.

Thoburn, J., Norford, L. and Rashid, S. P. (2000) *Permanent Family Placement for Children of Minority Ethnic Origin*, London: Jessica Kingsley.

Thomas, C., Beckford, V., Lowe, N. and Murch, M. (1999) *Adopted Children Speaking*, London: BAAF.

Timms, J. and Thoburn, J. (2003) *Your Shout!* London: NSPCC.

12 Contact in cases in which children have been traumatically abused or neglected by their birth parents

David Howe and Miriam Steele

Introduction

Although there is strong evidence amassing that adopted and fostered children benefit from contact with their birth mothers and other birth family relatives, including many who have suffered maltreatment, there are a few exceptional cases in which plans to maintain the parent–child relationship appear ill-advised, at least in the short to medium term. In this chapter, observational evidence is presented suggesting that placed children who have suffered severe maltreatment re-experience extreme states of emotional dysregulation each time they have contact with their abusive/neglecting carer. We also speculate that adoptive parents' capacity to help children recover a degree of post-contact equilibrium varies, with those who have unresolved states of mind with respect to loss and trauma posing the risk of being emotionally unavailable to their children at times of distress.

In contrast, adopters who possess high levels of empathy and mind-mindedness (the ability to recognise, acknowledge and reflect on one's own and other people's mental states) are not only more likely to be emotionally available to their children at times of need, but as a result of this availability they are also more likely to help the child develop increased resilience. And increased resilience might allow the child at some future date to handle renewed contact with an earlier maltreating birth parent.

We explain both the adopted child's negative reaction to contact and the atypical responses of some adoptive parents using an attachment perspective and the part that attachment plays in modulating stress (Eliot, 2001, p. 312).

Attachment

Schore (2001a) argues that attachment theory is, in essence, a theory of affect regulation. As caregivers help children make sense of their own and other people's behaviour by recognising that lying behind behaviours are minds and mental states, a whole train of psychosocial benefits accrue including the achievement of mind-mindedness, reflective function, and emotional intelligence (for more detailed descriptions of attachment theory and patterns of attachment see Cassidy and Shaver, 1999; Goldberg, 1999; Howe et al, 1999).

Bowlby (1988) argued that safety and staying alive are the bottom line of any organism's existence. In the case of vulnerable human infants, two things increase the chances of survival: being aware of danger and seeking protection at times of danger. In attachment theory, children monitor their environment for signs of hazard and threat. When children feel frightened or distressed, anxious or confused, their attachment system is activated, triggering attachment behaviour. The goal of the attachment system is protection, and once the goal has been achieved, distress subsides and the system terminates, making way for the corollary system, exploration of the world around them to be engaged. For most children, the need to feel close and protected is most likely to be found in relationship with one or both parents. Attachment behaviours, therefore, are designed to get either the parent to the child (crying, yelling and other distress signals) or the child to the parent (crawling, clinging). Once the child has captured the attention of the caregiver, other attachment behaviours, such as smiling and vocalising, serve to keep the parent engaged. With the attachment system satisfied, the child is then free to explore the environment without pre-occupying hindrance from unmet attachment needs, obviously important for the development of cognitive and social domains.

In this sense, parents and other closely involved carers become attachment figures, defined as people whom children seek as a source of protection and comfort at times of need and distress and with whom they can experience closeness and pleasure. The person most regularly involved with issues of care and protection is generally destined to become the child's primary or selective attachment figure. For most children the activation of their attachment system is acute and sporadic. In this sense, any activation is highly functional. However, for children who are mal-treated, either the availability of their carer at times of need cannot be taken for granted (neglect), there is no selective attachment figure (severe deprivation), or the behaviour of the attachment figure himself or herself repeatedly provokes feelings of anxiety and fear as children are threatened with harm or abandonment (abuse). In cases of maltreatment, children's attachment systems are 'in a relatively constant state of activation' (West and George, 1999, p. 138). There are few opportunities to feel relaxed and safe, to explore and make sense.

Attachment at the level of mental representation (internal working models)

Up to the point when language is acquired, babies can only communicate their needs and mental states behaviourally. Even so, their experience of how their carers react to these behaviours and how these reactions make them feel, begins to be processed by the child at an increasingly cognitive level. Internal working mental models of how the world of the self, others and relationships seem to work are gradually constructed. These *mental representations* refer to the kind of memories, experiences, outcomes, feelings and knowledge about what tends to happen in relationships, particularly with attachment figures at times of need.

For example, a secure child might develop an understanding that when he is distressed, more often than not his mother is available, sensitively aware and willing to respond. His existence and wellbeing seem to matter to her. He is loved and valued. In contrast, an insecure child might build up a picture that at times of need, her mother is reluctant to respond, or she reacts in a resentful way, or is overly intrusive. The child does not feel accepted unreservedly. Parental love seems conditional on good behaviour, or requires the child to meet the parent's own need to feel loved.

Armed with these mental models of how others are likely to behave and how the self is likely to feel, children can begin to *organise* their attachment behaviour to increase the availability, proximity and respon-siveness of their carers. They develop strategies to recover feelings of security when they feel anxious or frightened. In time, these mental representations begin to guide the child's expectations, beliefs, and behaviour in all important relationships. Children begin to enter into a "goal-corrected partnership" with their carer in which they learn to modify their own behaviour in the light of the parent's plans, intentions, beliefs and personality, but still with the ultimate goal of maximising, over the long term, the parent's willingness to provide care and protection.

There are three basic types of attachment organisation depending on the sensitivity and interest of the caregiver: secure, avoidant, and ambivalent. Each is designed to maximise care and protection, the goal of the attachment system. As long as the representational system remains organised, children can maintain functional relationships with others (George, 1996, p. 414). In effect, children develop strategies that help them adapt to their parent's caregiving characteristics in order to increase parental availability and the willingness to respond. So, 'as long as attachment is organized in relation to the function and goal of the attachment system, it is adaptive, that is, it facilitates and maintains "good enough" proximity and, therefore, protection' (West and George, 1999, p. 140).

The attachment relationship allows the child to recognise and regulate any intense arousal of the emotions while maintaining proximity (and therefore a feeling of safety) with the caregiver. Each pattern of attachment illustrates a different adaptive strategy in different caregiving regimes developed by children to help them stay close and connected to their attachment figure at times of intense negative arousal, whether or not they actually display that arousal in the presence of the carer. For example, the child who is classified as avoidantly attached, appears to show relatively little distress during separation from their caregiver, and shows little interest during reunion despite evidence to suggest that at a physiological level they are indeed aroused and their attachment system is engaged (Spangler and Grossmann, 1993).

Secure attachments

Children who find themselves in relationship with parents whose caregiving is sufficiently sensitive, loving, responsive, attuned, mind-minded, consistent, available and accepting develop *secure attachments*. Parents are interested in their infant's physical needs and states of mind. They are keen to understand their child, and to be understood by their child. This offers the prospect of a co-ordinated and co-operative relationship.

Children and adults with secure attachments are able to behave flexibly and openly within relationships. They provide fresh psychological inform-ation about their own mental states (what they are feeling and thinking) without too much distortion, defence or censorship. In other words, individuals feel secure when expressing their attachment needs to others. Their communication is accurate, honest and flexible. They can reflect thoughtfully and objectively about their own and other people's thoughts, feelings and behaviour. There is an underlying expectation and confidence that attachment figures will be unconditionally available and responsive at times of need.

Further, the secure individual does not have to manipulate his or her attachment behaviour (to heighten or dampen it) in order for the attachment figure to respond to his or her attachment needs. The result is the behavioural and psychological integration of attachment experiences, memories and affect such that the individual functions in a manner that is consistent with Bowlby's . . . notion of a goal-corrected partnership – a relationship that flexibly integrates the needs and perspectives of both the self and the partner (West and George, 1999, p. 140 This paragraph was emphasised in the original).

Insecure and anxious patterns

Insecure children experience normal anxiety about the location of the caregiver at times of need, but in addition they suffer uncertainty about the type and sensitivity of the response when they reconnect. Main (1990, p. 179) explains that insecure children are 'additionally controlled by the past behaviour of the attachment figure so that for these infants likely caregiver response as well as caregiver location must be continually taken into account'. This introduces a degree of hypervigilance into the minds of insecurely attached children, particularly in the case of those who have been maltreated. Insecurely attached children, therefore, find more of their mental time and energy is spent on issues of safety, security and monitoring, leaving less time for exploration and mutual, pleasurable intersubjectivity with their caregiver.

Caregivers who are unwilling (avoidant patterns) or unable (ambivalent patterns) to respond to or satisfy a child's normally expressed attachment needs create anxiety and insecurity in the parent–child relationship. In the case of the avoidant patterns, which are often characterised by caregiver interactions which cannot tolerate negative emotional states, in order to increase parental responsiveness, children unconsciously learn that they cannot display attachment behaviour in its full, rounded and unabridged form. Instead, they develop secondary attachment behavioural strategies. By suppressing their primary attachment strategy, children re-organise their attachment behaviour in an attempt to recover parental availability and interest. If the strategy works, the child has a way of relating to the parent, and increasing the amount of care and protection available. They then experience a 'secondary felt security'. And the behaviours and mental states associated with that strategy also become the preferred states in which to be, that is to say with which the individual feels most secure. In the case of the ambivalent pattern of attachment, the exaggerated distress and proximity-seeking behaviour on the part of the child serves to amplify the child's announcement that they indeed are desperate for the caregiver to respond as if they wouldn't be heard if they expressed their attachment needs at normal volume.

However, these adaptive strategies come at some developmental cost. Children cannot find or display their true and full psychological self to an anxious carer as this reduces availability, care and protection, particularly at times of need. By minimising affect (in the case of avoidant strategies) or exaggerating distress (in the case of ambivalent strategies), children defensively distort elements of their own and other people's psychological make-up. As a consequence, they fail to process, learn about and make good sense of either emotions (in the case of avoidant patterns) or how thought and behaviour affect people and their feelings (in the case of ambivalent patterns).

Disorganised attachments

Children who are parented by carers who are either frightening, frightened or both, experience distress within the context of the parent–child relationship (Main and Hesse, 1990). Abusive and hostile carers hurt and frighten their children. Depressed, drunk or drugged parents can appear helpless, and this can also alarm children. And carers who are beset by old *unresolved* losses and traumas from their own attachment experiences, can feel confused, fearful and numb when prompted by their children's attachment needs. This results in parental responses which can be experienced as toxic by children. A psychologically lost, fearful or panicky parent is also frightening for the child. Thus, if the carer reacts with fear or distress when caring for the needy infant, the child experiences the self as the source of the parent's fear. The infant begins to synchronise with the parent's dysregulated and distressed emotional state caused by the adult's own unresolved losses, fears and traumas (Schore, 2001b). At other times, parents may actually be behaving more or less appropriately, which can also be confusing to the child in terms of the vacillations and perturbations in knowing what to expect. The parent–carergiver relationship in these cases may provoke the child to be cast in the role of caregiver and protector often when they themselves would otherwise be looking for safety and comfort.

In these highly distressed and arousing parent–child relationships, co-regulation of affect is absent. The parent fails to deal with the child's distress. The child is left running in a parallel but unconnected state of unmanageable arousal. Their attachment behaviour goes unterminated If the arousal becomes too intense and unbearable, the child first becomes emotionally hyperaroused, and then may dissociate in an extreme form of defence. In these mutually dysregulating parent–child interactions, there is no intersubjectivity. Therefore the child is unable to find or explore her own psychological self in relationship with the distressed and out-of-control parent. Lacking a coherent subjective sense of self, the child cannot manage her own or other people's emotional arousal.

In essence, when the child's attachment system is activated, the maltreating parent's attachment system also becomes activated. It seems that whenever the abusive or neglectful parent finds himself or herself in a relationship in which the other appears vulnerable or in a state of need, old unresolved childhood feelings of fear, rejection, distress, or abandonment are unconsciously activated. Whenever the parent feels under stress in the caregiving role, he or she is liable to feel disorganised, out-of-control, and without a strategy to deal with his or her own arousal or that of the child. This results in caregiving behaviour which is either *hostile* or *helpless* or both (Hostile-Helpless states of mind – Lyons-Ruth *et al*, 1999). Either way, at the very time when the child needs to be emotionally understood, regulated, contained, and protected by the carer, the attachment figure is experienced as dangerous, unpredictable, or fearfully distressed.

For the child, each one of these parental reactions is frightening. The effect of a hostile/helpless carer further intensifies attachment behaviour in the child, which in turn leads to greater disorganisation of the parent's attachment behaviour. The result is an inexorable breakdown of the caregiving system. The child suffers "relational trauma" and is left in a state of mounting distress. Parent and child find themselves in a loop of catastrophic feedback, leading in each case to a state of emotional hyperarousal and behaviour which becomes hopelessly out-of-control (hostile, helpless, or rapid switches between the two). These are the mental states which we find in both maltreating parents and maltreated children whenever their attachment systems become strongly activated.

As Main and Hesse (1990) neatly put it, the child who is frightened by the behaviour or condition of the attachment figure suffers the simultaneous activation of two contradictory behavioural systems: fear and attachment (Main and Hesse, 1990). This results in the child experiencing two incompatible behavioural responses: avoidance *and* approach, escape *and* engagement. As it is impossible, either physically or psychologically, to resolve the two contradictory behavioural responses of approach and escape, the young child has difficulty in finding an appropriate strategy that might enable him to terminate the arousal of his attachment system. He remains in a distressed, traumatised and highly dysregulated state – which in itself is frightening. Maltreated children's attachment behaviour therefore remains *disorganised* and *disoriented*, with some children switching rapidly and incoherently between avoidant and resistant attachment patterns. In effect, they lack an effective proximity-seeking strategy. Toddlers might wander around aimlessly circling their attachment figure, helplessly whimpering and going nowhere. Some drift slowly away, only to bang their heads against a door or wall. Under extreme relational stress, others might freeze, or show trance-like, dissociated responses. And yet others begin to move towards their carer, only to drift off again, in a series of approach-avoidance responses, leaving the child hopelessly and help-lessly distressed.

What develops then is a strategy, that is, a habitual mode of resolving the excitation of the attachment system which is not really a strategy-less situation. However, the strategies the infant employs are non-optimal from an attachment/evolutionary preservative perspective. They are brought into action in a rather consistent way, and so they constitute a "strategy". For example, to "freeze" is inefficient in getting your caregiver near but it probably does serve to dampen spiralling affect which would otherwise be too overwhelming. Or the children who are classified "disorganised" by virtue of their attempts to leave the room when the caregiver enters have a strategy that one can make sense of, again despite it heralding the opposite of what it should, that is, bring the protection of the caregiver.

These deficits, distortions and disturbances place maltreated children at risk of a range of mental health, social and behavioural problems. For traumatised children, the world is frightening and dangerous, and yet no-one is able or willing to help them make sense of it. In more extreme cases, a coherent and continuous sense of self fails to form. The mind remains fragmented. The psychological self is troubled and anxious. "Relational trauma" adversely affects memory, perception, and the forma-tion of an integrated, coherent self-identity. These developmental impair-ments mean that social relationships are difficult, stressful and often puzzling.

Controlling behaviours

However, by toddlerhood, disorganised children begin to develop a fragile overlay of "brittle behavioural strategies" which see them trying to organise their own safety and regulation (West and George, 1999, p. 142). They do not feel safe when they allow the carer to be in charge of the relationship. After all, this is the relationship associated with hurt and danger, fear and pain. In the face of a caregiving failure or threat, children therefore try to control the parent, either through (i) aggression and compulsive self-reliance, (ii) compulsive caregiving, (iii) compulsive compliance, or (iv) combinations of any two or more of these behaviours.

These strategies are described as "controlling". They represent extreme attempts to get the distressed, vulnerable or "out-of-control" parent to refocus on the child's needs and anxieties. *Controlling* strategies empower children. They help them disown representations of the self as helpless, vulnerable and needing comfort. Such strategies allow some degree of mental and behavioural coherence to be achieved. However, these strategies are fragile. They break down whenever the attachment system is strongly activated, returning the child to highly disorganised, out-of-control mental states in which feelings of fear, danger, rage and despair once again flood the young mind. The strategies are brittle but work, once again at a cost to the child. For example, mothers diagnosed as clinically depressed show decreases in their own depressive states if they have children classified as "controlling/caregiving". However, as the mothers' depressive states decrease their children's depressive symptomology increase (Moss *et al*, forthcoming).

For the child, any significant arousal of the attachment system becomes associated with, and seems to them to be a precursor of fear, intimations of danger, and the eventual collapse into a disorganised state. In time, *any* activation of the attachment system can lead to a breach of the psychological defence, leaving the child feeling overwhelmed by feelings of alarm and panic, rage and anger, despair and helplessness. Maltreated and severely neglected children therefore tend to be in one or other of two mental states:

- a controlling, defensive mode (compulsive compliance, compulsive caregiving, compulsive self-reliance) with the fragile outline of an organised but very insecure attachment strategy, or
- an out-of-control, disorganised, helpless mode in which attachment behaviour completely breaks down.

Unless disorganised and controlling children enjoy relationships later on in life which help them develop a more trusting, reflective, and less defended state of mind, they are likely to carry these mental states with respect to attachment into all future relationships.

Stimuli that act as reminders of past unresolved traumas, including the maltreating parent, powerfully activate the attachment system leading to rapid deployment of one or other of the controlling strategies, or if the arousal is extreme, to a catastrophic breakdown of attachment behaviour leaving the child out-of-control, that is to say helpless, hostile, or both.

From colleagues (Perry *et al*, 1995) in neuroscience we learn that, once a child has suffered from repeated incidents of trauma, relatively little is required on subsequent occasions, or even in markedly less threatening contexts, to trigger the same kind of responses that the initial trauma provoked. Moreover, one often hears from carers of older, previously maltreated children, descriptions of compulsive repetition of patterns of attachment behaviour that children bring into their new caregiving experiences. For example, an adopted child might respond with extreme aggression or destructive behaviours even to the mildest of reprimands by the new carer. These can be explained in terms of the internal working models the child brings to the new and seemingly different caregiving context. These "old" and established internal working models can't simply be extinguished as the child moves from one carer to another. Their existing patterns at least bring a semblance of safety by providing the child with habitual modes of response, albeit with negative if not disastrous consequences. What often belies the hostile/ aggressive and destructive behaviour is the hopeless/helpless feelings from which they originate. However, from the new carer's perspective, these behaviours seem way out of proportion, supremely challenging and confusing.

Thus, in the case of children who have suffered severe maltreatment at the hands of a birth relative, contact can trigger old unresolved memories of the traumatic character of the relationship and intense activation of the attachment system. This leads to highly dysregulated behaviour which will be dealt with either defensively, or if the arousal is too great, the child will feel overwhelmed, helpless and out-of-control. In effect, contact can re-traumatise the child. There is then the real danger that the child experiences the placement as unable to offer a reliable or permanent sense of safety and security. The only way to survive the stress of repeated exposure to a previously maltreating carer and a placement that seems unable to protect you from such distress is to continue employing one or more of the controlling strategies, both with your new caregiver, and when in contact with your old, maltreating caregiver.

Sophie – aged 15 months

As a child, Sophie's birth mother, Kelly, suffered emotional rejection and physical abuse. She experienced depression in her late teens and was the victim of domestic violence by her alcoholic partner. Her first baby died of a heart abnormality when he was three weeks old. On two separate occasions, Kelly attempted suicide. Sophie was an unplanned and unwanted pregnancy. She was born five weeks premature, remaining in a special unit for the first three weeks before returning home with her mother. Although encouraged to visit her daughter daily and be with her as much as she wanted, Kelly's hospital visits were erratic and short. Even after the birth of Sophie, Kelly remained socially isolated from both her family and local community. The health visitor observed that Kelly 'had age-inappropriate expectations of Sophie'. Even though Sophie was only seven weeks old, Kelly thought that she should be able to hold her own bottle and became irritated when her daughter failed to manage this task, and agitated when she couldn't work out why Sophie was crying. She rarely held or cuddled her baby. Kelly mentioned that she felt most relaxed when Sophie was asleep upstairs.

It was also noted that Kelly was extremely dismissive of any sign of emotional weakness in both herself and others. For example, Kelly was reluctant to talk about the death of her son, suggesting a possible unre-solved painful attachment-related experience which she dealt with by strongly deactivating her attachment system. She returned to work two days after the baby's death saying she wanted to get on with her life. Whenever her partner became upset as he thought about the loss of his son, Kelly told him that his tears helped no-one, adding that she thought he ought to have got over the death by now, as she had, and that he should move on. She dealt with old hurts by avoiding, downplaying or dismissing their significance. This might also explain why she did not want to be pregnant with Sophie. Six months after her birth, Sophie suffered broken ribs and a fractured skull consistent with being thrown against a hard surface. Upon examination, Sophie was found to have a number of bruises and several healed leg and arm fractures.

Once she had recovered, Sophie was initially looked after by foster carers and then at 13 months she was placed with adopters. Her behaviour with her foster carers was described as lively and that she had an "infectious laugh". However, in new situations or when sudden and unexpected things happened (a loud noise, someone noisily barging into the room, another child accidentally hurting her), Sophie would either "freeze" or go into a "screaming fit" which could last for an hour or more.

While living with her foster carers, contact with her birth mother had been agreed at once a month. Observations during contact visits noted that upon meeting her mother, Sophie would stand motionless, staring blankly into the air, sometimes rubbing her eyes, suggesting some form of dissociative behaviour: 'She makes no moves towards her mother, never smiles, and if picked up she remains stiff and speechless, looking glazed.' Upon return to her foster carers, she screamed inconsolably for several hours, before curling up asleep on the floor exhausted. She also stopped eating for a couple of days. Kelly, the birth mother, is requesting that some level of contact is continued post-adoption.

Tom – aged 6 years

Tom's mother, Vicky, experienced neglect and emotional rejection as a child. She had spent nine separate periods in foster care, the last one lasting three years. As a young adult and mother she was ill with depression. She regularly found herself in relationships with heroin-addicted and violent men. In time, Vicky also became a heroin addict and in order to pay for her habit, she went out on the streets as a prostitute. Tom was born with symptoms of opiate withdrawal and was in a very distressed state for several weeks. As a toddler he was often left unfed, under-clothed and neglected.

In her role as caregiver, Vicky presented herself as helpless. For much of his pre-school years, Tom was left unsupervised. While she was out or away from home for days at a time, his mother would leave him with a series of very unsuitable carers. On one home call, the health visitor found Tom crying. He had cut himself badly while playing with a kitchen knife. His mother had 'crashed out' in her bedroom and when challenged about why she had not taken Tom to hospital, she replied, 'I can't get him sorted until I am sorted'. He also witnessed considerable domestic violence in which his mother would get beaten up by one or other of her partners.

Before being finally removed from his mother when he was five years old, it was noticed that Tom appeared to be caring for himself, even when his mother was around. He told one of his foster carers, 'I had to look after myself because my mummy had to sleep a lot'. Indeed, the foster carer reported that while he was with her he seemed to have little idea that it was her job to cook his meals, sort out his clothes for school and go to the shops for food: 'Tom still tries to look after himself. He will make his own meals, get himself off to bed, and tell me what to do.' When he was with his mother, his behaviour switched between making her drinks, worrying where she was, and being rude and dismissive towards her. Vicky would look on, smiling helplessly, saying what a grown-up boy he was and wondering where she'd be without him. 'He brightens up my day, he does,' she has said more than once.

Now that he has been placed for adoption, Tom's mother is keen to maintain contact. He currently sees his mother once a month. His behaviour during contact has been very consistent. 'He takes charge,' was how one contact supervisor described it. The first thing Tom does is ask Vicky for a large sum of money, which she promptly hands over. She says he deserves it after all he's gone through. He then dashes down to the local shop and buys either a video or sweets. Tom constantly bosses his mother about, often in a sarcastic and belittling way, telling her she's useless, that he knows more than she does, that she is a 'dozey bitch', before making another demand for more money or a present. Vicky continues smiling throughout these exchanges, making weak reprimands or laughing while observing how grown up he is. An observer described Tom as 'manic, unable to slow down, conflictual and contemptuous'.

On returning home to his new carers, Tom remains 'very hyped-up, argumentative, and very aggressive'. He has attacked the family's dog. He walks around on his toes with his arms stretched out wide with a wild, staring, menacing look in his eyes which frightens the younger children. 'It's like he needs to be big and dangerous,' said his would-be adoptive mother. 'I also think he's scared after he's seen his mum. He has night-mares, talks a lot about death, and worries that the house might get bombed and everyone gets killed.' He talks about getting lost and being killed by a paedophile. On three occasions he has smeared faeces over the bathroom wall. This agitated, post-contact state lasts about a week. He then calms down although he continues to ask when he is next due to see his mother. However, it is never quite clear to his prospective adoptive mother whether this is something which he views instrumentally as a time when he expects to be given presents and lots of money, or whether he worries that he might have to go home to live with Vicky. 'He does keep asking whether he's go to go back to his mum's again, and I'm never really sure whether he would like this or not because if I do ask him, he says nothing and just goes quiet.'

Under the stress of contact, Tom appeared to show a mixture of aggressive/punitive controlling behaviour, compulsive self-reliance, and occasional episodes of compulsive caregiving. On being returned to the care of his prospective adoptive parents, the assessment was that, from his point of view, his new carers might be seen to be unable to protect him from the highly dysregulating experience of being sent back to the care, however short-lived, of his distressed and helpless mother. In her care, all his old feelings of being alone, in danger, frightened, and without protection appeared to be unconsciously triggered. The intense activation of his attachment system left him feeling helpless and vulnerable, a disorganised state of mind which he defended against by becoming highly controlling and presenting himself as big and dangerous.

In both Sophie's and Tom's case, contact not only appears to be a disorganising experience in its own right, it also seems to interfere with the child's ability to trust the capacity of the new carers to keep them safe and emotionally well regulated. This anxiety is likely to result in the child maintaining a self-protective controlling strategy, or in the case of Sophie, the continued use of a dissociative response whenever she feels under stress. Either way, the continued use of controlling and dissociative behaviours interferes with children's ability to access their new carers' regulatory capacities at times of heightened distress and develop a secure attachment. These are also likely to impair children's psychosocial development.

States of mind of permanent carers

However, there is one more element we need to add to the picture. Recent findings from the Thomas Coram Adoption Project, London (Steele *et al*,

2003; Hodges *et al*, 2003) suggest that adopters bring their own attachment histories to the parent–child relationship. More specifically, the study investigated whether the adoptive mother's state of mind with regard to attachment, measured using the Adult Attachment Interview, was associated with their newly placed child's state of mind, measured using story stem techniques. The study sample consisted of 43 mothers and the 61 children placed with them all of whom had histories of maltreatment. The children ranged in age from four to eight years, with equal numbers of boys and girls. The mother's attachment strategies were classified as either secure, dismissing or preoccupied. In some cases, an unresolved mourning pattern was also present, indicating ongoing grief and disorientation concerning some past loss or trauma. The children's narratives were rated using a coding system organised under six general headings: quality of engagement, disorganisation, aggression, child representation, adult representation, and positive adaptation.

The study judged 71 per cent of the 43 adoptive mothers to be autonomous-secure, 23 per cent dismissing, 5 per cent preoccupied, with 21 per cent also being judged unresolved with respect to loss or trauma. Themes of catastrophic fantasy, child aggression, adult aggression, bizarre events, and death and injury (together giving an "aggressiveness" score for each child) were much more likely to appear in the stories of children whose adoptive mothers were judged to be "insecure" (particularly those rated as dismissing) compared to "secure" mothers. Children adopted by mothers whose attachment interviews were judged "unresolved" scored more highly for narrative themes to do with adult aggression, parents appearing child-like, and throwing out or throwing away, and scored lower for themes to do with children coping realistically with challenging situations, and receiving help from siblings of peers. Children of unresolved parents appeared less able to use an organised strategy to deal with the conflict depicted in the stories.

Quoting Tronick and Weinberg (1997), Steele *et al* (2003) note that children of parents who fail to (i) recognise attachment needs, (ii) respond to their children's attachment behaviour, and (iii) "repair" the disruptions that inevitably happen in any parent–child interaction, are at risk of more negative developmental outcomes.

This then may be one of the critical elements in the relationships of caregivers with states of mind dominated by unresolved trauma and loss. That is, the availability of the adult to engage with a child, especially one that may be expressing challenging and negatively tinged behaviour, may leave too many of the ruptures unattended. We know from Bowlby's early writings on affect regulation . . . that insecure parents find the child's negative emotions . . . the most difficult and meet such displays with a similar matched negative response, an averted gaze, withdrawal or display of concomitant anger (Bowlby, 1956). (Steele *et al*, 2003, p. 15)

Thus, when vulnerability inherent in "unresolved" adoptive parents interacts with maltreated children's vulnerability, the level of vulnerability in both is likely to heighten (Steele *et al*, 2003, p. 15). And returning specifically to the subject of adopted children who are dysregulated by contact with previously maltreating birth parents, we speculate that whereas autonomous-secure parents might remain emotionally available even when their child is in a disorganised/controlling state, unresolved carers not only fail to establish a degree of mental connection with their child post-contact, their unavailability compounds the child's feelings of danger and stress, serving only to increase the child's disorganised state.

We therefore suggest that in cases in which children with histories of maltreatment appear to be re-traumatised by contact, direct and indirect contact with the birth parent should stop, at least in the short to medium term. However, we speculate that autonomous-secure adopters are likely to become increasingly successful in helping their children feel safe in allowing co-regulation of their distressed affect leading to the development of more secure internal working models. With increased trust in the emotional availability of adults, improved self-esteem and the growing ability to understand and regulate their own and other people's affect, there may come a point when the children of autonomous-secure adoptive parents are sufficiently resilient to cope with and not become helplessly dysregulated by the intense activation of their attachment system during contact with a previously abusive or neglectful birth parent.

In contrast, adoptive parents with unresolved states of mind with regard to attachment may find it more difficult to help their children develop increased mental integration, improved social cognition and greater resilience. In these cases, renewed contact with earlier traumatising birth parents is likely to remain traumatising and so contact is not recommended. Placements in which vulnerable adoptive parents look after vulnerable children remain fragile. They are the most likely to break down. Every effort should be put into helping both carers and children resolve their experiences of loss and trauma. Not until vulnerable carers have shifted to more organised and secure states of mind with regard to attachment will their children let go of their own defended behaviours and controlling strategies. Only then should thoughts of renewing contact be contemplated.

Summary

- Permanently placed children who have suffered severe maltreatment may be re-traumatised when they have contact with the maltreating parent.
- Children may therefore experience the permanent carers as unable to protect them and keep them safe. This will interfere with the child's ability to develop a secure attachment with their new carers.
- Severely maltreated children who feel unsafe and insecure will continue to employ extreme psychological measures of defence which may lead to a variety of aggressive, controlling and distancing behaviours. These behaviours place great strains on the carer–child relationship and increase the risk of placement breakdown.
- Adopters who possess high levels of sensitivity, empathy and reflective attunement help children feel both safe and emotionally understood. These parenting capacities promote secure attachments and increase resilience.
- Secure and resilient children are better able to cope with the emotional challenges of difficult relationships, including those which evoke feelings of distress.
- In contact cases where children suffer re-traumatisation, the need to make the child feel safe, protected and secure becomes the priority. Contact in the medium term would therefore not be indicated. This decision does not rule out the possibility of some form of contact at a later date, but this will depend upon whether or not the child has

achieved levels of resilience, psychological autonomy and reflective function that will equip them to deal with the emotional arousal that renewed contact with a once traumatising parent will initially trigger.

References

Bowlby, J. (1956) 'Psychoanalysis and child care', in J. Bowlby (1979) *The Making and Breaking of Affectional Bonds*, London: Tavistock Publications.

Bowlby, J. (1988) *A Secure Base: Parent–child attachment and healthy human development*, New York: Basic Books.

Cassidy, J. and Shaver, P. (1999) (eds.) *Handbook of Attachment*, New York: Guilford Press.

Eliot, L. (2001) *Early Intelligence: How the brain and mind develop in the first years*, London: Penguin.

George, C. (1996) 'A representational perspective of child abuse and prevention', *Child Abuse and Neglect*, 20(5), pp. 411–24.

Goldberg, S. (1999) *Attachment and Development*, London: Arnold.

Green, J. and Goldwyn, R. (2002) 'Annotation: attachment disorganisation and psychopathology: new findings in attachment research and their potential implications for development of psychopathology in childhood', *Journal of Child Psychology and Psychiatry*, 43(7), pp. 835–846.

Hodges, J., Steele, M., Hillman, S., Henderson, K. and Kaniuk, J. (2003) 'Changes in attachment representations over the first year of adoptive placement: narratives of maltreated children', *Clinical Child Psychology and Psychiatry*, 8(3), pp. 347–63.

Howe, D., Brandon, M., Hinings, D. and Schofield, G. (1999) *Attachment Theory, Child Maltreatment and Family Support: A practice and assessment model*, London: Palgrave/Macmillan.

Lyons-Ruth, K., Yellin, C., Melnick, S. and Atwood, G. (2003) 'Childhood experiences of trauma and loss have different relations to maternal unresolved and Hostile–Helpless states of mind on the AAI', *Attachment and Human Development*, 5(4), pp. 330–52.

Lyons-Ruth, K., Bronfman, E. and Atwood, G. (1999) 'A relational diathesis model of hostile–helpless states of mind: expressions in mother-infant interaction', in J. Solomon and C. George (eds.) *Attachment Disorganization*, New York: The Guilford Press, pp. 33–70.

Main, M. (1990) 'Cross cultural studies of attachment organization: recent studies of changing methodologies, and the concept of conditional strategies', *Human Development*, 33, pp. 48–71.

Main, M. and Hesse, E. (1990) 'Parents' unresolved traumatic experiences are related to infants' disorganized attachment status: Is frightened and/or frightening parental behaviour the linking mechanism?' in M. Greenberg, D. Cicchetti and E. Cummings (eds.) *Attachment in the Pre-School Years*, Chicago: University of Chicago Press, pp. 161–182.

Moss, E., St.-Laurent, D., Dubois-Comtois, K. and Cyr, C. (forthcoming) 'Quality of attachment at school-age: relations between child attachment behaviour, psychosocial functioning and school performance', in K. Kearns and R. Richardson (eds.) *Attachment in Middle Childhood*, New York: Guilford Press.

Perry, B. D., Pollard, R. A., Blakley, T. L. and Vigilante, D. (1995) 'Childhood trauma, the neurobiology of adaptation, and "use dependent" development of the brain: How "states" become "traits",' *Infant Mental Health Journal*, 16, pp. 271–89.

Schore, A. (2001a) 'Effects of a secure attachment relationship on right brain development, affect regulation, and infant mental health', *Infant Mental Health Journal*, 22(1–2), pp. 7–66.

Schore, A. (2001b) 'The effects of early relational trauma on right brain development, affect regulation, and infant mental health', *Infant Mental Health Journal*, 22(1–2), pp. 201–269.

Spangler, G. and Grossmann, K. (1993) 'Biobehavioural organization in securely and insecurely attached infants', *Child Development*, 4, pp. 1439–1450.

Steele, M., Hodges, J., Kaniuk, J., Hillman, S. and Henderson, K. (2003) 'Attachment representations and adoption: associations between maternal states of mind and emotion narratives in previously maltreated children', *Journal of Child Psychotherapy*, 29, pp. 187–205.

Tronick, E. and Weinberg, M. (1997) 'Depressed mothers and infants: failure to form dyadic states of consciousness', in L. Murray and P. Cooper (eds.) *Postpartum Depression and Child Development*, New York: Guilford Press.

West, M. and George, C. (1999) 'Abuse and violence in intimate adult relationships: new perspectives from attachment theory', *Attachment and Human Development*, 1(2), pp. 137–156.

13 Conclusions: a transactional model for thinking about contact

Elsbeth Neil and David Howe

It is clear from the research presented in this book that there are no straightforward answers to broad questions about whether or not contact will be of benefit to specific children in particular permanent placements. However, we shall try and distil the research findings and present a way of approaching the question of contact based on an assessment of placed children's psychosocial needs and how these are likely to be affected by the thoughts, feelings, behaviour and attitudes of both their permanent carers and birth relatives. In particular, we need to pay attention to how new carers and birth relatives are managing the psychological tasks that are peculiar to adoption and permanent care, and how their management might affect the developmental needs of placed children.

Children are permanently placed with substitute families when it is judged that their developmental needs cannot adequately be met by their birth parents but they can be fulfilled by adopters and foster carers. In broad terms, contact with birth relatives is recommended if it appears likely to facilitate one or more of these development needs. Contact is therefore not a "good" in itself. It has to be viewed as a potential resource, a protective factor, a means to a developmental end, an experience that promotes placement stability and a sense of security. In some cases, the judgement might be that contact is acting as a risk factor capable of upsetting sound psychological progress and mental health.

However, a complication in applying this simple rule of thumb is that some developmental needs and the psychosocial tasks required to meet them are brought about by the permanent placement itself. As a result of the adoption or foster care placement, children and permanent carers have to deal with the particular issues of separation, loss, belonging, identity and genealogy. In these matters, the birth parents and family have the capacity to play a unique role. Contact clearly has the potential to help children deal with these developmental concerns, but it can carry risks. We therefore need some kind of developmental calculus that indicates when contact is likely to be developmentally either harmful or beneficial. Although there is the inevitable cry that we need more research, we believe there is enough common ground to be found in the previous chapters to give us strong pointers to what such a calculus might look like.

Kirk was one of the first to realise that people who decide to adopt have to cope with a number of potential conflicts. They have to approach other people to acquire a child. They are not certain about the status of the parent in adoption. And they are unclear about the status of their relationship with the adopted child (Kirk, 1964, p. 1981). To some extent, these issues can act as a handicap in people's performance of the role of parent, introducing a measure of uncertainty and anxiety into the parent–child relationship. Kirk pointed out that adopters are faced with conflicting obligations. They are required to *integrate* the child fully into their family. But they are also expected to tell their child that they are adopted and that in some way they are "*different*". There is therefore a tension between integration and differentiation that both parents and child have to try and resolve. Kirk also calls this 'the paradox of adoption'. From the children's point of view, they have to reflect on the fact that they have been both chosen (by the adopters) *and* given up by or taken from (the birth parents).

Brodzinsky developed Kirk's early insights producing what he called a "stress and coping" model of adoption. 'The basic thesis of the model,' explains Brodzinsky (1987, p. 30), 'is that the experience of adoption exposes parents and children to a unique set of psychosocial tasks that interact with and complicate the more universal developmental tasks of family life . . . it is assumed that the degree to which adoptive parents and their children acknowledge the unique challenges in their life, and the way in which they attempt to cope with them, largely determines their pattern of adjustment.' Thus, the adopted child has the same developmental tasks as the non-adopted child plus a few more in addition that are peculiar to being adopted. The successful negotiation of these extra tasks requires adopters to be responsive and empathic, accepting and flexible. Adopted children have to work out what adoption means to them and other people in order to work out who they are, both to themselves and others. If they are successful in this, self-esteem and self-confidence –

both major protection factors – increase. Although coming at matters from a different direction, Brodzinsky, and indeed Kirk before him, both recognise something fundamentally important in the ability of adopters (and we would argue, foster carers) to remain attuned, open, empathic, thoughtful and reflective when contemplating the psychosocial complexities of adoption (and fostering) as it affects both their child and themselves, and we might add, the birth parents.

In all of this, the aim is to help permanently placed children achieve optimum levels of psychological development by helping them to:

- build a relationship and establish a secure attachment with new carers;
- resolve feelings of separation, loss and rejection;
- form a coherent sense of self and a clear identity by achieving autobiographical completeness and a sense of genealogical connectedness (defined as ' . . . the extent to which children identify with their natural parents' biological and social backgrounds . . . the degree to which children identify with their natural parents' background is dependent upon the amount and quality of information they possess about their parents . . . Socio-genealogical knowledge is fundamental to our psychological integrity. It is essential to our sense of who we are, what we want to be, where we come from, and where we belong in the order of things' (Owusu-Bempah and Howitt, 1997, p. 201).

Although all three psychosocial tasks receive high value, primacy is given to establishing a secure attachment with adopters and foster carers, although in the case of some older children this would not preclude them also maintaining an established relationship with their birth parents. It is within the child–parent relationship that young minds form, where children learn to process complex emotional and cognitive information, cope with stress, and develop resilience. Children who are robust on all these fronts are best able to deal with the demands of difficult relationships including those with birth parents and birth families. In secure, responsive caregiving environments, degrees of resilience are likely to increase year on year.

This gives us our first hint that we need to think flexibly about contact. The needs and feelings of children, permanent carers and birth relatives will interact and change over time. The amount of openness that individuals need (or can tolerate) will vary at different stages of the placement process. Carers will affect how safe children feel about contact. Children will bring their needs and emotional history to bear on the relationship they have with their birth parent. New carers who meet birth parents may become more empathic and relaxed with their child. Birth parents who meet carers might feel less hostile to the placement. A relaxed carer might make a child feel more secure. A secure child might handle contact less anxiously. A less anxious child might help the birth parent accept the placement. And an accepting, more co-operative birth parent might help the new carers contemplate an even more open placement.

Relationships tend to work best when communication is open. When people communicate they convey information – about their thoughts, feelings, beliefs, hopes and fears. In turn, those who receive this informa-tion process it psychologically, and as they do, they are affected and changed. In other words, relationships are *dynamic*; they change over time. And they are also *transactional;* as information flows between people it changes their mental states, understandings, feelings and behaviour. Contact therefore might be viewed as a *transactional dynamic* that takes place between children, foster carers or adopters and birth relatives. Moreover, if communication is not too defensively distorted and remains open between children and their carers, and the placement and birth family, then the information exchanged is likely to help those involved develop balanced and realistic understandings of their own and other people's positions. In fact, Brodzinsky (forthcoming) defines the essence of openness as 'the creation of an open, honest, nondefensive, and emotionally attuned family dialogue, not only about adoption-related issues' and a willingness of individuals 'to consider the meaning of adoption in their lives, to share that meaning with others, to explore adoption-related issues in the context of family life, to acknowledge and support the child's dual connection to two families, and perhaps to facilitate contact between these two family systems in one form or another.'

At this point, we might notice that permanent carers who are good at recognising, reflecting on and communicating openly about their own and other people's mental states not only provide an effective caregiving environment for children's optimum development, they also tend to be those parents who best understand the purpose and potential benefits of contact. Given a choice, they are likely to feel positive about a more open placement: communicatively open-minded carers and structurally open placements typically go together. And as we have seen, even if it is not possible to have a fully open placement with direct contact, communicatively open carers still recognise the need to help their child think about and process information about the meaning of their placement, their birth family, and the feelings which both of these generate. Conversely, there is small but recognisable risk that permanent carers who remain anxious, emotionally defended and therefore less communicatively open, relaxed and psychologically reflective are more likely to have less secure children. They are also likely to feel less comfortable with open placements, contact, and considering the psychological tasks peculiar to adoption and foster care.

A note of caution must be introduced here. We are not arguing that adopters and foster carers who feel anxious about contact will necessarily make unsatisfactory parents, or that they will not be able to handle any contact that does take place. In fact, we would argue that anxiety about birth family contact is common, understandable but can change. The personal anxiety of new parents is likely to be highest at the pre-placement stage where they are dependant upon the assessment and approval of others for fulfilment of their parenting desires and when their future relationship with the child is not yet real. Anxiety about contact is also not just about personal insecurity but can also result from a healthy partiality towards, and somewhat possessive view of the child and a desire to protect him or her. Who, after all, does not want their love object to be protective and a little bit jealous of potential rivals? What we are arguing however, is that the long-term capacity to think about, talk about, and have contact with the child's birth family is a dimension that differs strikingly between individuals. People who remain very defended about these issues will find aspects of "adoptive" or "foster" parenting difficult. These defences may also indicate less optimal broader psychological functioning that is likely to affect other domains of parenting. In these cases, practitioners should aim to understand and help manage carers' anxieties, and increase their reflective capacities and emotional availability to the child. Success in these matters increases the chance of developing a more communicatively open placement, which in turn would help the child deal more effectively with issues of loss, identity and genealogy. These aims might be achieved in a variety of case specific ways. For example, helping a birth parent accept the placement might make the carer feel less anxious.

Contact with birth relatives is likely to be particularly helpful to children in dealing with issues of separation and loss, and the need to achieve an integrated sense of self, but there will always be the potential for some tension between the three basic psychosocial tasks. This could be especially true in cases where contact, although helpful in terms of maintaining family relationships and a coherent identity, is nevertheless judged to be inimical to the child's feelings of safety and the establishment of a secure attachment to the permanent carers. Again, because a secure attachment and a sense of permanence provides the optimum environment for a child's socio-emotional development, in the immediate term it has to outbid the psycho-social tasks of resolving feelings of loss and dealing with issues of identity if these involve contact with a dysregulating birth relative.

The value or otherwise of contact is determined by the views, thoughts, feelings and behaviours which the child, the adopters, and the birth parents bring to the conduct and management of the event. Because contact has the capacity to be a highly charged and stressful experience for one or more of the participants, their psychological strengths and weaknesses, including their coping skills, will be brought heavily into play. The more stressful is the child's experience of contact, the greater his or her anxiety. In conditions where anxiety is raised, a child's mental energies will be absorbed by defensive concerns, and the need to feel safe and secure. Under stressful circumstances, the amount of mental energy available to a child to extract developmental benefit from the contact (to promote a secure attachment, to help resolve feelings of loss, and to achieve a clear and continuous identity) may be severely reduced to the point where contact begins to have a negative impact.

Contact being a relatively complex "system", what each participant brings to the relationship will affect the outcome in ways which are not always easy to predict. The studies reported in this book describe a range of findings which illustrate the need to think about contact, not just at a point in time but also over time. People's needs and ability to access and process adoption and placement-relevant information change, therefore contact arrangements must remain flexible and fluid. Each participant has to deal with and will be affected by the feelings, thoughts and behaviour of the others. This sets up relationship dynamics unique to each case and suggests that looking only at the characteristics of one party is insufficient to predict outcomes. For example, a birth mother who refuses to accept that she is no longer the child's primary carer might have a particularly disruptive affect on a placement where an older child with an insecure relationship history joins newly-approved adopters who have little previous child care experience. In contrast, a birth mother with the same attitude might have little impact on a child who was placed as a baby with experienced carers; in this case the child feels absolutely secure in her placement. Should her birth mother say, 'I'm you're real mummy', the securely placed child is likely to reply indignantly, 'No, you're not!' and promptly tell her permanent carers who react by confidently reassuring the child.

The characteristics of children, permanent carers and birth relatives

Our suggestion for making contact plans for permanently placed children is that practitioners need to consider the psychological needs and position of each party in the triad: the child, the adopters or foster carers, and the birth relatives. How might they be vulnerable? What resiliences might they bring? What developmental risks and benefits for the child would each person bring to contact? How might each individual's psychological make-up interact with and affect the child's developmental needs? In thinking about whether or not to establish a contact network, we shall need to consider:

- the characteristics of the child;
- the characteristics of adopters or foster carers;
- the characteristics of the birth relative.

These characteristics represent a distillation of the main research findings reported in earlier chapters, although the use to which they are put remains the responsibility of the current authors.

Characteristics of children

Factors associated with beneficial contact

- Infant placement.
- Child does not have an established pre-placement relationship with birth relative.
- Secure attachment/secure placement (the child senses that the permanent carers are a secure and protective base available at times of anxiety and confusion).
- Healthy psychosocial development.
- Good social cognition/emotional intelligence.
- Absence of major behavioural and mental health problems.
- Established positive, or at least neutral relationship with birth relative (e.g. grandparent, sibling, birth parent).

Factors associated with difficult or detrimental contact

- Insecure attachment/insecure placement.
- Major behavioural and mental health problems (*risk*: reduced psychological resilience/reflective capacity to cope with the complexities of contact including emotional arousal, multiple families and multiple relationships).
- Older child has had a troubled/traumatic pre-placement relationship with birth relative; rejected child has lived with several different birth relatives (*risks*: managing relationships with birth relatives more complicated for older child; child experiences emotional dysregulation during contact).
- Child is re-traumatised by contact with birth relative (*risk*: child cannot experience new carers as able to keep them safe).
- Child does not wish to have contact.

Characteristics of adopters and foster carers

Factors associated with beneficial contact

- Possess "good enough" levels of sensitivity, empathy, mind-mindedness, reflective capacity, social cognition and communicative openness (psychologically undefended; secure/autonomous states of mind with respect to attachment).

- Permanent carer recognises the developmental benefits of openness and contact for their child even if they feel anxious about it themselves.
- Recognise, understand and acknowledge that their child will think and be curious about their background and birth family.
- Accept birth relative; able to see and present the birth relative's perspective/situation to their child.
- Convey a positive attitude towards the birth family including acknowledging the reasons and circumstances surrounding the need for the child to be placed.
- Resolved states of mind with respect to loss and/or abuse.
- Constructive and collaborative approach to problems.
- Constructive and collaborative approach to working with birth relatives.
- Early involvement in thinking about the role of the birth family and the possibility of contact.
- Full involvement in any contact that takes place (nature of involvement the child requires will vary from case to case).
- Actual experience of contact with an accepting birth relative increases empathy, understanding, confidence and feelings of entitlement for permanent carers who initially felt anxious, uncertain, and reluctant about contact. Reality dispels fears and fantasies.

Factors associated with difficult or detrimental contact

- New parents/carers are anxious about contact (this anxiety may be highest in the early days of a placement when their parental role and the security of the relationship with the child are not yet established).
- Low levels of sensitivity, empathy, mind-mindedness, reflective capacity, social cognition and communicative openness (psychologically defended) (*risks*: insecure placement/insecure child).
- Unresolved states of mind with respect to attachment, loss and/or abuse (*risk*: the prospect of contact raises high levels of anxiety in carer who becomes less emotionally available to child increasing the risk of an insecure placement).
- Permanent carer unable to contemplate open contact and lacks collaborative capacity.
- Permanent carers not involved in the contact arrangements (*risks*: child

is left to manage stress unaided, child has no "overlap" between his two families).

- Permanent carer critical/not accepting/not understanding of birth relative (*risk*: child unable to talk about their birth family and psychologically unable to integrate their two families; carers lack communicative openess; child unable to complete developmental tasks of loss and identity).

Characteristics of birth relatives

Factors associated with beneficial contact
- Birth relative has never been child's primary caregiver.
- Birth relative accepts and supports the placement (they recognise that the new carers are the child's *psychological* parents).
- Birth relative affirms new carers in their role.
- Constructive and collaborative approach to working with new carers.
- In the case of birth parents (and in some cases grandparents, siblings or other relatives who have had a significant parenting role) they relinquish their parenting role in favour of new carers.
- Birth relative relates to child in a non-abusive, preferably positive way.
- Contact allows birth relatives to see how well the child is progressing; provides them with an accurate, up-to-date picture; decreases their anxiety, anger and guilt knowing that they still have a part to play in their child's life.
- Birth relative is relatively free of (or is supported in managing) significant personal difficulties (e.g. mental health problems, substance abuse problems, etc) that can affect their capacity to maintain helpful contact.

Factors associated with difficult or detrimental contact
- Birth relative does not accept or support the placement and acts to undermine it.
- Birth relative continues to insist on occupying the role of primary and rightful carer; the child is discouraged from loving their new parents (*risks*: child experiences split loyalties; increases feelings of insecurity and the risk of failing to bond with new carers).
- Birth relative has seriously maltreated/traumatised the child (*risks:*

child is re-abused/re-traumatised during contact). Birth relatives who remain under environmental, relational and psychological stress may continue to feel helpless and out-of-control. Contact, with its loaded emotional agenda might therefore increase feelings of stress. However, some birth parents, once relieved of the stress of caregiving, find it easier to relate in a much more relaxed and constructive way with their child.

- Birth parent rejects child.
- Birth relative has significant personal/lifestyle difficulties (e.g. mental health problems, drug misuse, etc) that impede their capacity to maintain helpful contact.

Structural and communicative openness

Having identified what strengths and weaknesses each party might bring to contact, we next need to consider the various structural and psychological contexts in which children have to try and deal with the developmental tasks associated with being permanently placed with another family.

Two key dimensions define the character of contact in permanent placements. These dimensions run as core themes throughout the studies reported in this book. One dimension captures the *openness of the placement*, including whether or not there is contact. Brodzinsky (forthcoming) discusses this dimension in terms of the structural openness of the adoption or foster care placement, that is, the extent to which the child and his or her new family are in touch, either directly or indirectly.

The second dimension is the degree of *psychological and communicative openness* on the part of the permanent carers. That this is something distinct from (though possibly overlapping with) structural openness is not a new idea. It is implicit in the work of Kirk (1964, 1981) and explicit in the discussion by Brodzinsky (forthcoming). The research by Grotevant and colleagues has also extensively explored this dimension. They recognised that, within different structural openness groups, adoptive parents could adopt very different approaches to communicating with their child about adoption, especially with regard to the decisions they made about disclosing or withholding adoption-related information. Parental communication was not a fixed attribute, but could alter both over time and in response to different expressed needs from the child, once again highlighting the dynamics and transactions that take place (Wrobel *et al*, 2004). We would argue that openness and the ability to collaborate are promoted by relatively undefended states of mind, ones which are capable of sensitivity, empathy, and the capacity to see, understand and reflect on how things look and feel from other people's points of view, including those of children and their birth relatives. As we have argued, open and reflective states of parental mind help children feel secure. They promote children's psychosocial development, emotional competence and resilience.

Dichotomising these two dimensions into (i) open and closed placements, and (ii) open and closed communicative carers gives us a simple two-by-two grid, defining four basic contact positions. Of course, in practice each dimension is continuous, which is why all contributors to this volume remind us that any one case is unique and that contact decisions therefore have to be case specific. The following grid acts as a first step in trying to think more flexibly about the factors which define the nature of contact in any one case.

Table 13.1

Open and closed minds and placements

		Openness of placement	
		Placement open	*Placement closed*
Psychological and communicative openness of new parents	New parents open	Position A	Position B
	New parents closed	Position C	Position D

It has also been noted that there is a strong likelihood that communicatively open and reflective carers are those most likely to recognise the developmental benefits of a structurally open placement, including direct contact with birth parents (Position A). To some extent, the converse is also true: carers who feel anxious when contemplating attachment and emotionally charged relationship issues deal with their anxiety defensively. They are therefore less likely to feel comfortable with a structurally open placement (Position C) and, given a choice, may seek a placement with no birth family contact (Position D). New parents who exclude difficult and potentially distressing information from conscious processing have relatively closed states of mind. The result is a lack of communicative openness about adoption, permanent care, and other parenting and attachment issues, including the ability to think empathically and collaboratively about how best to meet placed children's special set of developmental needs.

For a while, debates about contact tended to polarise around the merits and demerits of structurally open versus closed placements. Missing from these early arguments was a full appreciation of the particular developmental needs of placed children; the capacity of new parents to understand and reflect on these needs, especially as they might imply some kind of relationship with the birth family; and the link between open-minded and reflective carers and children's feelings of security. Adding a developmental and caregiving perspective to whether or not the placement is structurally open gives practitioners an extra degree of freedom when thinking about children's needs.

For example, in cases where for whatever reason contact is not possible, the placement remains structurally closed. However, the child is likely to have a number of psychosocial and developmental issues around her background and birth family. A psychologically open carer would understand that, even though contact is not taking place, the birth family is likely to remain under some kind of active consideration in the child's mind. Issues of loss, identity, belonging, worth, connectedness, and security may well be concerns about which the child needs to talk. The carer has to establish a relationship with the child within which communication about such birth family matters is understood to be appropriate, safe and manageable. This is the situation to be found in Position B (Table 13.1) – a placement currently without contact, the psychological and developmental implications of which the communicatively open carer fully appreciates.

In light of the findings reported in this book, we can add two more refinements to the contact matrix described in Table 13.1. The first is to examine the position of children whose birth relatives either (i) accept the placement and wish to co-operate, or (ii) who do not accept the placement, find it difficult to co-operate, and in effect undermine the security of the placement. The way these two contrasting types of birth relative are handled by new parents, placed children and agencies depends on whether there is contact or not, and whether or not the carers are psychologically and communicatively open.

The second refinement recognises that the management of contact and openness is likely to vary depending on the age at which the child is placed. Older children are likely to have had a relevant relationship history with their birth family. This can play powerfully in the minds of new carers, children, and birth relatives. In contrast, children placed as young babies are less likely to have established a significant relationship with their birth family. Nevertheless, as we have been keen to point out, this does not mean that issues of loss, identity and the emotional significance of the birth family won't come "on line", developmentally speaking, at some time in the future. Structural and psychological openness therefore have to be thought about from the outset, even in infant placements.

When contact is conceived as a "right" or a "good" and not as a potential resource to promote children's psychosocial development, bad practice can result. For example, young children (particularly those placed as babies) are currently the least likely to experience direct contact, at least in the UK context (Neil *et al*, 2003). This poses long-term developmental risks around issues of loss and identity. What happens much more frequently is that older placed children with the most complex needs and the least developed socio-emotional skills are those most likely to have direct post-placement contact with birth parents. In short, direct contact is too easily dismissed for very young children (the complexity of the task is over-estimated), and direct contact is insufficiently planned, supported and monitored for older children (the complexity of the task for all three parties is underestimated).

Also underpinning a developmental perspective is the key point made by Beek and Schofield (see Chapter 8) who note that ideally children need to integrate their two families with as little tension or conflict as possible. From children's point of view, if there is 'physical and psychological overlap between the two families', their placement and contact experiences are likely to feel much more integrated. The most helpful way to achieve this is for children to experience their permanent carers and birth family members working together amicably and collaboratively. When permanent carers take no part in contact or have never met the birth relative, children have to deal with the complex emotions of contact on their own. They find it difficult to talk about the birth family with their carers, and their carers with the birth family. Beek and Schofield point out that it seems very odd that children, especially young children, are often taken to contact by someone they hardly know to a venue about which their permanent carers know little.

For children to see and experience their two families working together for their good, recognising their respect for each other and their respective points of view, experiencing them getting along sends children a powerful message: that they, too, can have good and positive feelings for both sets of parents, both families. Avoiding conflicts of loyalty helps children express their feelings more openly. Creating a climate of openness allows children to feel relaxed about asking questions to do with their identity, their origins, their background and their birth family. Their history is recognised; their birth family is valued. Children who have a good sense of who they are and where they are in life tend to feel secure, autobiographically complete and psychologically whole. As a result, self-esteem is raised and self-worth increased.

We are aware that thinking about contact and its potential impact on children, permanent carers, and birth family members, each with their own psychological needs and make-up, produces a complex picture. As one person's behaviour or attitude changes, so it affects the behaviour and attitude of everyone else in the "contact system". Thinking about contact transactionally and dynamically certainly opens up unexpected possibilities. Change the attitudes and behaviour of one member of the contact system and you are likely to change the attitudes and behaviours of all other members. Different combinations of the characteristics of each of the main players inevitably means that simple contact formulae do not work and that decisions have to be made on a case by case basis. However, by looking at the key components of the research findings reported in this book and presenting them in tabular form, we offer a way of thinking about contact which we believe is logical and systematic, and based on children's developmental needs considered in relationship to different quality caregiving environments. This approach generates four basic scenarios within the context of (i) placements which are structurally either open or closed, and (ii) permanent caregiving which is communicatively either open or closed:

1. Infant placements + co-operative and collaborative birth parent/ relative.
2. Infant placements + unco-operative and non-collaborative birth parent/ relative.
3. Older placed children + co-operative and collaborative birth parent/ relative.
4. Older placed children + unco-operative and non-collaborative birth parent/relative.

So, to repeat, the main purpose of contact is to help children meet their three basic developmental needs of attaining good mental health (achieved in the context of a secure relationship with sensitive carers); resolving issues of loss and trauma; and achieving a strong sense of personal identity and genealogical connectedness. These three tasks are most likely to be realised in placements which are structurally and psychologically open (Position A in Tables 13:1–13.5). Contact planning and support should therefore always look to help children, new parents and birth relatives get to this position by changing their behaviours, attitudes and understandings whenever possible.

However, as we have argued, of the three developmental tasks, the most important is that of achieving social and emotional competence in the context of a secure and sensitive parent–child relationship. If pursuing structural openness violates this developmental principle, even if the other two are enhanced, then contact is not indicated. Open communicative processes, which indicate sensitive and mind-minded parenting, are more important than open structural practices, although as we have seen, open minded carers are much more likely to recognise the value of structurally open placements. When contact is not possible, this does not mean that long-term loss and identity issues can be ignored; on the contrary if contact is not an available option, there is an even greater need on the part of the carer to attend to issues of loss and identity. The most common situations in which contact is contra-indicated include birth parents who cannot adjust to the idea that for their child's sake the new carers have to become the psychological parents, and birth relatives who remain a physical or sexual danger to the child. In these cases, the fall-back position (B in Table 13.1) is to ensure that the permanent carers are psychologically and communicatively open about both the placement and the birth relatives, even though the placement, at least for the time being, remains structurally closed.

Position D in Tables 13.1–13.5 (placements which are both structurally and communicatively closed) poses the risk that children will fail all three developmental tasks. Again, looked at transactionally and dynamically, an insensitive and communicatively closed placement increases the risk of a child feeling insecure. This might impair their social and emotional development and possibly lead to behavioural problems. When these insecure children begin to think about their placement, their identity and where they belong, as they inevitably will, they not only have reduced psychological capacities to cope with these developmentally challenging tasks, they have no-one to whom to turn to talk about their anxieties and confusions. Feeling emotionally distressed, these children might become behaviourally difficult, unco-operative and resentful. These are behaviours which insensitive and communicatively closed parents are least able to handle or understand, which only makes matters worse. Every effort therefore must be made to help children, carers and birth parents avoid the placement becoming both structurally *and* communicatively closed.

The following tables define the four "open–closed" positions for each of the four basic scenarios.

Scenario 1: Young placed child, birth parent/relative co-operative

Table 13.2
Young placed child, birth parent/relative co-operative

	Placement open	*Placement not open*
	1A	1B
New parents open	Contact likely to be straightforward and beneficial for child. Child's identity needs best met in this scenario.	New parents will promote child's identity needs even though no contact occurs. They may seek to open up placement, and birth relatives likely to co-operate, hence possibility of move to 1A. If no contact is possible, new parents will seek to meet child's needs by other means.
	BEST OUTCOMES	GOOD OUTCOMES
	1C	1D
New parents not open	Contact likely to be straight-forward and beneficial for child, and disconfirming of new parents' fears. Possibility that contact will increase security of new parents, hence possibility of movement to 1A. Intervention with new parents may be required to achieve move to 1A.	New parents unlikely to be confident in addressing child's identity needs, and unlikely to feel comfortable in opening up placement. New parents' insecurities remain unchallenged. Child's identity needs least likely to be met. Possible intervention could be work with new parents (hence possible move to 1B).
	GOOD OUTCOMES	NEED FOR CHANGE

In Scenario 1 it is assumed that the child is either placed in their adoptive or permanent foster home in infancy, or if placed older, that he does not have an established relationship with the birth relatives involved in contact, and he is relatively free of the kind of emotional or behavioural difficulties that could complicate his attachment to new parents. In other words, the scenarios in Table 13.2 all assume that the psychological task of forming new attachments can be more or less taken to be relatively straightforward. Thus we are talking here about children who are likely to start their new placements with few risks factors and who are likely to increase their resilience over time, primarily through the development of safe and loving relationships with new parents. We also assume in Table 13.2 that the relevant birth relatives of the child have an overall attitude of benevolence towards the child and support for him or her in their new family. Because the child does not have an established relationship with birth relatives, the purpose of contact is likely to be to facilitate the child's resolution of long-term issues of loss and identity.

When these conditions apply, it can be seen that good outcomes for the child are quite likely to follow from a number of situations. If contact is planned it is likely to be straightforward and beneficial for all parties, and is very unlikely to have any detrimental impact on the child's attachment to his new parents. Even when adoptive parents or foster carers feel anxious or negative about contact, their experience of contact is likely to disconfirm any fears that it may upset the child, interfere with the child's attachment to them or expose them to hostility or undermining behaviour from birth relatives. Thus contact could help new parents attain a more empathic view of the birth family (as identified in the research by Grotevant *et al*, Neil, and Logan and Smith) and hence bring about a move from 1C to 1A. Even when no contact is planned or possible, children may be able to successfully manage issues of identity and loss by other means, for example, if they can obtain relevant information about their birth family from records and can communicate with their new parents freely about their background. For some people however, even when these conditions apply, the lack of actual contact with birth relatives may be experienced as a frustration and loss (Grotevant *et al*, Chapter 2; Howe and Feast, 2000). What is likely to be the trickiest scenario for a child is a situation in which no birth family contact is planned and the new parents are not open minded or able to communicate openly about the birth family (Position 1D). In addressing identity concerns, a young placed child who has no memories to draw upon, will have neither the resources of the birth family, nor resources within the adoptive/foster family to assist him. The consequences are unlikely to lead to placement breakdown or serious developmental problems, but the child may feel unhappy about identity issues, may harbour feelings of rejection and loss, and may feel at a distance from adoptive or foster parents.

Compared to the situations in the following three Tables, contact in these situations is most likely to be a resource for all parties in managing adoption/fostering related issues, and therefore the possibility of contact should not be lightly dismissed. Most of the cases in Grotevant *et al*'s study (Chapters 2 and 3) apply to this Table, and as they report, most of the children were faring very well in all developmental domains. Although contact made little difference to socio-emotional development, it was associated with a greater level of satisfaction when the children were teenagers.

Scenario 2: Young placed child, birth parent/relative not co-operative

In Scenario 2, the child is again placed as an infant, but the behaviour and attitudes of birth relatives are different. In this case it is assumed that one or more of the following characteristics apply to the birth relatives: (a) they do not accept that the child is now part of a new family, (b) their attitude to the new parents is hostile or undermining, (c) their attitude to the child is hostile. These are all factors that can make the experience of contact uncomfortable or negative for the child and the foster carers/ adopters, though (as above) it is unlikely to affect the child's attachment to new parents. If contact takes place (2A and 2C), it could make for a tense or difficult atmosphere between the adults. What happens next is likely to depend very much on adoptive parent/foster parent character-istics. Neil's research (Chapters 4, 5 and 6) has shown that although many birth parents and grandparents started off by not accepting the child's placement, positive contact experiences helped them to move in this direction. This was especially likely when adoptive parents were welcom-ing and accepting of birth family involvement. Thus, many cases in her study could be said to have started off in 2A but moved quickly to 1A.

Adoptive parents or foster carers who feel less open about contact issues are much less likely to be able to demonstrate the kind of accepting behaviours that, in turn, can help birth relatives shift their position. It

Table 13.3
Scenario 2: Young placed child, birth parent/relative not co-operative

	Placement open	*Placement not open*
New parents open	2A Contact may be challenging for new parents, but this unlikely to have great impact on child or new parents (low potency of birth family/child relationship) unless difficulty is severe and sustained (where possibility of moves to 2B or 2C are possible). Possibility that adoptive parent's positive attitude will help birth relatives feel more accepting of placement, hence possibility of move to 1A. Intervention with birth relatives may also make move to 1A possible. Contact may still be of benefit to child in understanding reality of birth family. GOOD or MIXED OUTCOMES	2B New parents will still work hard to promote child's identity needs and will help child to understand why birth parents cannot or will not have contact, mediating potentially negative consequences. New parents may seek to open up placement, hence move to 2A (and later 1A) may be possible. If placement is to be opened up, work with birth family will be helpful. GOOD or MIXED OUTCOMES
New parents not open	2C New parents will find contact difficult (even if child doesn't) and unless something changes may seek to restrict/stop contact (move to 2D). Alternatively contact will continue but will have little benefit for child, as new parents cannot mediate the experience for them. Individual	2D New parents unlikely to be confident in addressing child's identity needs, and unlikely to feel comfortable in opening up placement. New parents' insecurities remain unchallenged. Child's identity needs least likely to be met. Possible intervention could be work with new parents,

	Placement open	Placement not open
	2C	2D
	work/support and or mediation with new parents and birth relatives needed to achieve move to 2A or even better 1A.	hence possible move to 2B and/or work with birth family (move to Scenario 1)
	CHANGE NEEDED	CHANGE NEEDED

is especially important therefore to support all parties in this type of case. If this does not happen adoptive parents are likely to end any contact. Foster carers have less power to take this course and so all parties may be left with an ongoing but unproductive and uncomfortable contact plan. When this is the case, the child is in a difficult position, firstly because contact itself is difficult. Secondly, because his adoptive/foster parents are likely to be personally stressed by contact, their capacity to mediate the experience for the child will be reduced (see Chapter 12). In this kind of situation, children may experience some stress as a result of contact, as children do in any tense situation, but we would not anticipate serious behavioural and emotional disturbances resulting from contact, unless problems were severe or persistent. This is because the potency of the child's relationships with birth relatives is low (as he or she does not have an attachment relationship with them), therefore the dysregulation described by Howe and Steele (Chapter 12) is unlikely to occur, and the contact is unlikely to make any negative impact on the child's capacity to attach to new parents.

In some cases it may be worthwhile persisting with contact, if the stress is low. Benefits to the child in the longer term could be that he or she develops a realistic understanding of the birth family (as Thoburn found could be the case, Chapter 11). In other cases, if birth relatives cannot be helped to adopt a more co-operative stance, then it may be that the child's needs in relation to loss or identity are best met by other means, open-minded adoptive/foster parents being the primary resource (2B). Stopping contact if it has been persistently difficult may not cause any particular harm to the child, as the child is (by definition in this group) not attached to the birth relative.

Grotevant's research (Chapter 2) illustrates that it is very worthwhile to attempt to move new parents and birth relatives to a collaborative position regarding contact. He found that where birth relatives and adoptive parents can exercise give and take on both sides and truly work together over contact, this brings about important developmental benefits for the child. Thus the positions where contact is happening but one or both parties are not really collaborating (1C, 2A, 2C) will never be as beneficial for the child as contact when both parties work together (1A). Work with new parents, birth relatives, or both may be required to bring about this change.

Scenario 3: Older placed child, birth parents/relatives cooperative

In Scenario 3, the complexity of contact is increased because of the complexity of the child's psychological world. Here we are assuming that the child is placed probably beyond the toddler stage of development (though as Howe and Steele's chapter reminds us, the psychological worlds of very young children can also be very complex); that they have formed an attachment with birth relatives prior to placement; and that the process of making relationships with new parents may not be straight-forward. Such children begin their life in new families with a number of risk factors and subsequent good developmental progress cannot be taken for granted. The factor most likely to build the child's resilience is the establishment of a close loving relationship with adopters or foster carers. Contact with birth relatives is likely to be a potent experience for children, but whether this is positive or negative will depend on the quality of relationships between the child and their birth relatives and the quality of the contact event. Even when children want to see their birth relatives, and have a good relationship with them, contact can arouse feelings of sadness or confusion.

In Table 13. 4 we are assuming that birth relatives have a co-operative and positive disposition towards the new parents and the child: they are a potential resource to the child in managing issues of loss and identity. When new parents also have an open and positive approach, contact is likely to benefit the child. Any complexity of feelings for the child brought about by contact with birth relatives is likely to be handled sensitively

Table 13.4
Scenario 3: Older placed child, birth parents/relatives cooperative

	Placement open	*Placement not open*
	3A	3B
New parents open	Contact likely to be a positive or mixed experience for child, but both birth family and new parents will collaborate to help mediate experience for child. Contact unlikely to undermine child's stability in new placement (and may enhance stability) and will have likely benefits in terms of identity and loss issues.	Lack of contact may be problematic for child, but new parents will help mediate this experience, in some cases by opening up placement, a move likely to be supported by birth family (move to 3A). If no contact is possible, new parents will seek to meet child's needs by other means.
	BEST OUTCOMES	MIXED OUTCOMES
	3C	3D
New parents not open	Contact is likely to make child feel divided loyalties, as they will pick up on discomfort of new parents. This may counter potential benefits of seeing co-operative birth parents. The experience of contact with co-operative birth parents may be enough to move to 3A, but if not, intervention with new parents will be needed.	Lack of contact may be a relief for new parents, but problematic for child. New parents may reinforce or create negative views of birth family in child having negative immediate or long-term consequences (divided loyalties may interfere with new parent–child relationship – worst case scenario child may feel unable to invest in new relationship). Work with new parents needed to move to 3A (if contact is possible) or 3B (if contact is not possible).
	CHANGE NEEDED	CHANGE NEEDED

by both birth relatives and adoptive parents. The support and approval of birth relatives may help the child settle in their new family (3A).

In contrast, if the child is unable to continue relationships that are important to him or her, this could make them unhappy or even reluctant to invest in new relationships (see Thoburn, Chapter 11). Adoptive or foster parents with an open attitude and sensitivity to the child's needs are likely to respond to the child's distress by attempting to open up some contact with birth relatives (see Chapters 8, 10 and 11). Where this may not be possible for any reason, again the new parents will be psychologically available to the child to help him express and manage his feelings of loss. On the other hand, if the child's new parents themselves feel anxious about birth family contact, they may not pick up on the child's signals, or their own attitude towards the birth family may inhibit the child from expressing their feelings. As Thoburn (Chapter 11) has discussed, in some cases this could lead to children taking the matter into their own hands in adolescence and seeking out their birth family without the knowledge or support of their adoptive or foster parents, a scenario that she found rarely had a good outcome.

Where contact does take place, but new parents do not have an open attitude (3C) the potential benefits of any contact may be offset by the disadvantages brought about by the child picking up on the discomfort of the new parents, and hence feeling divided loyalties. In some cases adoptive or foster parents, having found the birth relatives to be supportive of their position, will feel less anxious about contact (moving to 3A, see Beek and Schofield, Chapter 8), but if this is not the case some help and support for the new parents may be required in order that contact can be more comfortable for the child. As Beek and Schofield highlight (Chapter 8), it is important that foster carers/adopters are not kept on the margins of contact arrangements, but that there is some overlap between the two families either in terms of the new parents being present at meetings, or a third party (e.g. a social worker) acting as a "bridge" between the two families. How the contact is actually set up and managed may determine how comfortable the new parents feel about it.

Scenario 4: Older placed child, birth relative/parent not co-operative

Table 13.5

Scenario 4: Older placed child, birth relative/parent not co-operative

	Placement open	*Placement not open*
New parents open	4A Contact likely to be a mixed or negative experience for child, but new parents will try to mediate the experience. Therapeutic work with child may also be helpful. Positive attitude of new parents may help birth relatives change (move to 3A), but if not, work with birth parents will be needed to achieve this. Whether contact is to net benefit or detriment of child will need to remain under assessment. If birth relatives' lack of acceptance is interfering with child's safety, security or attachment in new placement, stopping contact may be advisable (move to 4B). MIXED OUTCOMES	4B Child may be upset and/or relieved at lack of contact, but in either case new parents will try to mediate experience for child and help them develop balanced view of birth family. In some cases, opening up placement may be helpful (move to 4A), but this would be best attempted by first working with birth relatives. Therapeutic work with child may be desirable. MIXED OUTCOMES
New parents not open	4C Contact is likely to be difficult for all parties. Child is at risk of feeling divided loyalties and feeling unsafe or dysregulated, and new parents will lack capacity to contain and manage	4D Lack of contact may be a relief for new parents, but child's views may vary and differ from new parents. New parents may reinforce or create negative views of birth family in child having

Placement open	Placement not open
these feelings. Contact likely to be of net detriment to child and intervention with new parents (move to 4A or 4B), birth family (move to 3C) or both (move to 3A) may help. New parents may be struggling with other aspects of placement and general support may be indicated including direct work with child.	negative immediate or long-term consequences (divided loyalties may interfere with adopter–child relationship – worst case scenario child may feel unable to invest in new relationship). If safe contact is not possible, work should be attempted with new parents to move to 4B. If child wants and needs contact, work needs to be attempted with birth relatives, child and new parents to attempt move to 4A or (preferably) 3A. Move to 4C not advised (i.e. instigating contact when birth relatives not co-operative and new parents not comfortable).
POOR OUTCOMES – CHANGE URGENT	POOR OUTCOMES – CHANGE URGENT

In Scenario 4, the child again has complex psychological needs. In addition, the birth family may have attitudes or behaviours that undermine the child's position within the new family or threaten his or her safety. It cannot be assumed that the birth family will act as a resource for the child. This is the most complex set of circumstances in which to have contact, and whatever the attitude of the new parents or the structural openness of the placement, it can never be taken for granted that contact will be straightforward or beneficial. The findings of several authors (see Chapters 7, 8, 9, 10 and 12) remind us that contact can expose children to harm as well as good. There is therefore a strong argument for supporting all parties and closely managing any contact that does take place.

If contact does take place, the experience for the child, at best, is likely to be mixed. However, decisions to stop contact are often difficult to make. As several authors in this volume remind us, children may very well have strong wishes to see birth relatives, even though these people may continue to disappoint them, let them down or even hurt them. Whether or not to overrule a child's wishes in such circumstances is a hard call to make. Wilson and Sinclair (Chapter 10) argue that many children do distinguish between different relatives: they may wish to see some but not others. Furthermore, they found that in abuse cases children had better placement outcomes when contact with the abuser was restricted. Howe and Steele's chapter puts the case that when the child is emotionally highly dysregulated by contact, meetings should stop, at least until the child is in a better position to cope.

Thoburn (Chapter 11) makes the point that some children simply will not commit to a new placement if they are denied contact with existing attachment figures, and that overruling children's wishes and feelings may do damage to their sense of self efficacy: there may be risks in having contact, but there are also risks in not having contact. What is very effectively described by Beek and Schofield (Chapter 8), Wilson and Sinclair (Chapter 10), and Thoburn (Chapter 11) is how confident and open-minded foster carers and adopters can balance these competing risks by allowing children to remain loyal to birth relatives by promoting some controlled contact, but at the same time supporting them in dealing with the hurt or disappointment that can follow from contact. This can allow children to reach a realistic understanding and appraisal of their birth family without making them feel they are disloyal to either family. In some cases therefore, where children have contact and can be supported by their new parents (4A), contact may be a 'bumpy ride' (as Thoburn has put it) but in the long term, benefits could outweigh disadvantages.

Situations that indicate that contact is likely to do more harm than good are those where the contact appears to be having a detrimental impact on the child's attachment to their new parents. This (as described by Howe and Steele) could be either because it undermines the child's sense that their new family can keep them safe and secure and/or because the child's emotional distress brought about by contact has a knock-on effect of undermining the new parents' psychological equilibrium. This latter point will be much more likely to apply in situations where the new parents do not have an open attitude towards the birth family, as both parent and child will be upset by the contact (4C). It is also important that the frequency of any birth family contact should not be such that the child and new parents are cannot spent time together consolidating their position as a new family (see Selwyn, Chapter 9).

When contact cannot or does not occur, the child must come to terms with feelings about their past and their birth family by some other means. Where children are supported by sensitive carers (4B), and possibly therapeutic support, they can achieve a good outcome. When children don't want contact with birth relatives, 4B may be a better position than 4A. When contact does not occur and new parents are negative about contact and the birth family (4D), a child who has positive feelings for his birth family will find it hard to express them and a wedge may be driven between children and their new parents. Where children themselves have very negative views of their birth family, these are unlikely to be moderated by new parents. The child is then left with a one-sided view of their background: it is all bad. What will such a child think about herself? Where birth relatives cannot help children with identity issues, it is even more imperative that they receive help with these issues from their new parents. Thus, for children in both 4C and 4D, intervention to increase the capacity of new parents to support the child in dealing with issues of loss and identity is needed. It may also be helpful for the child to receive therapeutic support from outside either of their families to deal with these concerns.

Because none of the possible outcomes of this final set of scenarios is optimal for the child, working with birth relatives to help them adopt a more collaborative position should always be considered. In some cases it may be that certain members of the birth family cannot offer much to the child but other relatives can. Neil's study (Chapters 4-6) found that grandparents had fewer difficulties than birth parents, that they were more able to sustain contact over time, and that such contact was in almost all cases a positive experience for all.

Conclusion

The experience of contact can change the psychological position and outlook of children, permanent carers, and birth relatives. It is not without its hazards, and in some situations it is simply too risky to proceed. But in more cases than was once thought possible, it appears to confer benefits all round. A more open mindset by all parties, including placement agencies and courts, driven by an understanding of placed children's special set of developmental needs, opens up a whole range of possibilities. People who thought they could never feel relaxed about contact find themselves able to meet, collaborate and understand. Less anxious carers become more emotionally available and communicative with their children, who, as a result, feel more settled and secure. And birth relatives, who angrily feared the loss of their child, find that they can still play an important part in the life of their son or daughter without the need to threaten the caregiving role of their child's new psychological parents. Contact, particularly face-to-face contact, provides children and families with the chance to share information, keep up-to-date, gain knowledge, and hear feelings without the filter of time or third parties. The more people know about each other, the greater their understanding, tolerance and compassion is likely to be. This is fertile ground for the growth of strong, young minds and well-adjusted adults.

References

Brodzinsky, D. (1987) 'Adjustment to adoption: a psychosocial perspective', *Clinical Psychological Review*, 7, pp. 25–47.

Brodzinsky, D. (forthcoming) 'Reconceptualising openness in adoption: Implications for theory, research and practice', in D. Brodzinsky and J. Palacios (eds.), *Psychological Issues in Adoption Theory, Research, and Application*, New York: Greenwood.

Howe, D. and Feast, J. (2000) *Adoption, Search and Reunion*, London: The Children's Society.

Kirk, H. D. (1964) *Shared Fate*, New York: Free Books.

Kirk, H. D. (1981) *Adoptive Kinship*, Toronto: Butterworth.

Neil, E., Beek, M. and Schofield, G. (2003) 'Thinking about and managing contact in permanent placements: the differences and similarities between adoptive parents and foster carers', *Clinical Child Psychology and Psychiatry*, 8(3), pp. 401–418.

Owusu-Mempah, J. and Howitt, D. (1997) 'Socio-genealogical connectedness, attachment theory, and childcare practice', *Child and Family Social Work*, 2(4) pp. 199–208.

Wrobel, G. M., Kohler, J. K., Grotevant, H. D. and McRoy, R. G. (2004) 'The Family Adoption Communication (FAC) model: identifying pathways of adoption-related communication', *Adoption Quarterly*, 7(2), pp. 53–84.

Contributors

Susan Ayers-Lopez, M.Ed., Project Manager, Center for Social Work Research, The University of Texas at Austin, 1925 San Jacinto Blvd., Austin, Texas 78712, USA

Mary Beek, Senior Research Associate, School of Social Work and Psychosocial Studies, Elizabeth Fry Building, University of East Anglia, Norwich NR4 7TJ, UK

Dr. Harold D. Grotevant, Distinguished University Teaching Professor of Family Social Science and Adjunct Professor of Child Psychology, University of Minnesota, 1985 Buford Avenue, St. Paul, Minnesota 55108, USA

Dr. Susan M. Henney, Assistant Professor of Developmental Psychology, Psychology Department, Worcester State College, 486 Chandler St., Worcester, MA 01602, USA

Dr. David Howe, Professor of Social Work and Dean of the School of Social Work and Psychosocial Sciences, Elizabeth Fry Building, University of East Anglia, Norwich NR4 7TJ, UK

Janette Logan, Senior Lecturer in Social Work, Department of Applied Social Science, Williamson Building, University of Manchester, Manchester M13 9PL, UK

Dr. Ruth G. McRoy, Associate Dean for Research, University Distinguished Teaching Professor, School of Social Work, The University of Texas at Austin, 1925 San Jacinto Blvd., Austin, Texas 78712, USA

Dr. Elsbeth Neil, Lecturer, School of Social Work and Psychosocial Sciences, Elizabeth Fry Building, University of East Anglia, Norwich NR4 7TJ, UK

Professor Sir Michael Rutter, Social, Genetic & Developmental Psychiatry Research Centre, Institute of Psychiatry, P080, De Crespigny Park, London SE5 8AF, UK

Dr. Gillian Schofield, Senior Lecturer, Director of the Centre for Research on the Child and Family, School of Social Work and Psychosocial Sciences, Elizabeth Fry Building, University of East Anglia, Norwich NR4 7TJ, UK

Julie Selwyn, Director of the Hadley Centre for Adoption and Foster Care Studies, University of Bristol, 8 Priory Road, Bristol BS8 1TZ, UK

Professor Ian Sinclair, Research Professor and Co-director of the Social Work Research and Development Unit, University of York, Heslington, York YO1 5DD, UK

Dr. Carole Smith, Senior Lecturer in Social Work, Department of Applied Social Science, Williamson Building, University of Manchester, Manchester M13 9PL, UK

Dr. Miriam Steele, Graduate Faculty of Political and Social Science, New School University, 65 Fifth Avenue, New York NY 10003, USA

Dr. June Thoburn C.B.E., Emeritus Professor of Social Work, School of Social Work and Psychosocial Sciences, Elizabeth Fry Building, University of East Anglia, Norwich NR4 7TJ, UK

Professor Kate Wilson, Director of the Centre for Social Work, Law and Social Sciences Building, University of Nottingham, Nottingham NG7 2RD, UK

Julie Young, Research Associate, School of Social Work and Psycho-social Sciences/School of Nursing and Midwifery, University of East Anglia, Norwich NR4 7TJ, UK

Other BAAF titles on contact

What is contact? **NEW**
A guide for children
Hedi Argent
Explains for separated children the many ways they can keep in touch with birth relatives and significant others.
2004   26 PAGES FULL COLOUR   A5   ISBN 1 903699 59 2   £3.95

Contact in Permanent Placement
Guidance for Local Authorities in England and Wales and Scotland
Good practice guide highlighting factors to be taken into account when considering contact within permanent placements.
1999   20 PAGES   A4   ISBN 1 873868 66 9   £4.50

Staying Connected
Managing contact arrangements in adoption
Edited by Hedi Argent
Contributors discuss research and current practice in making, arranging and sustaining contact, illustrated with many direct quotes from families and children.
'... a valuable source of information for practitioners' Quality Protects Magazine
2002   244 PAGES   A5   ISBN 1 903699 12 6   £12.95

See You Soon
Contact with children looked after by local authorities
Edited by Hedi Argent
Explores planning and managing appropriate contact from a variety of viewpoints.
'A mine of useful information, research and views.' Community Care
1995   210PP   A5   ISBN 1 873868 30 8   £10.95

Adoption with Contact
Implications for policy and practice
Joan Fratter
The experience of adoption with contact in the cases of 32 children with special needs.
1996   281PP   A5   ISBN 1 873868 37 5   £9.95 (PREVIOUSLY £11.95)

Contact
Managing visits to children
Peg McCartt Hess and Kathleen Ohman Proch
UK edition of US handbook containing valuable guidance on good practice.
1993   88PP   A5   ISBN 1 873868 12 X   £3.00 (PREVIOUSLY £5.95)

ADOPTION & FOSTERING

All available from BAAF Publications tel 020 7593 2072 or email pubs.sales@baaf.org.uk. Full details of other BAAF publications at **www.baaf.org.uk**

Registered charity number 275689